Real Pet Sitting

Scenarios and Advice from a Professional Pet Sitter
with Seventy-Eight Pet Sitting Scenarios

THE PET SITTER'S HANDBOOK

Geri Laverie

PAGE PUBLISHING, INC.
New York, NY

First originally published by Page Publishing, Inc. 2014

ISBN 978-1-63417-147-2 (pbk)
ISBN 978-1-63417-148-9 (digital)

Printed in the United States of America

CONTENTS

The purpose of the writing of this book is to inform the reader. The only nature is to help guide you in your quest to become a professional pet sitter, the most valuable guardian of animals. This book contains advice, life experiences, and information related to pet sitting. The publisher and author disclaim liability for any problems arising from pet sitting.

Consultations with your client's veterinarian for any health concerns contained in this book is highly recommended.

DEDICATION

I'd like to thank my children for their support and the sacrifices that they have made for me throughout the years. When everyone was skeptical, they stood by their faith in Mom. They never complained about the fast food or hectic schedule that made up our days.

To my daughter Jessica, who would come to my rescue when I couldn't do another sit due to exhaustion, most times at the last minute. I appreciate all that she has done and for being my right hand girl. For the two beautiful grandsons she has blessed us with, I thank you. Thanks to my son Scott, for without his optimistic attitude towards this business and his help, I might have given up. For my son James and his wife, Holly, for protecting our country and making it back from Iraq safely, I give you guys a special thank you. And although the miles have separated us, their support and confidence have made this all worthwhile. And for the special granddaughter and grandson that makes our lives and future brighter. We are truly blessed. I must also give a special thanks to my mom, who wasn't so thrilled when I started up this business but has helped me tremendously both in the business aspect and when it's time for me to let some steam off. Although she is no longer with us, her inspiration and strong work ethics follow me.

Thank you to all my relatives and friends for their constant inspiration, support, and for listening to my never-ending pet tales. I'd like to thank all my loyal clients who have taught me so much. They are the reason I am successful and strive to be the best. For your generosity around the holidays and the pleasure of caring for your pets and for being a part of my extended family, I thank you.

INTRODUCTION

When I first decided to open a pet sitting service, I really had no idea the adventure I was about to begin. The one thing I was sure of was that I would be working with animals, a lifelong dream. The road has been bumpy at times, and I have to admit that there were times I thought of giving up and selling the business, shaking my head, wondering what in the world was I thinking! Some may think *What a cute little job to have* or *How hard can it be to walk dogs?* At first one might think the business is a great way to make a living. This might be true, but believe me, it does come with a huge price tag. Think about what a tremendous responsibility we have in caring for another's pet and home. I'd like to give you a brief example on just how many of the pets we care for depend on our expertise when it comes to recognizing signs of stress or illness.

Recently I got a call from a woman who was extremely upset. It seems her in-laws had left the country for six months and must have gotten a good deal from her hairdresser for pet sitting their one geriatric cat. They had been gone for three months into this vacation when the daughter-in-law had only stopped in for a two-day stay to find the cat in dire condition. Did I forget to mention this woman was on the verge of tears as we spoke? She immediately took the cat to a vet. It had lost half its body weight, was dehydrated, and was seemingly depressed. She had gotten my number from a friend of the family who had used my services in the past. This new client had already decided to drop the hairdresser and hired my services at two visits per day at least for the next couple of weeks until the cat was in better condition.

At that point we were to do daily visits. There were another three months left for cat care, and I had to speak with the owners along with the daughter-in-law so we'd all be on the same page. She went on to explain that the hairdresser never had a cat, but her in-laws wanted a good deal because of the length of the vacation—penny-wise and pound-foolish in my opinion. This poor cat suffered at the hands of an inexperienced person looking to make extra money and her owners looking to save a couple of dollars. As you can see, pet sitting involves much more than caring for pets. When pet sitting, we are responsible for all the many things that can happen while the client is away, including pet illnesses. This is why I felt it necessary to include a section on this. Now I don't want to intimidate you into thinking that you are not up to pet sitting, but be aware that you will have to do your homework, and being overly cautious wouldn't hurt either. My area has exploded with new pet sitters and dog walkers; some are very good at their craft while most haven't a clue on what they're doing.

This being part of the reason behind my thoughts on putting together a book. This is not just a book on how to start and run a successful pet sitting service. Anyone with some business sense can pull that off. This book was written to make each and every one aware we must educate ourselves on pet illness, signs of stress and show a genuine concern for the pets in our care. We must remember that our clients view us as professionals and expect us to not only care for their pets but identify problems that they themselves may not notice. Knowing what to do in an unpredictable situation isn't always an easy call. This is why I tried to include all the situations I have encountered throughout the many years of caring for animals. Every day is an adventure with new learning experiences even for an old-timer like me. I came in with a basic knowledge of animal behavior.

I was always aware of even the smallest changes of the pets in my care. I learned from my clients when it came to past and present illnesses of their pets and tried to see possible trouble with a situation before they spiraled out of control. Pet sitting as a profession is not a walk in the park by any means. We have real responsibilities with the possibilities of problems arising that can have some very serious consequences if you do not have the basic knowledge required to care for animals coupled with the added responsibility of being held liable for many things that could go wrong in the client's home, some of which are out of our control, not to mention the hectic schedule, working holidays, long hours in all types of weather. You will miss out on family gatherings and have rushed dinners, barely tasting the food you've just gobbled down. You will experience tying to schedule a time to shower and attend to your personal needs in the busy months.

I almost forgot to mention, if you have pets yourself, how guilty you will feel at times you are not there for them. When I first started my business I felt like I was cheating on my dogs and felt bad about having to go see a client's pet while mine were looking at me with those sad, puppy-dog eyes and wanting to come with me. You will be faced with many different personalities, dogs that won't let you out of the home, dogs that won't let you in, attack cats, illnesses, home emergencies. The laundry list goes on and on, not to mention all the drool, poo, vomit, and other pet messes you will clean up, pet hair on everything along with dogs suffering with diarrhea and more poo. Having a strong stomach will be a plus when getting into this business. Add to the fact that many of the pets in your care were never taught basic training and will not behave on the leash, jumping and mouthing at your arm or leg, and have no manners in general will be a test to your patience. Imagine driving fourteen hours a day when business is peaking, getting to your assignment on the other side of town and remembering leaving your keys for this particular job on the kitchen table! This will add stress to your day and throw your schedule off.

This is basically a 24-7 business with a sure chance of burnout unless you set some strong guidelines for yourself. Now that I've given you a good reality check, the opportunity for at-home pet care is still growing even in the decline of our economy. I started my career as a professional pet sitter back in January of 1994. There was only one other pet sitter at the time in my area, and she had only been in business a year or two when I started. Within another couple of years she had moved out of the area to be closer to her daughter. When I first brought the idea up, most people thought I was nuts, saying, "No one will pay you to care for their pets." Well, I refused to listen and loved the idea of being my own boss. Being with animals and getting paid for it, the opportunity is there. It will not be easy by any means. You will be juggling a hectic schedule and wear all the hats that apply to business. When I say we wear all the hats, this means that we are dog walker, pet sitter, in charge of collections, accounts payable/receivable, logistician, graphic designer, printer, janitor, secretary, adjudicator, therapist (when client needs counseling about their pets), psychologist, advertising/sales executive, and CFO.

It is pretty intimidating if you sit down to think about it, and I'm glad I never did this when I first started out. It's not as hard as it sounds. If you're serious about pet sitting, the will and determination to make it work will take you far. The potential is great in this profession but not glamorous by any means. Yes, I said profession, not to be taken lightly if you are serious about your business and intend to make this a career choice. Most pet owners are concerned about the care of their pet; if this was not the case, they then could have hired the teenager next door or their hairdresser for less than what they would pay for a pet sitter. In return, the client expects much more from a professional, trusting our knowledge and experience when caring for their pets. Your success or failure will depend on how serious you are about making this business work, and with this you will assume great responsibility. I suggest you build your business slowly, to grow accustomed to the new lifestyle you will be taking on. Growing too fast will not give you a chance to feel your way around, to know your strong and weak points. Knowing what you can handle will be to your advantage.

My hopes are that this book will give you some insight into both the pros and cons of pet sitting, that it might serve as a guide to some of the problems you might encounter. I hope to share with you what my many years of pet sitting has shown me and possible solutions to some of the situations you might have the pleasure of dealing with. Hopefully save you from some of the pitfalls I experienced in the beginning and during the years that followed. Come to think of it, our learning experiences never come to an end when working with animals and their owners. Whether you plan to keep it small with twenty loyal clients or you have as many independent contractors or employees as your workload will allow you need to think ahead. Even if you thought of franchising your pet sitting business, you need to think about your long-term goals. And in my opinion, you have to truly care about your clients' pets, taking the time to choose your independent contractors or employees carefully, if this is the case. Background checks, training, and continued support for your sitters will let you know when a sitter needs some time off, a pep talk, or a good-job pat on the back. These pet sitters will be reflecting your business in either a positive or negative way. Big or small, you must plan for the future because this will be beneficial to your business. Asking yourself where you will be a year, four years, and ten years from now will give you goals to reach for.

It is definitely possible to make a decent living as a pet sitter. For many years I have been a single mother who carried all the bills. It hasn't been easy at times, but for the most part I always managed to keep a roof over our heads and put food on the table. I've always described my business as a roller-coaster ride, a little scary at times but a lot of fun. Please remember, if you are going to depend on pet sitting as your sole source of income, it will be best to have some sort of reserve built up to carry you through the lean times. Or if you are currently employed, it would be best to keep your present job and take on assignments that will fit into your schedule until your business has grown some.

I never said it would be easy, and until you build up a loyal client base, it will be somewhat difficult to pay all the bills and still be able to get you promotional materials together. You will find at times that pet sitting and dog walking can be either feast or famine. This type of business will take time and require a lot of work, as you know. One thing that you will find very different from the business world with set hours is that pet sitting tends to be a constant split shift—early morning, midday, evening, and then late night visits. And let's not forget to mention that holidays and weekends are usually required, with never a dull moment. A pet sitter's life can be very hectic at times.

When starting up your pet sitting business, it would be to your benefit to look into all aspects of doing it right—legally. This will save you time and money, more than likely some aggravation along the way too. I've included examples of some of the many experiences I have encountered along the way in hopes of guiding you and your business. By learning to recognize the signs of illnesses in pets, which, in my opinion, is extremely important to make a really great pet sitter and reading books that can help you gain knowledge. Remember, knowledge is power. Any remedy in this book should be checked with both your client and reputable veterinarian to make sure the pet will not have a bad reaction and for permission. I have learned from my clients and my own animals that sometimes it just takes a simple remedy to make the pet comfortable.

CHAPTER 1

Safety and Security

I would like to address an important aspect to this business as it's not all fun and games. Both personal and business security have always been a top priority for me, being a woman and with the crazy hours I sometimes have. I found it necessary to attend a personal-safety course offered by the NYC Police Department, which was free. Of course, this became necessary for me as my car was broken into twice, and one of my daily dogs walking client's house was broken into which was a very scary experience for myself. So I wasn't about to wait around until something jeopardized my personal safety. I want to give you some tips on how to keep yourself, car, and client's home safe as possible as many things can happen while performing our job.

Car Safety

Most pet sitters will admit to the fact that their car is their home away from home. I know it is for me, and my car is an extension of my office. Having important paperwork and keys for many homes are just a start. We need to carry cash or credit cards for meals and gas for the car. Constantly going in and out of homes, we might be easy targets for thieves. I know I have been. On two separate occasions my car was broken into. The first time was partly my fault, but I really didn't realize how fast some thieves work. I had just stopped off to go into a store, wasn't gone but about five minutes, and someone had broken the passenger-door window and grabbed my purse, which I stupidly left after I took what I needed for my purchase. It was winter and snowing. I was in the middle of a busy schedule and had to make four more stops with a broken window with snow coming in. Needless to say, this was very stressful for me. I had to put a stop on credit cards. My driver's license was also in my bag, and I was worried that someone then had my home address as well.

The second time was only three weeks later, and I suspected the same person along my route. Only this time they got nothing because I did get smart after the first incident, but they did break the driver's-side window this time. Again it was nighttime. It was not snowing but freezing cold. I was driving to finish up my stops with a black garbage bag that was not put on so well flapping in the wind.

Here are some tips to keep your car safe from thieves and to give them a hard time from stealing your belongings or, worse, your car! Chances are slim but still possible.

- Always park your car in a well-lighted area if at all possible.

- Close all windows and lock the doors. Although this didn't stop my thief, but at least you did your part.

- If you have an alarm, activate it. If I feel nervous about my environment, I will sometimes set the alarm off before going over to the car to scare anyone away. I also want to add my car did have an alarm but not a motion detector, so by my thief breaking the window the alarm wouldn't go off unless the door was opened.

- All valuables, jackets, and other belongings, should be placed out of sight, preferably in the trunk or, if you have an SUV, hidden well inside the vehicle.

- If you use a commercial parking lot or community garage, leave only the ignition key with the attendant. Never leave your house keys attached.

- Do not keep your license or registration in the car as a thief can then get your home address, and you might come home one day to find your home burglarized. I thank God every day I did not have to go through this ordeal.

- If your clients have a garage, ask if you could use it while they are away and lock both the vehicle and garage. I would also like to add that you always double-check the garage before leaving the client's home, making sure the remote worked correctly and that you did not accidently hit the open button when leaving and the door is closed.

Car alarms are great while out on assignments as my vehicle has been saved a few times by the alarm going off, I'm sure of it. If while on a sit your alarm goes off, observe activity around your car from a distance. If you see a suspicious person, call your local police departments. Don't try to handle the situation yourself because safety should be your first concern. Another problem that might arise could be when your car breaks down; this is why maintenance is very important for your vehicle. Always make sure you have your cell phone, and it should always be charged in case of an emergency.

Giving weekly checks on tire pressure, oil, brake, battery, power steering fluids, radiator coolant level, and window wash fluid will help keep you safe along your route. In the event you do break down, always keep a well-charged flashlight and flares in the car, lock the doors, turn your flashers on, and stay in your car until help arrives. I will sometimes go out just to raise the hood and if a Good Samaritan stops and offers to help. I just ask if they could tell the nearest service station about my problem, or I have already called for help, especially out on late-night runs in secluded areas of my town and my little voice tells me to be cautious. In the winter months you should keep emergency supplies such as a shovel, a bag of kitty litter for weight, a traction mat, and a blanket so you don't freeze while waiting for assistance. If you ever get a flat tire in a dangerous location, drive slowly to the nearest service station, even if it means ruining a tire. At least you will be safe.

Getting flat tires seems to be my most common problem. I would suggest avoiding shortcuts in unfamiliar territory or areas that might not be safe. Staying on high-traffic roads is your safest route, and I always try to avoid getting lost. If you are ever in a situation that you are getting harassed or being followed by another driver, you can drive to the nearest police station or other public area. Park as close as you can, and I wouldn't worry about parking legally. Make sure you get yourself inside fast. When out at night and driving, be cautious of any vehicle that might bump into your car. Don't get out but explain to the other driver without getting out of your car that you will be driving to the nearest service station to exchange accident information. Or just call the police and stay in your locked car until they get there. I watch way too many crime shows, and sometimes when driving late at night, my mind begins to replay these shows, and it's better to be cautious.

Residential Security

When you take on an assignment, you are not only responsible for the client's pets but their home as well. Many clients will leave their home vulnerable by leaving a window or door unlocked. And I most certainly won't take on a job where a door is left unlocked or a window is left open. I have had both situations come up and did not feel comfortable with either. The door being left unlocked was not to the main house but a separate area for the dogs. That didn't last long before I had access to the main house and the door was left locked. The second was a client early on in my career that wanted her cat to be able to come and go as he wished. I was very uncomfortable with that situation, and the client insisted on leaving the window open. So I closed and locked the window with the cat indoors and opened the window on my last visit. I would be worrying about the cat's safety and mine as well. This client wasn't a client for long because I decided to make this part of my policy. Needless to say, she wasn't happy, but I was.

Most times the client is busy getting their luggage packed and attending to last-minute chores, not realizing that they had left that window unlocked or forgot to lock the garage door, which can be another way of getting into the home. The first thing I do when entering a home, be it a new client or regular, is check the windows and doors. I can't tell you how many times my clients have left a window or door unlocked. One of my biggest fears since I started this business was worrying about some unsavory character following me and getting a brilliant idea of breaking in after I leave or knocking on the door after I've gone in and trying some rouse to get into the home by either posing as a repair person or as someone with car troubles. This is one of many reasons to never answer the door while on assignment or do so by speaking through a window, giving the appearance of not being alone. Let Duke show them whose home.

At one point we had a rash of push-in robberies back in 2008. The robbers pretended to be police officers, flashed fake badges, and they got the woman who was babysitting to come to the door and pushed her in and then proceeded to rob the house. This was documented in our local newspaper. Never hesitate if you feel threatened of any suspicious circumstances. Use your instincts! If you're feeling something is just not right, then it's probably not. You have to be aware of your surroundings. If you see a suspicious car parked nearby, be cautious. If you go to a home that has a window or door that is opened that was not on your last visit, don't go in as the intruder might still be in the home.

This scenario actually happened to me on one of my daily walks for a client. I went into walk her beautiful golden retriever, Dakota. When I entered the home, I was aware of a problem immediately as her cats were freaked out. Learning to read your pets' expressions and behavior will give you extra clues as to what is going on in the home. Continuing to walk into the kitchen, I saw that the back kitchen window was wide open. Now this was a window that she always left open with the screen in place for the cats to look out of in the nicer weather. I had mentioned this to her in the past, but she did not listen to my concerns. Dakota was usually asleep in the bathroom, and I did go and check on him. He was fine and asleep as usual. When I went outside, I saw that what the thief had done was pull up a lawn chair, open the kitchen window, lean in, unlock the kitchen door which was right next to the window, and just walk in. I went back in and was going to check upstairs to see if anything was off, and halfway up the stairs, I got an uneasy feeling and decided not to go up.

Keeping your cool will help you think straight and make good decisions. Sometimes it's not so easy when you're faced with a break-in. Of course, when these things happen, most times things just don't seem to go right, adding to the stress. When I called the client's work number, she had changed positions and never notified me of the phone number change, and I was unable to get in contact with her immediately. Dakota was fast asleep in the bathroom, so I woke him up and took him out to let him do his business on a shortened walk. I also knocked on all the neighbors' doors, and on this particular day, no one was home. I went back to the office and started making phone calls and finally got in touch with the owner, who went home immediately. The police were notified, and they were able to get prints off the window and door. I later found out that the thief had fed Dakota a box of doggie treats and had taken a shower in the client's home. More than likely he was still in the home when I went in. That's pretty scary. So I did a number of things wrong. The first was not leaving right away to call the police. The second was attempting to go and investigate the upper level, and the third was not having an updated client telephone number.

You can bet I do keep all telephone numbers current if at all possible. You should never enter the home when confronted with this type of situation. Wait for the police. I would also suggest that you go to a neighbor's home while waiting for the police if they are home. Have your cellular phone charged and in your possession at all times, making sure to be aware of your surroundings. Thankfully, break-ins don't happen often but can happen to any pet sitter at any time.

Another incident that had happened in my area was back in September of 2007 with the appearance of the Ninja Burglar. This burglar would dress all in black including a black ski mask similar to a ninja. He would come into homes even if someone was home, as homeowners actually ran into this guy. He'd slip in, stealing jewelry, computers, cameras, and cash—whatever he could grab. If the alarm sounded, he would smash it, and all this was happening in neighborhoods I was working in. He had broken into several homes and was dubbed the Ninja Burglar; I swear I am not making this up. He was front-page news in our borough for some months. I was definitely on the alert, and thankfully I did not have to deal with another break-in.

You must also follow the client's instructions for setting the alarm when leaving the client's home if an alarm is being used. If a break-in occurs and you fail to set the alarm, you could be held liable for anything that was stolen. See if the clients will be using timers for their lights or if they will want you to either alternate lights or put a certain light on during your evening visit. This will give the appearance of someone being home. Keeping safe when entering homes is easy if you train yourself to carry your phone with you at all times, even in the home. When entering the home, you must make sure the door is locked after you enter. When going for your walk, make sure you lock the door as you leave. Pay attention to your inner voice when you have a bad feeling. Stay off the phone and don't listen to music; this can make you vulnerable, not being able to hear your surroundings. I have always kept my keys between my fingers if I felt unsafe. This, no matter how small, could be used as a weapon to defend yourself. And if you have a large key ring with all your keys attached, this should work well to ward off an attacker.

Personal Safety

In this section there are actually two safety issues, one being related to dog walking, keeping both your dog and yourself safe, the other being personal safety, going into different homes at all hours. Some people are under the impression that crime only happens in bad neighborhoods—not so. We actually had a burglar who regularly visited upperclass neighborhoods and would go into the homes while the owners were home, as I just spoke about. Try to do most of your visits before dark when possible, but keep in mind, crime can strike at any time.

I also like to ask the clients if anyone else will have access to the home. Even if they say no one else will be coming in, we did have an occasion that a brother and two of his friends came by for the weekend, and on the morning visit one of my ICs (independent contractor) walked into the home finding three guys sleeping on the couch and living room floor. My IC was scared and called me and refused to go back in the home. I contacted the clients, and she said that she remembers him saying he might stop by but forgot to mention this. So be prepared for anything unusual. And don't hesitate to walk out if you feel the least bit uneasy about the situation.

When going on consultations, always let someone know where you are going. Leave them with an address you will be at and let them know if you're not back within an hour to call your cellular phone. If at all possible, do your initial consultations in the daylight. If that's not possible due to client's scheduling issues, visit the area in the daylight to see what the neighborhood looks like. See if the address is legitimate and the home looks lived in. Earlier in my career I had set up a consult, verified the consult before driving over to the home, speaking with a man needing someone to care for his dog while on vacation, only to find out that the house number was nonexistent, and when I called the telephone number I had to speak to someone not an hour earlier, no one answered. Nothing happened, but I did waste my time and wondered why someone would do such a childish prank. I guess I'll never know.

If you're feeling uncomfortable about the consultation for whatever reason and would like to see if the client is a sex offender in the United States, you can do a search by visiting www.nsopr.gove.

In Canada the National Sex Offender Registry (NSOR) provides the Canadian Police with information about crimes, and the public does not have access to the registry. By visiting the Royal Canadian Mounted Police at www.rcmp-grc.gc.ca you will be able to find useful information on keeping yourself safe. In the United Kingdom the Violent and Sex Offender Register (VISOR) is a database of offenders and not available to the public. Please contact your local force regarding any concerns you might have in this matter as they might have literature or safety classes that you could attend.

Unfortunately in Australia the general public is not provided with access to sex offender registries by the federal or state governments. When I was doing my research, I did find MAKO/Files Online, which is a free public pedophile / sex offender registry. The website address is http://www.mako.org.au/prelist.html. Be alert to your surroundings and think about your safety at all times. You must avoid dangerous situations because this is your best protection. I think women are particularly vulnerable as we are out at all times of the day or night and are usually thought to be the weaker sex, but men are not free of worry either. I have been extremely lucky in respect to my personal safety, but I still take note of my surroundings at all times.

Also, while you're on your assignments, I would suggest that you do not answer the door or telephone. I have never done this for a couple of reasons. One is I don't won't want to be a victim of a push-in robbery, and it's not my job to be an answering service while the client is on vacation. I also don't want to get blamed for not getting any important messages while the client is away. I have only been asked one time if I would answer the phone, and I told the client this was not part of the service. Another situation you might encounter is someone (husband, older son, or other male relative) will be home while you're coming in to care for the pet, sometimes due to illness or because they don't trust the pet care to their spouses or children. If the situation makes you feel uncomfortable, you must be straightforward with your client and tell them they will have to make other arrangements as you are bothered by the fact of someone being home while you are coming in.

I have worked through situations like this, and although I did feel uncomfortable at times, nothing ever happened. When making your rounds, you should vary your daily routines, avoiding predictable patterns and times you will be visiting homes. When you arrive at an assignment, lock the doors to your car before going into the client's home. Make sure to lock the door to the home once you're inside; also make sure that the doors are locked when you take the dogs for a walk. You wouldn't want someone to be waiting inside when you come back.

When you have finished your sit, make sure the door is locked. I always double-check as some locks are hard to lock, or sometimes it's hard to figure out what direction to turn the key to lock it properly. I always have my keys ready to open the door, but not only for that reason as the keys can be used for protection in the rare event that you might be attacked. Before getting back into your car, look inside and always be aware of your surroundings. I can't stress this enough.

Dog Walking Safety

I've always said that you never know what to expect while out on a walk. So many different scenarios can happen. Always make sure you have complete control of your dog before crossing a busy street. Never get pulled into traffic by an enthusiastic dog. Beware of some suspicious character getting close to your personal space. When walking a dog at night, try to wear bright colors. Have a portable blinking light that you can attach to the leash or your clothing. I found a collar and leash that has lights running through them. Use these especially in dimly lit neighborhoods where there are no sidewalks; it makes it easier to be seen by cars coming along. Just this week, I found a small flashlight that has a neon light on the end that you can set for a constant light or to blink and comes in various colors.

Know the area that you will be going into. If you scout your neighborhood before going in, you will be aware of any questionable characters. This will also be helpful on your walks in case of any stray or loose dogs that might pose a problem on your walk. If you carry a pocket alarm, whistle, or anything that's makes a loud noise, this will not only deter people but would also scare away loose dogs. You should be able to find one that can attach to your keys in a local hardware store or locksmith. Don't walk your dog through a park or secluded road at night. Stay on the lighted roads, away from bushes and alleyways. Someone walking a big Doberman pinscher or German shepherd more than likely wouldn't be targeted. But as we know, they're not all big dogs, and I do know some tough little Chihuahuas, but I'd prefer not to take a chance with my safety.

Always be aware of your surroundings, like someone walking a short distance behind you. They might be up to no good. Keep a safe distance. Way back in the day I was followed home from a fast-food restaurant, never being aware that I was being stalked. Although I did notice the man behind me and turned around a few times and heard the footsteps getting faster, it never registered that I was about to be jumped. At one point I even saw him jump behind a car to get closer, and I still had no clue. Well, before I knew it, I was on the ground with him sitting on top of me, holding my arms down.

I'm not sure what you've heard about what to do when an attack happens, but I heard a professional say to do whatever the attacker wants to avoid being injured. But I can tell you that no one knows how they will react to a situation like this until it happens. I fought tooth and nail, screaming the whole time, until he finally gave up and ran away. No one ever came out of their homes to help or to even see what was going on. So if I'm ever presented with an attack again, I will, more than likely, do whatever it takes to get away and keep myself safe. I suggest you do the same, using whatever works to hopefully get some assistance or scare the attacker away.

There are some questionable characters out there, and when walking a smaller dog, your safety could be in jeopardy if you don't pay attention to your surroundings. Although I'm not a dog trainer, I will insist on the dogs in my charge to be somewhat well behaved. I have found that the majority of my clients have spoiled dogs; the owner will often let them get away with unacceptable behavior. If I have a weekly dog walk, it doesn't take much time for the dogs to understand that there are certain rules to be followed. On the other hand, an unruly dog of a client that goes on vacation every once in a while will be harder to train, as they usually regress when the client comes home and will forget what you have taught them.

Being safe does not only consist of personal safety but safety from injuring yourself while walking a dog. If you have a daily dog walk with a high-energy dog that likes to pull, there are a few things that can be done. Carry an extra-long training lead for dogs with high energy, take them to the park, and let them run that energy off. I have a strict rule that I will not let a dog off its leash (liability issues), and this gives me the ability to let the dog run without losing control. I also wanted to add that I will not take any of my dogs to a dog park for liability issues as well. My job is to make sure that the dog is kept safe at all times. I heard from a local vet that since we have had dog parks open on the island, the incident rate of dogs coming in with wounds from other dogs has gone up considerably. This is due to the stupidity of their owners. Knowing they have an aggressive dog does not deter some owners, and others must pay the price.

Carrying treats around comes in handy. Whether you have a puller, barker, aggressive personality, or even a non-walker, treats usually work 95 percent of the time. You will have to get the dogs to focus on their walk. A dog that pulls can do damage to your hands, joints, and muscles. And after all these years, my wrists and hands are feeling the effects of walking unruly dogs. When they start to pull, make them sit for a treat or do an about-face, walking in the opposite direction. Another technique is when the dog starts to pull, give a tug on the leash (a quick pop of the leash), say no, then let go. This one is my favorite. Or you can give a tug, turn around, and go the other way. Do this every time the dog starts to pull. It may take some time for a thickheaded dog to get the hang of this, but in the long run, it will be worth it. I have had many a dog that will try to control the walk by pulling on their leash and then wrestling it as they would while playing with a sock. What I do is give them a firm no (in a growl tone) and then ignore them. Some of the thicker-headed dogs will require a few corrections in the same manner, but they too get the message that this is not acceptable behavior. While they continue this behavior with their owners, they will not do this with me.

Another option that can be used is the anti-pull harness, which gives correction under the dog's front legs. The reason this no-pull harness works so well is because the skin under the dog's front legs is sensitive and rather thin. I have compiled a list of the various harnesses and collars, which is a section that you should review as there are many, and some of your clients might be using them, or you would be able to suggest a certain harness/collar. You would be wise to also learn how to put these on a dog and either try them on your own dog, a friend's/ neighbor's dog, or a stuffed animal.

This will give you the opportunity to become accustomed to the various collars and harnesses and how they work. Many years ago, before I started my business, I attended a dog training class with my Labrador retriever. Believe it or not, he was a quick learner and a very low-key Lab, a pleasure to walk. My trainer showed me a little technique, and at the time I didn't know why because my boy was well behaved. But he said that with this technique I could control the largest and strongest dog. This technique is called high collar, and what you do is to place the collar as high on the dog's neck as possible. The lower portion should sit directly under the dog's jaw, while the upper portion of the collar should sit directly behind the dog's ears. I have used this technique to control the strongest pit bulls and Rottweiler's, and honestly it only takes a few times before they get it and the dog starts to pay attention to my basic commands.

To get an ill-behaved barker to be quiet, you can also use the tug on the leash (a quick pop of the leash) with a "Shhh, shhh." This works quite well. Another method is getting the dog's attention with a treat and by repeating the dog's name and saying *cookie*, *treat*, or some word of your choice. But whatever words you choose, remember to use this word every time you're trying to get the attention of your dog because repetition is the key. While doing this, wave the treat, and when the dog turns to look at you, give him a piece of the treat if he listens to your command. I will withhold any treat until they pay attention to my commands. Repeat this as many times as necessary, but it usually doesn't take much time before the dog will get the idea that by turning to look at you means getting a treat. This has totally distracted him from whatever unacceptable behavior he was doing.

I seem to get my fair share of aggressive dogs, not aggressive to people but other animals or dogs. When a dog gets into an aggressive mode, this might be one of the most difficult situations to deal with. So I like to block any views of what might arouse the dog. If we see a cat, squirrel, or dog, I try to either get behind a car, garbage can, tree, or anything to block their view. They still smell the other animal, but if they don't see them, this lessens their aggression. This could be used in conjunction with a treat as a reward, but I have found this is not always necessary, and the dog in your care should listen to you if you have treats or not.

When confronted by a non-walker (a dog that refuses to walk), treats will work if the dog is food-motivated. I have a beautiful white German shepherd that gives me a hard time on our walks. He happens to be the largest German shepherd I've ever had the pleasure of meeting. When Snowy doesn't want to walk, we don't move. So what I have to do is throw treats in front of him just to get him to walk. This does work and takes a little longer than your average dog, but we get the job done.

Another tactic you can use is by giving gentle tugs (a quick pop of the leash) to get them to move along with you. At the same time offer the dog a piece of treat and use a calm, happy voice. This, however, will not work with strong-willed breeds as they sometimes become resistant. If the dog continues to plant themselves firmly, say nothing and offer no treat. Try this a few times to get the dog moving. Patience is needed with these personality types. You might think that a dog that won't walk could not pose a problem, but what if they decide to do this while crossing a busy street? Yikes!

Many years ago I walked a Saint Bernard who would just decide to plop down, and treats worked to a point. But she was smart and would get up to get the treat then plop down again. I learned not to take her for very long walks and to take plenty of treats with me. The tone of your voice is a very important part of getting your dog to recognize good and bad behavior. Following any of the quick training methods along with your tone will help keep you in control of your dog. The first tone imitates the sound or tone a mother dog makes, which is a high-pitch whimper. Using a happy, high-pitch voice will make the dog happy to please you. The second tone is more like a "Grrrr," making your voice sound like a growl, which in dog language means stop. Early on in my career I was once told by a trainer that dogs will listen to a man more than a woman, and I can see his reasoning. The meaning of this is that men have deeper voices than a women and have more force in the tone. I have found that just using a "Grrrr" sound and meaning what you're saying to the dog works wonders for a woman. These tones are just basic dog language. Don't be weak or wishy-washy when giving your dog a command as they will sense this.

Consistency in your commands is essential in order to get your dog to understand what is expected on walks. If you are not consistent, the dog you are walking will become confused. Using the same words for basic commands along with your speech and leadership for both good and bad behavior will make walking any dog a pleasurable experience. You must remember that it will only be a few seconds after bad behavior where any type of correction will be associated with the behavior, so in order to get your point across, you have to act immediately. I also let them know how disappointed I am with them, and we all know how dogs want to please not only their owners but their favorite people, dog walkers!

Body language is very important when working with dogs. Humans rely on speech to communicate, but dogs use body language as opposed to speech. How you present yourself and the way you reach for your dog will influence how your dog interprets your intentions. And just like people, dogs vary in personalities, and each dog will require a different message. Some dogs will only respect you if you are the leader, so you must make yourself appear taller. While other dogs will need a friendly approach and need a more relaxed approach (bent and rounded shoulders) coming from the side rather than head-on to encourage a timid or nervous dog. You must be gentle and nonthreatening with a soft tone to your voice. Every assignment is unique, and the more experience you acquire, the easier it will become to determine what body language will work for the dog you are caring for.

You must also be on your toes when on your walks as things can develop very quickly. Say you turn around for a second to look at something and at the same time your dog sees a squirrel and decides to chase it. By not seeing this coming, you will be caught off guard and pulled down. I have heard of a grown man getting pulled down by a 100 lb. dog under the same circumstances. I used to walk a 110 lb. Rottweiler named Bruno, who caught me off guard while I was bending down, picking up his business. He was a very sweet dog but was sometimes people-aggressive; he saw a young woman walking down the street and took me down along the grass, off the curb, and onto the street. The whole time I was yelling his name, and finally he heard me, turned around, and came up nose to nose with me, as if to say, "What are you doing down there?" He did not have a clue as to what he had just done.

There are so many things that can happen on your walk, and with these simple training techniques along with the tone of your voice will help keep you safe on your walk. Another issue I'd like to address is the wearing of headphones (listening to an iPod) while walking a dog. I would love to walk down the street listening to music, but I want to be aware of any jingling collars coming towards us or any unusual noises. You should also be aware of cars that might be honking at you while crossing the street. You won't be able to do this while listening to music. Instead, listen to nature's music, the gentle breeze blowing through the trees, birds singing on a beautiful day, or even the falling rain and thunder. That's what I really enjoy about walking dogs—getting back to nature.

Talking on your cell phone while on a walk is a definite no-no with me because this will distract you. If I was walking dogs, talking on my phone, and we got ambushed by a loose dog, I wouldn't have seen this coming. In all the years of walking dogs, I have been involved in six dog fights while walking dogs. This situation is very stressful, and if you're not prepared for the attack, you are caught totally off guard and could even get knocked down by the commotion. That would not be to your advantage. Now you're on the ground, rolling around in the middle of a dog fight—not good. While we are working, our full concentration should be on our pets. Please wait to call someone back. After all, that's why they invented voice mail.

Safety on the Assignment

Dog Related

I have gone on interviews where the dog was friendly but, on arriving on my first visit, has turned into the Tasmanian Devil. I carry extra umbrellas in my car for the first time I enter a new assignment if I'm feeling a little nervous about the dog. This has helped me several times in getting in or has aided me upon entering. We used to have a dog named Lulu. She was a rescue that was saved from being put down. Normally I wouldn't have taken the assignment, but the client was an old friend from high school, and Lulu was sometimes good to me. I had three other sitters refuse to go back to her. As she got older she became very grouchy. She was food-aggressive, and even if there was one kibble left in her bowl, I was in for a hard time. I had asked my client several times to take up her food before she went to work, but do they listen? I always used the umbrella by putting it through a small opening of the door. If she went after it, I would do it a few more times before she stopped. Once she stopped, I would slowly slide in the house. Then there was putting on her leash. She would want to go for her walk but would give a strange sideway stare, and you would have to be quick in getting the leash on. There were many times I know she would have loved to have bitten me but didn't. She did manage, however, to bite my daughter two times. Learn to read your pet's signals and body language.

Other times, by using an opened umbrella, you can use this for keeping distance with a dog whose trust you have yet to win over. If a dog charges you when entering a home, stand your ground and give a firm growl type of no as this has worked for me in the past. They will then retreat to watch you, maybe growl from a distance. I talk to them, constantly asking if they want to go out or go for a walk or if they are hungry, whatever makes those ears pop up—a definite sign you are winning them over. Never look directly at the dog or stare. Turn and look away.

Once you've gained their trust, they turn out to be very nice dogs. Your body language will also play a big part in how the dog views your presence and intentions when entertaining the home. Eye contact should be minimal, and if you blink your eyes, this is a calming signal to dogs. Yawning is also another calming signal. Yawn and look away; both have worked well for me in the past. Take your time on the assignment; never walk quickly through the home until you have established your intentions to the dog. Some of the dogs will let you in the home but be leery of letting you hook them up to their leash.

I like to use a British slip lead made by Mendota. They are very well made and last for years. These leashes make it easy to slip over the dog's head without having to get too close. Once the dog realizes you are here for good things, like going for a walk, they should be happier to see you by the next visit. I never just walk into the home on the first visit. What I do is open the door just a bit and start talking to the dog. This gives them time to settle down. I then get myself through the door and stand close to the door, talking to the dog the whole time. Never go over to a dog that is hiding under a chair or behind a couch. Give them time to come to you. Fear is usually the number one reason a dog will bite. Always close the inside door after entering a home, never leaving to chance that the storm door is secure enough to keep your dog from getting out. After I'm in the house for a few minutes, I slowly make my way into the kitchen and start cleaning dog dishes and get their dinner ready. I will then feed them. This helps with the bonding between you and the dog. Never go near the dog while they are eating until you're sure of the beast you're dealing with, as some dogs could be food-aggressive.

On the other end of the spectrum, you will have a dog that runs to you and the door. Make sure that when going in you don't make it easy for the dog to slip by you and escape. What I do is put one leg in and then slide my body through, giving virtually no room for the dog to escape. This is easier to do with larger dogs as the small ones are sometimes quicker. Something to ask on your interview is, are they escape artists? This is something that the clients might forget to tell you, and you wouldn't want to find out the hard way.

Cat Related

Cats can be just as territorial as dogs. Most times they will hide until they feel it's safe to come out. But I have had to deal with some pretty aggressive cats, and they have extra weapons that dogs do not carry: those sharp claws. I had a month-long sit for one of these cats that wanted me out of the house every time I came in. This was actually the assignment in which I found out how helpful an umbrella was. The first few visits I used my clipboard, pillows, whatever I could use to keep myself safe from being attacked. By the third visit I noticed they had an umbrella outside their door, and I used it, and it worked like a charm. I would then have to corral the cat into a bedroom and close the door to perform litter-box cleaning and feeding. Once done, I would let him out and slowly back up with my opened umbrella. I thought that after a week he would accept me, but I spent a whole month trying to make friends with this not-so-social cat. I did finish up the assignment and was delighted when the job was over. Cats are interesting to care for, but not easy by any means. If you've ever witnessed a cat fight, you will notice a certain body posture and a definite vocal warning to their competitor. And most books on the market are geared towards the dog's behavior while the cats are often neglected; I believe this is the case because they are so hard to figure out.

But just like dogs, cats will "talk" in their own language. A happy meow is short and tends to go from high to low meow. An angry meow tends to start low and escalate to a high-type meow, almost sounding like a scream. There are also many variations of the meow from the soft meow to the more demanding meow. The growl, which is just as dogs do, warn that they have had enough and you better go away. Or you're really in trouble if the cats starts to yowl accompanied by a glaring stare at you, which could mean you're about to be attacked. We all know that a purr means contentment, and a very loud purr means the cat wants attention or contact. Also keep in mind that purring in an older or sick cat is done to comfort itself when it is in pain or ill.

All this talk could be just that, and until you become familiar with the cat in your care, it's best to give them some space. Body posture in cats is also the way they communicate. We've all enjoyed watching kittens play, how they puff themselves up and walk or hop sideways. These are all ways cats will try to make themselves look bigger. Puffing their fur makes them appear bigger than they actually are, and when they swagger or hop sideways, this is a sign of a dominant cat. It's like a game of cards—bluffing sometimes works. A cat's tail is also a flag on how his emotions are going. An upright tail is a sign of a friendly, content cat. A quivering tail is a sign that that cat is very pleased to see you. If the cat's tail is upright but has a little hook at the end, this means he is friendly but unsure of your presence or the surroundings. If his tail is thrashing about, it could mean a few things. He could just be excited, irritable, or angry. If his tail is between his legs, this means he is being submissive to you. His tail is all puffed out means he is angry, and you'd better go get your umbrella! Some calming signals that work well with dogs will also work with cats. Sometimes yawning, looking away, and blinking at a shy cat will help to calm his fears. I have tried this with a couple of aggressive cats and have not had any success with trying to calm them down but have had success with shy or timid cats.

Cats are very emotional creatures, despite what some people might think, and if you watch cats' facial expressions, you can see the different moods they can have. The more you care for cats and just observe their behavior, you will notice that they are more complex than one could ever imagine. They experience fear, anger, happiness, sadness, and the desire for that female in heat or the bird out the window.

Next time you have some food that has spoiled in the refrigerator, let your cat have a smell and watch the look of disgust that will come across his face. They rely on their keen sense of smell and taste to avoid eating bad food. I told you they were interesting creatures. Try your hardest not to get bitten by a cat as a cat bite can get infected very quickly. When this happens, the bite should be cleaned and disinfected thoroughly. Keep up with your tetanus shots, and if you do get bitten, don't hesitate to see your doctor because you will need antibiotics for the infection that will surely set in.

Another disease to worry about when caring for cats and you get bitten is CSD (cat scratch disease.) It is caused by Bartonella henselae infection and is spread by coming into contact with an infected cat's saliva. Almost half the cat population carries Bartonella henselae at some point in their lives. Two to three weeks after getting bitten, swelling or a blistering occurs near the scratch or bite and could leak fluid. Other symptoms include weakness, fever, headache, and a general discomfort. I believe they have a special test that your doctor can perform to see if this is the case.

One of my son's friends who lived in the neighborhood had contracted this when he was about twelve years old. His mother had a dozen cats at the time, and these were both inside and outside cats. The doctor had said that children and older people or people with immune problems are more susceptible to this disease.

If you're a woman and become pregnant while pet sitting, you must be aware of another disease called Toxoplasmosis. This is a disease that can be contracted from cat feces while cleaning litter boxes. Of course, this can also be gotten from gardening if outside cats happen to use your garden for their bathroom. You might unconsciously touch your mouth after cleaning a litter box. A cat that has caught a bird or rodent could potentially be carrying the disease. If you plan on continuing to care for cats while you're pregnant, protect yourself by wearing disposable gloves and make sure you wash your hands thoroughly after taking off the gloves. You might want to opt for having someone else taking over while you're pregnant to play it safe.

Another thing I would like to mention is that some of the cats in your care can get overstimulated from grooming or from being touched too much. When this happens, they might turn and bite. Try to do short petting or grooming sessions; this will be better for the kitty. I sometimes find them wanting more without getting them overstimulated. I would also like to add that you should take caution with clients' homes that feel safe in leaving a second floor window open with just the screen for the cat to look out of. Being we are not in the home for most of the day and we all know how cats can become rambunctious at times, I feel very uneasy about these scenarios and will close the window just enough to prevent the cat from hitting the screen too hard and possibly falling out. I do this despite what the client requests, as I would be devastated if this ever happened on my shift.

Whenever I first start a cat sitting assignment, I will look around for potentially dangerous situations. If your client has blinds, please make sure to put the cords up out of the reach of the cat. This can be done by winding up the cord and placing it on the upper part of the blind. Kitties sometimes like to play with the cord, and being no one will be in the home for a good part of the day, we don't want any accidents to happen. If by some freakish accident the cord gets caught around the cat's neck and tangles, the cat could choke to death.

Be alert to cats that might slip into the refrigerator as well. One of my own cats has done this several times, and it doesn't matter how much food I pile into the fridge. He always manages to jump in to investigate, usually while I'm busy cooking and going in and out of the fridge. If you go into a client's pantry, closet, or garage, always check to see if a cat has managed to slip by and get in. You could close the door and not see the cat going in while turning around, close the door, and the cat is then locked in. This same thing can happen when the client is getting ready to leave for vacation, so if you can't find a cat, check all cabinets, closets, rooms, and the like. Cats are curious by nature and never seem to learn, even after they have gotten themselves stuck somewhere they shouldn't be. Life is just one big adventure for cats.

One last concern—if your client has a collar on their cat, check to see if it is a breakaway collar or elastic or stretch cat collar. If they get caught on something while jumping or running, they can choke if it's a regular collar. If that's the case, I will take the collar off the cat altogether and leave a note for the client as to why I have done so. If my client insists the collar be left on, I will loosen it considerably so in case they get caught on something, the cat should be able to pull its head out. Some plants can be toxic to cats as well, so it would be wise to educate yourself as to what plants can harm the cat and dogs as well. In turn you will be able to educate your clients if they have some in their home. Anything that could be a potential danger should be removed, and a note to the client should be left. If you've voiced your concern and the client pays no heed, what could I tell you, but at least no problems will come into play while on your assignment.

CHAPTER 2

Pet Sitting Scenarios

This section is what I felt warranted the writing of this book. It has taken me roughly three years to put together all the problems and situations a pet sitter might come in contact with. I wanted to put together a book that would help guide the new pet sitter (even the seasoned pet sitter) and make them realize that when things go wrong, and they will, they are not the first to experience the stress and heartbreak that can come with the territory. One must remember these scenarios are bound to come up, and my experience will hopefully help you. But every situation and every pet is unique. Finding a way to work through difficult situations is not always easy, and it is quite possible to get frustrated when confronted with these scenarios. I have found myself sometimes trying a few different ways of dealing with difficult pets. Sometimes it is trial and error to find a solution to a problem. And honestly I really don't think there is a right way of doing things. What will work for one pet doesn't necessarily mean this will work on another. I have always compared pets to children; they will try to get over on you if you let them. They will test you to see how far they can go. A pet sitter must be a strong leader if we are to get the pets in our care to cooperate. Now I am not saying you must be forceful in order to get them with the program but rather to be patient with even the most stubborn of pets.

Administering Medications

If you've ever owned any pets in your lifetime, you will have a pretty good idea on how to administer medications to an animal. The problem, however, lies in the pet you're trying to medicate, and just like humans, some of us are horrible patients. Especially if the pet is not feeling well, they can be grumpy and uncooperative. Also keep in mind that, unless you've know these pets for a while, you might have a tough time ahead trying to medicate some of the pets in your care. Before taking on any of these assignments, remember to get as much information from the owner as possible.

I have found that dogs are easier to "fool" than cats. Unless the pill packaging states not to, in most cases you can crush a pill into a powder form or pour out the content of a capsule and mix with a tablespoon of wet food for dogs and a little less than a teaspoon for cats. By giving them a tiny amount of food with the medicine in it, you can ensure that they will eat it all. You can crush a pill in a small plastic baggie with the back of a spoon if you don't have a pill crusher on hand. Pill crushers can be found in your local pharmacy or online and don't cost much.

I usually give them their medicine before I feed them, making sure they eat all the food with the medicine in it, and then I ask them if they want more. Keep in mind this will not work with dry pet food. Some medicine is bitter tasting, and pets might pick up on this, especially cats. If you're working in a multicat household, you will have to confine or watch the cat, making sure the cat eats all the food with the medicine in it. I have also used cream cheese, plain yogurt, butter, baby food, tuna, and pill pockets for tricking cats into taking medicine. Lately many of my clients have switched to liquid medications to give orally or a cream that is applied to the ear for cats; this is much easier to administer. A pill popper or pill gun (also known as animal pill dispenser or medicine dispenser) is a plastic tube with a soft rubber end, where you put the pill then push the plunger on the back of the pet's tongue, releasing the pill, and close the pet's mouth, stroking the neck and chin till they swallow. These pill guns make it easier than fumbling around with a pill on your fingers and can be found at Fosters & Smith, Petco, or your vet usually carries them. For cats I usually coat with a little butter for taste, and this also makes it easier going down.

For medicating cats you can use a large towel and wrap the cat with only its head sticking out, preventing the cat from scratching and running away. I have had some that wouldn't stand for this at all. If a cat is totally uncooperative, trying to medicate may just stress the cat out and cause additional problems, so an alternative method is required. Once this is done, you can pry the cat's mouth open and push the pill to the back of the mouth and hold their mouth closed, stroking their neck to make them swallow. Another trick to make them swallow for both cats and dogs is to blow air into their nose. This works like a charm. When medicating some cats you might have to forego this technique altogether because some get so stressed out, and you may end up doing more harm than good. And this is where tricking the cat will work best.

Another way of medicating cats is to kneel behind the cat and hold them by the scruff of the neck (like the mama cat would do when they were kittens). This is sometimes hard to do because you will then have only one hand free for medicating, using one hand for holding the pill and prying the cat's mouth open, but it is possible. You would then tilt the cat's head upward and, using your fingers, open the cat's mouth and toss the pill to the back of the tongue, close their mouth, and rub their neck or blow air in their nose. Give extra praise and treats to the cat so that you will build a positive experience when medicating the cat. I have also been known to take the cat by surprise, getting all their meds ready and heading straight to the victim. If they're half-asleep on a couch, windowsill, or bed, I will grab them before they know what has happened. To tell you the truth, this actually works the best. By not making a big issue about the whole process and getting it over with right away, all is forgotten in a matter of minutes.

Now you might have to medicate a cat that usually hides. You will have to make a judgment call on an assignment like this. I have taken on some with really difficult cats, but the stress level involved for both the pet sitter and cat is not a good scenario. If the cat can be left in a room where no other pets will be, you could add the medicine to the food and go in before you leave to make sure that they have eaten it. Pill pockets work well in a situation like this, and what I usually do is leave the pill pocket with the pill inside close to the cat and go about all my chores, checking before I leave to make sure the cat has eaten the pill pocket. This is done only if no other pets have access to the meds. Feeding is done after the cat has eaten its medication to make sure they won't fill up on their food. Most times I will suggest to the client that they board the cat at the vet for the duration of their vacation. When at the vet, they are confined to their cage and have extra help to get the medication into the cat. Sometimes boarding a fearful or shy cat can be very stressful for the cat, so this is a very tricky scenario.

When medicating dogs the majority of them are very easy to care for. Most will gobble up their medicine if hidden in some type of treat. Some might even be agreeable to you just opening their mouth and tossing the pill in the back of their throat. Using the same technique as with the cats holding their mouth closed, either rubbing their throat or blowing air into their nose will get them to swallow the pill. A lot of my clients will use the pill pockets and will just stuff the pill inside the treat, and they will gladly eat their medicine. Liquid medicine is just as easy, using a needleless syringe from the corner of the mouth and squirting it in the cheek they will swallow. Now some dogs can be pretty slick and eat the treat and spit out the pill. If you have a smart dog that does this, you can squirt a little water in the side of the dog's mouth with a needleless syringe while still holding their mouth shut. This will make them swallow and wash the pill down. And as always, give lots of praise and extra treats to make medicating a positive experience.

Another trick is to have a couple of treats (without meds in them) and give to the dog and along the line sneak in the one with the medication in it. Make it a game for the dog. They love it. If the dog is uncooperative, you can crush their pill or open the capsule and add a small amount of food. I have used peanut butter, cottage cheese, butter, liverwurst (forms well around pill and is extra smelly to entice the dog), cheese, cream cheese, baby food, plain yogurt, pill pockets, and hot dogs. I prefer to use something that binds well to the pill so they just eat it without knowing what's inside. I have had to make do with something the client has in their refrigerator and improvise when nothing else is available.

I also will give insulin injections but only if the pet is cooperative and stable, meaning they have been on insulin for some time. And I prefer to offer this service to existing clients because I am already familiar with the pet and the pet is comfortable with me. I will still take on new clients whose pet needs injections, and I can usually tell at the interview if the pet will be receptive to me and take these assignments on a case-by-case basis. I actually stayed away from giving injections for years but had no choice when of my longtime client's cat developed diabetes. The client showed me how to do this, and because the cat was already familiar with me, it turned out to be a positive experience, so I added this to my services.

If you're thinking of adding injections to your services, always feed the pet first before giving the injection. I have noticed that most pets are used to their routine regarding their injections and know that it is necessary. But remember to go over instructions with your client and keep up to date on any changes that might come up. Diabetic animals will sometimes have their medication increased or decreased until they are stabilized. Have the client give you a trial run to go over the how-to part of administering the injection to make sure that you are comfortable. I do charge extra for medicating, and injections are priced higher because of the risks involved, one being insulin shock, while pilling is a few dollars cheaper. These fees are added onto the price for the visit, so these assignments are very lucrative for me.

The one thing I do not offer is subcutaneous injection, and although I have had clients wanting to teach me, I declined. With subcutaneous injections, you will have to sit with the cat for some time, and I'm just not comfortable sitting with a cat that has a needle in them. So any of my clients needing this service will either have a vet tech come in or board their cat. You will also have other types of medications that will at times need to be applied to the eye. Eye medications are usually an ointment or drop and can be applied the same as oral medications, wrapping the cat in a towel. With both the larger and smaller dogs (most cat clients as well), I prefer to kneel and get them between my knees with their back in front of me because I am comfortable doing it this way. Drops are to be administered right in the eye, so you must use one hand to pull the lower lid down and add the proper amount of drops required. The same goes with an ointment; pull the lower lid down and squeeze a small amount of ointment into the eye. When the pet blinks, it will go over the entire eye.

Another medication that you might need to administer is for the ear. Follow the same procedure for wrapping a cat in a towel. With both the larger and smaller dogs, I like to kneel with the dog's back facing me. You will then lift the ear. If it's a floppy-eared dog, place the required medication in the middle of the ear opening. You will then need to rub the base of the ear to draw the medication down into the deeper parts of the ear. Whether it's a cat or a dog, they're usually not too happy with medicating the ear, especially if they have an ear infection—even more reason that you will need to get the meds in. Some might even become aggressive because of the pain involved if an ear infection is severe. Stick to what you feel comfortable with; your clients should understand and make other arrangements if you're not comfortable with this scenario.

I recently had a long-term cat client that was extremely hard to medicate and requested that they board the cat. They insisted that the cat stay in the home as the last time they boarded a cat of this personality type, the stress from being boarded killed the cat. This is a tough scenario to deal with because you are faced with a "damned if you do and damned if you don't" situation. So I explained to the client I couldn't be held liable if the cat didn't receive required medication, and their reply was "Do your best."

Since this point on, especially with new clients, I have added to my policy page that a cat that is difficult to medicate will be taken to the vet regardless of what the client requests. I would also like to point out that if you are sharing an assignment with either another sitter (as I sometimes do a split shift with my daughter or son), family member, or friend, make sure who is to be the primary caregiver assigned to medicating the pet.

If you have any other type of pet in your care that needs medicating, such as rabbits, reptiles, or fishes, you will have to live and learn from your client; have them show you and write down specific instructions for you. In addition, always verify with your client before they head out of town if there have been any changes in medications, dosages, and such. I can't tell you how many times I have asked this question and the client will say, "Oh, I almost forgot to tell you, Scruff's dosage has been changed. He now takes two pills once in the morning and one pill at night."

Aggressive Behavior

There may be many reasons why a pet can become aggressive. And I have been surprised at times because sometimes the nicest pet can turn aggressive for no apparent reason. But we must remember that we are dealing with animals, and some of this aggression goes way back to their natural instincts. One of the types of aggression that can be easily recognized is territorial, and anyone coming into their space, be it their yard or home, can trigger this aggression.

Usually, once the dog becomes familiar with the person, they will be less threatening. I cared for an Akita, and every time his owners went away, they would call about a month or two before they left to have the dog get used to me coming in and hooking him to the leash to go for a walk. I was always cautious with him, and he actually would do a happy dance when I came in after some time. So these types of aggressive behavior can be worked through.

Pain induced aggression is exactly what its name implies. If the owners say that their pet has suddenly had a change in personality and started to become aggressive, this could be from an illness that is causing pain that has not yet been diagnosed. The pet associates the person closest to them with the pain and may lash out in aggression. It could be arthritis, thyroid disease, or something as simple as a toothache. What I usually do is advise the owner to make an appointment with their vet to see if there is something more than just aggression.

Now there's another type of aggression that I usually refer to as the Jekyll and Hyde personality, but the proper name is known as idiopathic aggression. With this aggression there is no known cause, and it can occur at a moment's notice. Maternal aggression can occur with a normally docile female dog that has given or is about to give birth. If you ever have an assignment that would involve a mother dog and her pups, be respectful of her space and caring for the litter.

Prey-driven aggression will come out when a car drives by or a squirrel scurries across the grass. It is a natural instinct to chase a moving object in most breeds, but this can become dangerous if they become so agitated and try to attack the moving object. Misdirected aggression can occur when the adrenaline gets pumping due to a dog fight. If you intervene, you can get bitten because the dogs are so involved in their fight that they may turn and bite you.

Food-guarding aggression usually starts when the dog is young and, if not corrected for this bad behavior, can worsen as the dog matures. Anytime the dog has a treat, food, even human food, will arouse this aggression. I have had a few of these aggression types, and I'll tell you, how do you feed a dog that's possessive of his food?

Well, it is saved for the last chore and put down as I am leaving. I hope and pray that before I come back the dish is empty because sometimes one little morsel of food can trigger this aggression again.

Punishment-induced aggression develops when owners physically punished the dog in the past, most times severely. Most of the dogs I've cared for with this type of aggression have been rescued, and their past is not known. There comes a day when the dog will not tolerate this and lash out. Even if the dog sees a hand moving too fast he will see this as a threat and may try to bite. This aggression can be eliminated through a trainer that is familiar with working with this type of aggression and lots of TLC.

Dominance aggression is seen in dogs that think they are in charge. When things aren't going their way, they start to show signs of aggression. I have a client who has a sweet but bossy golden retriever that shows this very aggression with his family. He also tries to pull this when I come in, but I will have no part in his behavior. When he starts to show aggression because I've taken something he owns or thinks he owns, I simply ignore him, which doesn't get the normal reaction he gets from his family members. So I believe a big part of dominance aggression comes about when they are allowed to get away with it, and I find it can be easily corrected.

Interdog aggression is a power struggle that occurs in households with multiple dogs. Fights will break out over toys, treats, or sleeping spaces, and it can happen quite often in multi-pet households.

Fear aggression is the number one reason a dog that you are caring for will bite. They will shake and cower in fear and, if they feel cornered or threatened, will lash out with aggression. That is why you should always wait until the dog is receptive to your advances before trying to hook them up on a leash or going to pet them. So with all these many different types of aggression, I have sometimes had dogs with multiple aggression issues. It is difficult dealing with aggression while on an assignment, and it is not always noticeable on the consult. So if we are already involved in an assignment and the aggression doesn't cause any real threat to the pet sitter, it is quite possible to work through this scenario. But be prepared and know that all dogs are not cute little dogs. Learning about dog behavior will be of great help to you when you are on your assignments.

Arranging Multiple Assignments Requiring Medication

As of late I have gotten so many new clients with pets that need to be medicated, older pets, mostly cats, as I decided some years ago to gradually switch over. These newer clients brought with them challenging scenarios, and although I have given many pets medication throughout the years, never have I had so many. So medicating isn't so much the problem as figuring out my schedule to keep them within their time frames for medication. Thyroid medications and insulin can be toxic if given at intervals that are to close in time. So what I usually do is to question the client as to what time they have been giving medication and try to keep it in that period. I said try because schedules get disrupted all the time. In a way it's the same as a regular assignment, but you must remember that when giving medication, it's better to be late giving the pet their medication than early.

Take for example this past week, one very sick cat with liver failure, two diabetic cats, and two cats requiring thyroid medicine; all needing medications at certain times. From the beginning I put the cat with liver failure at the end of my schedule. One reason being this job required extra time, second being if anything were to go wrong, we had to make a visit to the vet or, worse, he would pass. I would then have the extra time needed without stressing about my other assignments. One of the cats requiring thyroid medication was put on a larger dosage before the client left, and I had a three-way phone conversation with the vet and client to discuss dosage, time frame, and the like. The client also wanted to make sure that I was comfortable with this and I agreed. So I set my schedule and made sure that I would adhere to the times I had set.

These assignments can be rather complicated when it comes to scheduling. I had mentioned earlier in administrating medications that dogs can be fooled easier than cats. And I can tell you that some of these cats were not good patients at all; they would see me reach for the medication and take off. When you have a schedule that includes medicating pets, especially cats, always factor this in when putting your schedule together, always scheduling for the unexpected.

Benefits of Power Naps

When you first start out in your pet sitting business, more than likely you have well thought out your plans. But as you start to pick up more clients with no time off, you will find that somewhere during the course of the day your body will start to crave sleep. I have found that with my very hectic schedule I need a power nap, and it always seems to be around the same time each day. I call them power naps because even if I only get a fifteen-minute nap, I feel better and have more energy and power to finish up my day. I will either take a quick nap in my own home or while caring for a cat after I've done all my chores. I place myself on the couch with a cat in my lap or on my chest, very peaceful for both myself and the cat. Rarely can these power naps be taken when caring for dogs with walking, feeding, and, most times, some type of mess to clean up.

With early morning stops and going from dawn until late at night, I have learned that these naps are very beneficial to my health, giving me the strength to handle whatever comes my way. If you walk a lot of dogs weekly in the hot sun, you'll need a power nap.

Walking dogs in the winter, trudging through all the snow, cleaning off your car, and shoveling multiple houses to make it possible to get into the home, you will definitely need a power nap. I have found the extreme cold and heat really wears me out. Driving anywhere from eight to eleven hours a day is very tiring as well, so don't be afraid to take full advantage of these power naps. You will feel much better no matter the length of the nap.

Boarding Pets in Your Home

When considering boarding in your home, you should first check with your local state regulations and laws. Every region differs, and what might be legal in some states may not be legal in others. I had checked with my local state laws and found that in order to board in my home, I first would have to be properly zoned, which I was not, so following through with getting a kennel license wasn't even a consideration. But in my area there are many pet sitters doing so, and in my opinion, they are taking a big chance because New York has some of the strictest laws pertaining to animal boarding and care. Heavy fines are involved if you are found out, and it's not worth the penalty you will be forced to pay. Also, kennels are full of abandoned animals that their owners never came back for. So this would be another reason to think this through, or you might end up with additional pets. Please check your local state laws before diving into boarding in your home, a concept that many pet owners would prefer as you would not be entering their homes.

Many years ago I spoke with a woman on the phone who had decided to do this and found out she was not able to get back into her own home. The dog she had taken in had decided that he was going to take over. She was looking for advice, and all I could give her was to see if she could corral the dog into the basement until the owners were contacted to make other arrangements. Animals are unpredictable, and there are reasons that certain laws were designed to protect humans and animals alike. Another concern would be health issues if you do not require documentation of health records from your clients; kennel cough is tough to get rid of. It is highly contagious for there has been cases on the island were vets have actually called the kennels and told them they must close their facility for a few weeks to disinfect and get it under control. The vet had done this because of all the dogs that were coming in with kennel cough who were recently boarded in that particular kennel. So aside from legal regulations, there are also health and safety concerns that should be kept in mind before you decide to board in your own home.

In addition, if you have followed through with your region's laws and plan on boarding in your home, I would suggest having your client show proof that their pet is current on their vaccinations and licenses. If you have pets of your own, you would have to also have to make sure all will get along. Be prepared for dogs that will want to mark your home, and destructive behavior is something else to consider. Most clients will want to be ensured that their pet will not be left alone for a good part of the day. If you are also going to do pet sitting assignments while boarding in your home, this might be difficult to juggle. The pet that is left in your care should not be left outdoors unattended, even with a secure yard. Some dogs are great escape artists, and a lost dog could send you into crisis mode. A few years ago I picked up a new client who had left her dog at someone's home for pet care. Her dog is an active small mixed breed, and he managed to escape and was lost for three weeks. I would have hated to be this pet sitter trying to explain what happened to her client's dog. So I have been caring for him ever since he was returned home, and it was a happy ending, to say the least. If you are boarding in your home, this will make your life a little easier as far as traveling to clients' homes, but problems can still creep in.

Burnout: How to Survive

I can honestly say that I have felt the effects of burnout many times during the years I have been in business. I have worked through these times by taking multiple power naps, begging my daughter to take over for a while or just praying for a slow week. To get a break from the hectic routine isn't always easy, especially if you're a sole proprietor. I sometimes don't know my own limits and have just recently taken a look back on how much I've worked in the past, and I don't know how I did it. When I took my daughter into the business, things became a little easier, but I still did the majority of work.

From my experience, dogs can lead you down the road to burnout fairly quickly. In and out of the car, up and down stairs, being dragged down the street by some very enthusiastic dogs can take its toll. During busy times, besides dog walking and pet sitting, we must also find time to do our bookkeeping, accounting, marketing, and selling our businesses. We must dedicate unreasonable amounts of time to our business, but there are ways to take the pressure off ourselves. Someone once said to me to do what you do best and find some help for the other aspects of the business, which makes a lot of sense when you come to think about it. If you find yourself dreading a certain aspect of the business, putting things off, and for me it's the billing and record-keeping aspect that I sometimes put off longer than I should, you might consider hiring outside help. This is a part of the business that my mother had helped with until her health failed, so I have been thinking of delegating this task to a professional. Others might have difficulty in finding time to fit office work into their schedules; entering client information into the computer is time-consuming. Maybe you know someone who would be willing to help out in the office in exchange for dog walking service. Freeing up your time by having the extra help for office duties should give you the opportunity to take some needed time off for just spending free time with family and friends.

By handing some of these extra tasks over to someone, you are going to reduce your stress level, which I believe is a part of feeling the effects of burnout. Wearing all the hats is harder than it looks and can be overwhelming at times. When you free up your time to do what you do best, it allows you to expand and grow your business and in turn will increase your revenue. Even if you have to pay for some of this help, you will find that, instead of feeling burnt-out, you will begin to enjoy your business again.

As soon as my kids were old enough, I got them involved in the business, which lowered my stress level and, in turn, my burn-out. Another option would be to hire people who are happy to be around animals and would gladly trade their time for some experience. Helping these people will build a strong bond, and if they decide to become independent contractor or employee in the future, you would have that extra help, if you so desire. These interns or assistants could also help with the phones, office filing, and answering e-mails for free, but at the same time they are gaining knowledge and experience—a fair trade, in my opinion.

By clearing your plate of monotonous tasks, you can spend that extra time in areas of your life that need attention. I would also like to mention the benefits of scheduling a week off every so often. This is something I have only recently learned to do no matter how much I need to work; I've learned it's just as important to take that time off. Burnout is not only physical but mental and emotional as well, caused by prolonged stress and is definitely possible when caring for animals. Our clients may sometimes seem like they do not appreciate us. Find clients that do. This will help with burnout. If you're feeling overwhelmed and exhausted all the time, you're heading down the road to being burnt-out. Believe me, I have been there more often than I would admit to.

Take the time to care for your physical and mental health. Pet sitters spend so much time caring for others' needs, both our clients' and their pets', we sometimes forget about ourselves. We must give ourselves a raise at least once a year. If you're not being paid enough, you will begin to feel undervalued and overworked. I have often felt the high pressure of getting to an assignment on time either knowing the dog will not wait to go potty or the client was too demanding. To fire these clients will help with easing burnout as this is a factor.

Dog walking is often very monotonous and, after a time, will not be challenging. As I said earlier, dog walking alone will lead to burnout. A cure to this problem is to mix your schedule up—walk a few days and have someone else help out. I will constantly look for ways to change things up by taking a different route to the home or a new route while walking the dogs as it's the small things that change things up. Pet sitting, in my opinion, is a very demanding job; this is why so many pet sitters talk about burnout. We take on so many responsibilities without help, we don't get enough sleep, and we try to be too many things to so many people and their pets.

Of course some personality traits can add to your chances of getting burnt-out quicker than most, one being a high achiever, which, although might contribute to burnout, if you care about your business, I feel it's a needed trait. Being a perfectionist and the need to be in control are also causes of burnout. So try to let go by getting that extra help. Take care of yourself as well as your pets. Take the time off that so many other people do. Your clients will understand your needs if they appreciate you. If we let ourselves get past the breaking point when we get burnt-out, it can take a tremendous amount of time to recover. When you're exhausted and you keep pushing yourself, you will be of no help to anyone including yourself. Slowing down is our only option.

Rearrange your business to help with burnout. This will make you find a new enthusiasm for your love of animals. After all, this is the reason why we've all gotten into this profession to begin with.

Calling Clients After Visits

You might find that some clients request you call or text while visiting their home. I never took this personally, like they didn't trust me, but rather felt that these clients felt more relaxed after hearing all is well. I actually had a daily dog walking assignment for seven years where I spoke to my client Monday through Friday. We became very good friends, and I never felt like she was checking on us. This was my assignment, but my daughter also helped when I wasn't able to go in. She wanted us to call from her home phone, and we did. This is actually a really good idea that I plan on implementing when I expand my business. I always worry, and this will ensure that I will know what time the assignment was done, that all went well, and, by using the client's home phone, that no games can be played. Texting is another request. A quick text saying their babies are fine makes the client secure and less stressed while vacationing. Including a picture of their pet will make the client feel at ease. I have always tried to make the client happy, and if this is all they want, I've never had a problem with this.

Car Accidents and Car Trouble

I have had my fair share of car accidents during the course of my pet sitting career. And when looking back, I wonder how in the world I worked through these situations. Most were minor accidents, but I did have one major accident with a two-and-a-half-month-old car that was totaled. One thing that I always carried on my car insurance was a rental car. This was a must when the car ended up in the auto body shop for a couple of weeks. After all, just because my car was disabled doesn't mean my clients won't need service. So when shopping for car insurance as a pet sitter, make sure you have an adequate number of rental days in case your car needs repairs.

As many of the accidents were minor and the car was still drivable, I'll tell you about the last one I had about four years ago. And I know that you're thinking how bad of a driver this pet sitter must be. I sometimes spend weeks on end driving ten to fifteen hours a day at times, and with the amount of traffic in my region, I wonder how I hadn't had more. My last accident, and I mean my last, was on a winding one-lane road. This is also a main bus route with hills and curves. This night it was drizzling, and as I traveled up the hill, around the bend came a NYC bus. The problem was he was partially in my lane with nowhere for me to go. And I can tell you what words the majority of people that are about to crash their car say, and those words are "Oh shit!"

In a spilt second I had to decide, do I let the bus run through me, or do I swerve and hit the guardrail to avoid being crushed by a bus in my little car? Well, I opted for the second, and although I avoided the bus, I hit the guardrail, and my brand-new car was totaled! I was okay but still have problems with my knees to this day. One is worse than the other, and they mostly bother me when it's damp weather. But I was walking and talking so my guardian angel was there to protect me. I still had more stops and called my daughter to come finish up the rounds while I waited for the tow truck. Luckily, I have Allstate Insurance, and in New York State they have a policy that if you total your car before the third month, they replace it. If this had happened two weeks later, I would have been out of luck. So until all the insurance issues were settled and I was issued a check for a new car, I was driving around in a rental.

Having a backup sitter for emergencies is essential whether you have a car accident or have a car become disabled. Your business won't stop because of these little problems that can creep in. I have also made a card up on my computer that states I'm a pet sitter and who to contact in case I was ever incapacitated and couldn't speak. I would also suggest having an excellent insurance policy for those times when life throws you those little curves and you crash your car. Having your brakes and tires checked regularly will help in bad weather but won't prevent another car from running a stop sign or neglecting to stop when you do, as both have happened to me as well.

Maintenance on your vehicle is very important in keeping your business running smoothly. I always get new tires before the winter months set in. Have regular tune-ups, change your windshield wipers from time to time, and keep up on oil changes to make sure your car is ready and won't break down while you're out on your assignments.

Catching Fear-Aggressive Cats

Catching a fear-aggressive cat on an assignment pet can be just as stressful for the cat as it can be for the pet sitter. Keep in mind that too much chasing and trying to get the cat will put the cat over the edge, and this can sometimes make it impossible to catch the cat. Not only that, cats are rather sensitive to stress, and this can push a cat into an illness or, if the cat is ill, worsen the cat's delicate condition. One suggestion I have is to try to close off all the rooms in the home that the cat can have access to. If the cat is in a bedroom or den, I would then close off that room to try to catch the cat.

On one assignment the cats had the full run of the home. This particular cat needed to get to the vet because he was so difficult to medicate. So first I had to locate the cat, and fear-aggressive cats can be masters at finding the most secretive hiding spots. I finally located the cat in the finished basement and then had to move one of the litter boxes up to the main living quarters for the other cat. I put some food (but not much in case I had to resort to using a trap to catch the kitty) and water in the basement for the cat. I had to bring a cat carrier for I could not find the client's. This is why we have to be prepared on assignments, having our own tools of the trade because the client will either not have what we need or we can't find it in an emergency. Most of my clients are instructed to leave a carrier somewhere for me so that I don't have to go searching their home.

On my next visit I spent some time trying to get the cat in the carrier. It took about fifteen minutes, and I finally had him cornered in the furnace room. What I did next was to speak softly to the cat and use an umbrella to gently nudge him into the carrier. He originally didn't want to go, but I guess he viewed the carrier as a safe spot. Once he went in, I closed the door, and we were on our way to the vet. In retrospect, he really wasn't that hard to catch for I have had some very difficult cats in the past. Sometimes you might need to call in a recruit to help with catching the cat. My daughter and I have worked as a team for some of the tougher cats. For example, if the cat is under the bed and you're by yourself, every time you reach in the cat will slink farther away or out the other side, playing a cat-and-mouse type of game with your intended victim. If one person stays on each side of the bed and by using an extended umbrella or broom, you can try to push him towards the other side or out from under the bed. Grab the cat by the scruff of the neck and tip the cat carrier on its end with the door on top. You can then lower the cat in. You might need some help from your assistant with the cat's back legs as they will put those claws out and resist tooth and claw. Your assistant will have to get them to let go of the edge of the carrier and then shut the door before the cat leaps out, and this requires perfect timing. This brings me to the fact of being careful not to get bitten. We have some animal handling gloves that help catching a fear-aggressive cat but can sometimes make it awkward when trying to grab the cat by the scruff of the neck. While reading this, you might think that it doesn't sound that hard. But the reality is cats can sometimes look like they have wings because they seem to fly through the room, up on cabinets, between your legs, and over the couch. I'm sure you get the idea.

Remember, every situation is different as is every cat, so if in the event you start to see signs of stress from the cat, it would be best to stop all your efforts. You would then have to use a trap to catch your fear-aggressive cat. These are the same traps that are used to trap feral cats. I myself have purchased one for the abandoned cats in my neighborhood but have actually used this to trap one of my own fear-aggressive cats.

She had gotten out of the house when my daughter's friend who was staying with me moved out. The door was left open, and I didn't even realize she was out right away. I searched and searched my house, and she was nowhere to be found. I heard something on the side of the house and decided to put the trap out. I put some food in the trap after it was set, and it took a total of five minutes to get her. If this was on an assignment, I would have then brought the trap to the carrier and transferred the cat from the trap to the carrier. Be careful not to lose the cat when closing the door. You must be very quick, or the cat will be out, and you will have to start all over again.

Cats That Hide

Oh, the elusive cat! If you plan on working with cats, you will begin to notice that you might be spending much of your time trying to locate a cat that is hiding from you. And contrary to what most people think, cats are more difficult to reason with than a dog.

You will open the door and, like a flash of light, they're gone. They manage to find the most unusual places to hide. Sometimes they're above you, looking down from a tall bookcase or refrigerator, and other times they are under a bed, hiding in the box spring. I have found them hiding in couches with no visible entry. Closets seem to be another favorite hiding place. As time has gone by, I have learned not to become too alarmed if I don't see the cat on the first visit, but one thing is for sure, finding the cat is very important.

The reason for this is that the cat can get itself into a place and not be able to get out or is suffering from an illness. Even if the cat is not very social, it is still necessary to find them, and what I like to do is make them run out of their hiding spot. This shows me that the cat is feeling well enough to take off. This can be done with a broom handle, or sometimes just reaching for them will do the trick. But beware; a cat that is hiding is usually fearful and might strike out at you. You will have to be as quick as the cat in a situation like this. Most times the client will let you know that their cat is fearful, and you might not even see them. I always tell them that I will have to find them to make sure all is well and ask if they would close off some rooms in a larger house to keep my search time to a minimum. I ask where their favorite hiding spot is and if they could leave a flashlight for me to check under the bed, couch, and the like.

Cats are pretty slick, and as soon as you find them, they might just switch their hiding place. If in the event that I don't find a cat after a visit or two, I have been known to call the client. Some sitters don't want to disturb their client on vacation, but I won't hesitate to call if I feel the need to. Not one of my clients was ever upset that I called. As a matter of fact, they actually feel better knowing that I cared enough to call. I even had one instance that the client had neglected to tell me that one of their cats had died. I spent a couple of visits frantically searching for this cat, and this is now a part of my questioning when they call to book a sit. Now, I don't come out and say "Have any died?" But I ask if they are all in good health and if they have the same number of cats. You might even find out that they have an addition to their cat family and forgot to tell you.

I remember many years back on one of my searches, after looking all over the house, I opened the sliding closet door and out flew over my head onto the dresser, knocking all the perfumes and hairbrushes to floor, a rather stressed-out kitty. She was very upset that I had found her spot and, just like that, disappeared into the woodwork again, leaving me to clean up the mess she had created. The only consolation that I had was that she was healthy and very athletic.

On another sit, a few days into the assignment, I couldn't find the cat that was normally friendly. After searching the house and starting to get into my panic mode, I opened the pantry door. There she was, sitting and meowing in her very low voice, eager to be let out. The cleaning lady was in the day before and had locked her in. So here's another instance why other people coming in only creates problems.

On some assignments you might not ever see the cat at all, but by monitoring the litter box and food intake, you can detect a problem. If there are quite a few pee and poo in the box, all the cat's plumbing is working fine. This will only work if there is one cat in the house. If there are more than one cat, you might suggest to the client to confine the fearful cat in a separate room to keep an eye on the hidey cat. Believe me, there's nothing like looking for a cat in a two-story house with lots of hiding spots as you begin to wonder if the cat evaporated into thin air. As you can see, hiding cats are definitely a challenge, and they must be located, even if it's only for a fleeting moment. After some time you will find yourself starting to think like a cat and become rather experienced in cat psychology.

Cleaning Messes in Client's Home

When messes need to be attended to in a client's home, I will always use their cleaning products. This is a question that I ask on my consult, and I always ask where their supplies are kept along with needed paper towels, mops, brooms, and dustpans.

Some of my clients are well stocked while others are not, and I have had to improvise many times, which is a reason I carry cleaning tools in my car. On rare occasions I myself have run out of supplies or forgot my dustpan at another client's home and had to use a piece of cardboard or something flat lying around their home to get the dirt up. I never use my cleaning products on furniture or rugs for fear of damaging their belongings. If nothing is left for me to clean with, I will use an old rag and plain warm water to get the spit-up, poo, or vomit out of their rugs and furniture. This will get the mess out without damaging anything. I would leave the client a note that I cleaned the mess up as best I could.

Cats will sometimes leave something to be cleaned, and if you're going over once a day, these messes will become dried up and hard to remove. What I usually do is check for any messes and put a warm paper towel to set on the spit-up while I'm feeding and cleaning the litter box. This will usually soften up the mess, and you might have to go over it a couple of times with a clean rag, but this gets the job done. And believe me there will be many messes to clean up while out on your assignments.

Your clients will appreciate coming home to a clean house after vacationing. I recently got a new cat client because his last sitter had left all the messes for him to come home to. It was only a few hair ball messes and one vomit, but he wasn't happy. Cleaning up excessive hair left by a pet has always been part of my service as well. Both cat and dog hair can accumulate after a week, and I know I wouldn't be happy walking into my home after a week's vacation and find hair all over the couch, even though it's expected in a home with pets. I will vacuum up main areas where the pet spends most of their time, including rugs, chairs, and couches. But I will not go overboard vacuuming the client's home. In my opinion, cleaning messes from pets while performing our duties makes for a happy client.

Coping with the Loss of a Pet While Client Is Vacationing

Every time I care for an older pet I ask the man above to let all go well while I'm in charge, but unfortunately this isn't always the case. Even if we're aware of a pet's health, we are never prepared (or at least I'm not) to talk about stressful situations as this happened to me one time while caring for two cats. This assignment was going well, visiting the cats once a day, and one cat greets me at the door, but I couldn't find the other cat? Looking around in all the spaces he would be, I noticed him lying next to the bed, not moving or noticing me. Well, he was gone, and my stress level went up to code red immediately. I called the client, and thank God he answered. He said he would call his vet and call me back. When he called back, his vet wasn't available, so I called mine and brought the cat down to have all the preparations made. It was a very sad and stressful day.

The client had admitted that the cat hasn't been to the vet in some time, and the cat did look the same as he always did. When I was telling a friend about this incident, she had said to me, "Time to get out of pet sitting." It really didn't comfort me too much, and I almost felt like she was trying to say this was my fault. But the reality of it is that cats mask their illnesses very well and most times pass very quickly. Not only that, but if you're pet sitting for seventeen to twenty years and have never had a pet pass on your shift, consider yourself lucky. As I have said, we take on great responsibility when caring for another's pet and home.

Recently I took over an assignment where another pet sitter was involved. This was a rather complicated one as the owners were out of town for six months. For the first three weeks the neighbor who normally cared for the cat had pet care. The neighbor had a lot going on in her life and couldn't commit to six months of pet care. So the owner hired her hairdresser for the remainder of the time, and she had never owned a cat and didn't notice certain signs of illness from the cat. The son and daughter-in-law stopped by as they were traveling cross country and were appalled when they saw the condition of the cat and immediately took him to the vet. He was dehydrated, jaundiced, had an infection, and suffered from liver failure. He was a mess. The vet said that cats develop liver failure when they are not eating, and this could have been an existing condition before the client left town. The neighbor had used my service many years ago and recommended for the son to call me, and this is where I came in. I actually spoke to the daughter-in-law, who was very upset and pleaded with me to help as they were extending their stay to help with the cat. I have to admit, I was debating on whether to take this job on after meeting with the son and seeing the condition of the cat because he did not look good at all. But as you probably already guessed, I took on the assignment, billing in two weeks increments because I was doubtful of the situation. The neighbor would come in at least once a day, and I was to come in twice a day for medication, feeding, and such. I had no problem with this particular neighbor coming in because at this point the cat would benefit from the extra attention.

The cat started to hate to see me come in for I was the one who administered the medicine, but he was improving. The cat's appetite was great. I was monitoring his pee and poo in his litter box. Things seemed to be going fairly well, considering all this poor cat went through. The son came back to get blood work done, and there were still problems, but I was optimistic. His infection was still there, so they continued his antibiotics for another two weeks. A couple of days after his blood work was done his appetite started to decline and so did his pee in the litter box. I continued my twice-a-day visits, and the neighbor would come in between 10:00 p.m. or 11:00 p.m. We were leaving notes as to what went on, and when I came in one morning, he had passed. This was very upsetting for me as I had become very attached to this poor little kitty. I was crying when I called the owner, who, of course, did not answer. I called the vet, who I had numerous calls with throughout this ordeal, and the neighbor, who came right over. This was a special situation, and this was the reason I had no objections to the neighbor coming in. The neighbor turned out to be a big help when a crisis broke out. I brought the cat to the vet while she proceeded to contact the owner, who, in turn, called me. The client was very happy with my service even though the situation turned out badly. I did all I could, making sure the cat got each and every dose of medicine and making sure he was comfortable with lots of TLC.

So after all these years I am still confronted with situations that I knew could happen and still wasn't prepared for when it finally arrived. Sometimes there is no explanation on why the cat died, and other times we know that cat is in failing health. Of course, I felt extreme guilt with the cat that showed no signs of illness and kept asking myself how I could have let this happen. I was beating myself up for days about this, saying, "I should have seen something but didn't. Why?" I found it very hard to cope while blaming myself all the while. The owner was very understanding saying he was old and admitted he hadn't been to the vet in some time. It still didn't make me feel any better because I'm some sort of "super sitter," and these things can't happen. But they can at any point, and the longer you're pet sitting, the better your chances are for running into this situation. Even a seasoned pro as myself found it hard to cope with sudden death. As far as my sickly cat, I suspected problems but still had a hard time coping with the loss. Maybe the longer I pet sit, more situations like these will toughen my skin, maybe not. It has affected me greatly, and all I know is that if I can't find the cat after being in the home for fifteen minutes, I begin to panic. This type of situation is very draining mentally, physically, and emotionally. At the end of the day, after you've went through a death of one of your client's pets added to your full schedule, being exhausted is an understatement.

So be vigilant in your assessment of the pets in your care, and if you are ever presented with a situation such as this, try to stay calm, call your client, and try not to beat yourself up too badly because it is part of the job. I've often wondered how vets cope with losing a pet that they are supposed to make well.

I have been told by clients who knew the time was near what I should do. I even had a request that if the cat passed while they were away that I was to wrap it in a towel and place it in the freezer. More often than not I will bring the cat to the vet, and either the vet will put the pet on hold until the client gets back or the client will call and I will sign for the pet to be cremated. And if you care for older pets as I do, this will always be foremost in your thoughts. So when interviewing and an older or sickly pet is involved, this topic should be brought up, just in case.

Another thing, when a client is away and vacationing, they could experience extreme guilt when it comes to their pet. They feel horrible that they weren't able to be there in their pet's hour of need. I have spent time on the phone reassuring my client that their pet went peacefully and that no one knows when their time is up, including animals. I tell them not to be too hard on themselves as their vacation was planned and there was nothing that could have been done differently.

Try to ease their guilt by telling them how much you enjoyed caring for their pet and how lucky they were to have such a wonderful pet in their lives, how lucky this pet was to have them as their owners and what great care they took of their pet, including hiring a pet sitter to look after them.

Daily Walks

If I counted how many daily clients I've had through the years, you might be amazed. And now that I'm starting to remember how many walks I've done, my head is starting to spin. The first fifteen years of my business the majority of my business was daily walks. Within the last couple of years I've had clients retire, dogs go on to Rainbow Bridge, changes in income, and an array of changes on my daily dog walking schedule. With so many newer sitters in my area as of late, most are focusing on dog walking. This is fine with me because in the last couple of years I have started to focus on vacation, handicapped pets, and cat clients. The many years of dog pulling have affected my hands and wrists, not to mention the traumas that can occur while out walking dogs. Although I could get some independent contractors to help with the walks, I find the liability issues too stressful for myself and prefer to keep this a family-owned-and-operated business with enough work for daily dog walks to keep us busy, at least for now. When I decide to grow the business, this time I will have employees instead of ICs so that I can have more control on how the assignment is handled and to be able to train my employees. There is so much that can go wrong while walking on the streets. Even since the original writing of this book I have experienced many changes from Hurricane Sandy. So selling the business might be my next option. I am sure that one day I will sit down and write that down on paper as it is too long to put in this book.

I have had dogs pull me across grassy fields, down stairs, and across parking lots, and I've had dogs who have been involved in dog fights. I've had to deal with stupid people who just don't get it. They think because their dog is friendly, all dogs are. I had many that would let their dog run up to me while holding three out-of-control beagles that wanted nothing more than to attack their "friendly" dog, saying "Oh he's just a puppy." They just don't get it. Not all dogs get along. I had some macho men insist that their dog meet the dog I was walking, and when I went on to explain how this was not my dog and I couldn't take a chance on the safety of my charge, I was told how obvious it was that I knew nothing about dogs. Problem being is I do know about dogs and their behavior. As much as we love them and most think of them as family, we must remember that they are still animals. Animals are just like people some of us do not get along, to the fact that animals are unpredictable and work on their instinct. We must always use caution when approaching other animals. It is my responsibility when I have a dog in my control that the first priority is to keep them safe. If their owners want to take the chance and socialize their dog, that is their business. I had a client a while back, who had a senior basset hound, a very easygoing old dog. She was out with him on a walk and stopped to talk with her neighbor a few houses down, who also had her dog with her. They were chatting; the dogs were both on their leashes and seemed to be getting along. Out of nowhere the neighbor's dog attacked Huckleberry without warning, and he didn't even fight back. The poor boy ended up with fifteen stitches. This would never have happened on my shift because my job is keeping the dogs safe.

Although my client said there was no warning, I guarantee you there were signs. Dogs have a silent body language. If you watch them, you will start to read what they're saying. Their whole body speaks. A dog that stares too long is showing signs of aggression. Ears that are erect and a stiff body is another sign. Read books on the behavior of dogs, and of course, the more time you spend with dogs, the more you will see their silent language and get some hands-on schooling. But please be cautious when someone says their dog is friendly; they are animals and are unpredictable. And these things happen in the blink of an eye.

When you focus on daily dog walks, keep in mind your weeks will consist of a constant routine. Your clients will expect you to be there every day regardless. It can become very monotonous day in and day out. The one positive point to daily dog walks is the steady paycheck. Now imagine doing this for fifteen years with a steady flow of at least eight dogs per day, not to mention the occasional last-minute requests. Coupled with vacation clients, I was working an average of twelve to thirteen hours per day. When my daughter needed time off, I added her walks to my list. And of course she did the same for me and often told me when she did my walks, "I don't know how you do it!"

Now let's throw a twist into the mix. You have a client who is in the health care field, and their schedule is just as crazy as a pet sitter, maybe worse. Would you take a walk that needs to be done at 8:00 p.m. Tuesday through Saturday? Nurses and doctors have pets too. Or a fireman or police officer may have unusual schedules as well. These are all scenarios that can come up, and having help in these instances is a great benefit. But at times there doesn't seem to be enough help to go around. Take this weekend, it's the Fourth of July, my daughter has gone away overnight, and I got slammed with bookings from my steady clients. Both Saturday and Sunday we had twenty stops in all. My son will help out from time to time but has two other steady part-time jobs, and of course, my IC is unavailable. So I ended up doing the majority of the sits myself. No Fourth of July for me.

For the last few years I only use my own leads. These are British slip leads with a collar built in so this can adjust to any size dog. But before I switched over to these leads, I would always check the dog's collar before hooking up to the leash. If the collar is loose, I would adjust it, making it tighter, so the dog would be less likely to slip their collar. Then I would loosen the collar after bringing the dog back in the house, making sure it is loose enough that if the dog gets hung up on something, it will come off easily and lessen the chance of the dog choking to death. Another thing to be careful with is double-checking what you have hooked the leash to. Make sure it is hooked up to the leash ring and not the flimsy hook for their ID tags. These rings will not hold up to a dog pulling and could break. If you plan on using a flexi lead, make sure you have a firm grip on the handle as they can sometimes pull the handle out of your hand, causing it to bounce along the ground, make a loud noise, and possibly scare the dog, making them run away. I advise against this type of leash for many reasons besides the one just given. I have been given burns from the leash as they went behind my legs. If they are out too far, it becomes difficult to reel them in if a dangerous situation develops or another dog approaches.

If this daily is not a walk but the dog goes potty in the yard, make sure each and every time before you let the dog out that all gates are closed and secured. Check the perimeter of the fence to make sure no escape is possible and always stay with the dog while they are in the yard, as I have had some jumpers that could go over a four-foot fence. You are also able to observe if the dog eats anything, injures its leg, or runs into wildlife that could be dangerous. Hawks are a threat to smaller dogs and cats as well. Snakes bite, and I had a dog that ran into a bee nest and ended up getting hives due to allergic reaction. You might not be able to stop some of these situations, but you will know what the problem is.

I would also like to suggest that you do not listen to music on your walks, and the same holds true for talking on the phone. You should devote your full attention to the dogs in your care. So many things can happen in an instant that you should be prepared for whatever can come up. When you're listening to music or talking on the phone, you are distracted, and this is the time when things can go wrong. I think a city setting is more likely to have the unexpected happen, and from my experience it happens in an instant. I have spent many hours on the streets, walking one, two, sometimes three dogs at once, and although I have had some things go wrong, the outcome could have been much worse if I was not prepared and aware of my surroundings.

If you have dogs that tend to go crazy when they see another dog, squirrel, or anything that gets them going, I'd like to tell you what I do. First I try to block their view, but sometimes this is not possible. In that case I plant my feet firmly on the ground and hold on to the leash, preparing myself for the pulling and jumping. This helps in keeping your balance. When you're walking and the dogs are going nuts, it's easier for them to pull you down. Once the situation has calmed down, you can continue with your walk. Treats can be used to distract them, but this doesn't always work when the dog is all riled up.

I would say the majority of my dogs were fairly well behaved, but keep in mind that a client will sometimes hire you to walk their dog because he is absolutely horrible on the leash. They want the dog to get walked but failed to do basic training, and the result is an ill-behaved dog. If I spend enough time with the dog, we have an understanding. I'm the top dog and spend much of the time correcting bad behavior. Sometimes this happens very quickly, and other times we have a battle of wills with frequent time-outs by making them sit and calm down. After some time I usually win, but in the rare exception I have an extremely stubborn dog, I then practice dog psychology. Every dog is different, so I have to see what works for that certain personality.

In New York City we have dog walkers that take a multitude of dogs for a walk at the same time. I've often wondered how they do it without any incidents, and a friend of mine had said that in Manhattan the dogs must be well behaved in order to live in the buildings. Many years ago I spoke with a sitter on Staten Island who would travel to Manhattan to walk dogs. She had told me it was worth it for her and picked up her charges along the way, followed a route, and then brought them back home in order of pickup. The first one out was the first one back home. She had a really nice paycheck for an hour's work. But in reality she still had to commute to New York, and each way could take up to an hour and a half, maybe less if you manage to get the boat on time. And I couldn't imagine myself doing multiple dogs on the island, except if they were from the same household, because we usually get the bad dogs.

Sometimes housemates must be walked separately. The fact being they are either ill-behaved or very large, and I know my limits on what I can handle. Even when we walk dogs that live in the same build-ing, we walk them separate for that very reason, and the client feels confident in our abilities to know nothing will go wrong. If you take multiple dogs out together how do you handle all those dogs when something goes wrong? Someone will not get saved from a disastrous situation. Sure, I could pack a whole group of dogs into a van and take them to a dog park and make a pretty penny, of course I could. But in my opinion you would need additional sitters, one for every two dogs in case trouble breaks out. So we specialize in individual walks with less liability and individual attention to each and every dog.

I will always yield to another person with a dog, either crossing the street or keeping my charge by my side, depending on the size of the dog. Some dogs can pretend to be good while the other dog is walking by only to lunge at the dog, so beware. I always respect other people without dogs because not all people are dog lovers, and some could have a fear of dogs. So I will do the same, holding my charge close to me, and move to the curb or street if it's a low-traffic area. And I never let another person pet the dog in my charge unless I'm certain of the personality I'm dealing with, as some dogs can be funny in situations with strangers. I just explain this is not my dog and I'm not sure how they will react. All this I learned from many years of finding out what can go wrong. Being quick in my thinking, anticipating what might happen next, is my only saving grace.

My daughter had a walk with a dog when she first started out in the business, and a neighbor had wanted to pet him. So she let her. Well, sure enough he bit her. If she had listened to my advice about not letting people or other dogs close, this would never have happened. It wasn't a bad bite, but it was still a bite, and from this point on she paid attention to what I told her. I also share a walk with my daughter with two Shar-Pei males. This breed is very loyal to family but can be stand-offish with strangers. I was bringing them back into the apartment complex, and the general rule with these guys is to keep them distant with anyone passing by. Well, this day there was an older gentleman that got out of his car and started coming towards us to ask about the dogs. I told him they weren't mine, and he proceeded to tell me he had a hundred-pound Rottweiler at home. Well, I was watching my guys and noticed one of the males getting ready to lunge at this man, and I held my grip. I had told this man, and he wasn't hearing what I was saying. I know my dogs and their body language. He went in and told the doorman that the dog just tried to bite him, and the doorman told him, "Don't you know you're not supposed pet a dog you don't know?" This doorman knows these dogs as well, and he usually alerts us on incoming dogs and certain situations because he watches the surveillance cameras. Always be cautious with your dogs and situations that can develop very quickly.

If you have any walks in an apartment building, make sure that you wait away from the elevator. The reason being is that when the elevator door is opening, you will never know who is coming out, and if this person has a dog with them, you will want to ensure that there will be no incident. Again, keep in mind that not everyone is an animal lover, and some of these people might be going on an interview, to work, and the like. Be considerate.

Always be respectful of other people's property by not letting your dog pee on their lawn or bushes. Either bring them to an empty lot or, what I usually do, walk on the street if it is a slow-traffic area. This way I will keep everyone happy, including my dog. I suggest always cleaning up after your dog whether your city laws require this or not. There's always a possibility later in time you might end up stepping in the mess you've left behind, and in my opinion, it shows that you are a respectable business owner.

Also be aware of dogs that are garbage hounds. These dogs are so quick to pick up an old chicken bone, half-eaten sandwich, or whatever else they might find along the way. These dogs are very crafty as well because you will think that they are just sniffing, and what they are doing is scouting out the old food. They pounce on the garbage so quickly, and most inhale it so you can't get it away from them. When this has happened, I usually leave the client a note in case of an upset belly or bad reaction of some sort. Most times I will try to get it away from them, but be cautious because way back when I first started my business, I almost lost my finger because the dog acted negatively. Some dogs revert back to their primitive instinct when it comes to food. I used to walk a couple of beagles, and this one dog was so food possessive and quick that he managed to eat a saran wrapper from the meat that the garbage men left behind. I took a chance and only grabbed a small piece before he got nasty with me and gobbled it down. I left a note for his owners, who were quite aware of Hank's personality and his distinct love of garbage. I told them to make sure that the saran wrapper came out because I was afraid it might cause a blockage in his intestinal track. Always let your clients know of anything that was picked up along the way. They will appreciate your honesty, and most know of their dog's behavior.

Most clients have their own preference when it comes to leashes and collars, and sometimes I respect their wishes unless I'm not comfortable with the dog (e.g., a dog that I feel will slip their collar or harness or the client has an old or fraying leash/collar). Over the last couple of years I only use my own leashes (Mendota slip leads) because of past problems and let the client know this. The majority of my clients don't have a problem with this. These leads are great because they fit all sizes of dogs with an adjustable loop for collar, and the lead is built in. Of course, the smaller dogs that need a harness are an exception to the rule I've made.

I'd like to tell you a short story of a client we picked up with a young boxer. The only clue that I had to what might happen on this assignment was the client had said to me "Good luck" on the consult. My son and I shared this walk, and from day 1 I knew she needed my leash. The client had a harness on her, and she was a backer (a dog that tries to get out of harness/collar by backing up). Well, this particular client was a complainer. Whenever my son went in, he had a complaint, which I knew was totally unjustified. That was the beginning of the end of this client; I knew every time my son went in he would call. I was fine, but my son had to go. I had given my son strict instruction to use our lead, which he did. One day on his walk with her he ran into the neighbor who used to walk the dog, but the dog slipped her harness and got away. That's when we were called, and this client never said a word to me on the interview of the incident of her slipping her harness. What kind of dog owner that cares about their dog would not tell the dog walker to be careful about her slipping her harness? Well, the neighbor told the client that my son was using the choke collar on his dog, and of course, I got a call complaining of my son using this collar-lead combination. I went on to tell him I also used this type of collar-lead combination because we never lose a dog! I also went on to tell him that I've had dogs slip their collars and harness and would not take this chance with his dog. This was his second chance to clue me in on his dog slipping her harness, which he did not do. And at this point I had already found out through the neighbor and figured he either didn't give a damn about his dog or was trying to set us up for problems. So he's gone, and although I feel bad for his dog, I have no control over stupid people and their actions. We have to use our instincts when dealing with not only animals but people as well. If it doesn't feel right, lose the client.

So however you decide to set up your policies for walks, make sure you have thought out your plan of action well in the event that something could go wrong because when we're working with animals, at some point something will go wrong.

Daily Walks in Summer and Winter

When walking dogs in the summer, there are several things you should keep in mind. Always check the ground to see how hot the pavement is. If you step on the ground with bare feet and your feet get burned, so will the dog's paws. Keeping the dog cool will be difficult, so try to walk in the shade if at all possible, even if it means crossing the street or walking to the park if there is one nearby. I normally walk my dogs on the street except in the summer months when the sun has cooked the ground. One of my clients keeps a spray bottle of water in the fridge for our walks. Spraying on the fur doesn't necessarily cool the dog down being in a humid environment. The water does not evaporate, so it doesn't work well but helps. What I like to do is spray their belly and snout, and spray in their mouth. Spraying their feet will also help due to the fact that there are blood vessels and skin over the bones; this helps cool them down as well. Sometimes after we go back I will spray them down with the hose, but be sure to dry the dog off if going back into an air-conditioned house. They do sell cooling scarfs for dogs, and you might suggest this to your client, but let them purchase them as this could run into some money if you were to buy for all your clients. Short walks are needed for the warmer months. Always watch your dog to make sure they are not panting excessively—a sure sign of heat exhaustion. Older dogs are more prone to feel the effects of the heat, so be extra cautious when walking seniors. Puppies are also affected by extremely hot weather, and although they are young and healthy, they will not be able to tolerate the heat for long periods.

Do not let an overheated dog drink large amounts of water as this will not cool the dog down; a few laps of water is all that is needed. If a dog drinks a large amount of water and is panting excessively, this will cause the dog to take in a lot of air as well and might cause bloating.

Panting is a dog's way of cooling down, and a small amount of water is all that is needed to make this more effective for the dog. When the dog has started to pant less, you can then give more water, but not too much as what goes in will come out, and you might come back to a puddle on the floor if you allow your dog to drink too much.

Winter has its drawbacks as well, and some dogs can tolerate the cold very well while others do not. I have many dogs that gear up when the colder months come. It takes extra time getting jackets and boots on. But the same as summer, when the cold weather is severe, the walks should be shortened. I actually like when the dogs have boots to protect their paws from the salt that the city puts down, and most "dog owners" like it as well. If the dogs walk on the salt, it can irritate their paws and must be wiped off after your walk. You should not have to worry about frostbite while out walking if you keep the walks to a minimum. Basically letting the dog do their business and back to the house is all that is required in extremely cold weather. I've found that the smaller, short-haired breeds really hate the winter, and a quick relief is all they need.

I have had some clients in the past who would insist on a regular walk in a foot of snow with temperatures in the teens. I realize that they do want to get their money's worth, but come on! Most times the dog can't wait to get back inside, where it's nice and warm, except for the cold-weather breeds that can go for hours in a very cold environment. So I explain that even though our walks are shortened, we spend time inside snuggling or most times drying off. Keep in mind, all that snow that sticks to the fur turns to water when going back into the home. I charge by the half-hour or on dailies offer a twenty-minute walk and include all that is done in this time frame. Common sense is all that is needed when walking dogs in summer and winter months.

Dangerous Breeds

Pet sitting is no different than any other business; there will be both good and bad in all the breeds you will come in contact with. Most people tend to generalize what breeds are dangerous, and I can tell you that I have had pit bull that thought they were golden retrievers. I have had cocker spaniels who thought they were pit bulls. So while pet sitting I wouldn't be quick to judge an assignment on breed standards. I have cared for a variety of breeds over the years, and it's quite possible that I have been lucky. But I'm a firm believer in being the top dog in any assignment and never push any of my dogs by force. When speaking about dogs, often you will hear me refer to dogs and children in the same sentence. So by using psychology in any situation caring for a so-called dangerous breed, you should not run into any problems if you treat your dog with mutual respect.

Many years ago one of my first assignments was a daily walk involving three pit bulls. At that time I knew a little about the breed, mostly negative publicity. But I learned from my client and his dogs. I was always cautious while caring for them. The client had gone on vacation by the beach and had some kind of shellfish, which the younger dog had gotten into. It turned out to be toxic, and they lost her. After that the older girl was never the same, and there were days she refused to go for her walk. I would never force her to get off the couch and explained to my client her mood changes since the loss. More than likely she was suffering from depression from losing her housemate, and I couldn't take the chance of getting bitten by forcing her to go out. If she wanted to, we would go; other than that I would only take the male out if she refused.

Personally I would rather care for a pit bull than an Akita or Chow as the two latter breeds can be a handful for a sitter. They are good with family but difficult to care for if it's not done on a continuous basis, such as daily dog walk. Recently I got a call from a woman who needed service; her dog was a Presa Canario. I am familiar with this breed for I had seen a television show on the case of a California woman that was killed by two Presa Canario / Mastiff crosses in 2001. There was also another case in 2006 where a woman was killed by her own Presa Canario. The woman was surprised that I knew so much about the breed (I never mentioned the bad publicity), and I was hesitant about taking on the assignment but agreed to at least meet the dog. This breed can weigh between 100 to 160 pounds, is hard to train, has a strong character, is dominant to other dogs, and is suspicious of strangers. The day I was to meet with the woman, she called to say she didn't require my services for her brother would be able to care for the dog. I breathed a sigh of relief for I was having second thoughts about even going to meet the woman's dog. My inner voice was telling me not to go, and I was glad that things turned out the way they did.

If you have a fear about a particular breed, then I would suggest not taking on the assignment, as the dog will sense this. But I will suggest you get the AKC's *Complete Dog Book*, which is in its twentieth edition. It contains all the pure breed dogs with breed history, character traits, and pictures, so you will have an idea as to what type a dog a prospective client has if you're not familiar with a breed. I have always enjoyed learning about the different breeds, and this is a great source for learning. I know that all the dogs we care for will not be pure breeds, and if someone calls to say they have a designer breed like a puggle, you will know that this is an energetic smaller dog. Both the pug and beagle have a high energy level. You will be able to know what you're up against if someone says they have a mixed breed, part pit bull and Labrador retriever: you're in for a fun filled walk. I can tell by looking at a mixed breed and what its main breed is if the dog has a black tongue or black spots on their tongue and texture of coat. Chows are known to have black tongues as do some Shar-Peis, so if the dog has a fluffy coat and black spots on the tongue, more than likely it is a chow mix. If instead the dog had some prominent wrinkles on its face with short coat and the black tongue, more than likely the mixed breed had some Shar-Pei in him.

The Center for Disease and Control website cites that the pit bull is considered to be the most dangerous of all the breeds. I attribute this to the careless and callous owners of this breed who promote fighting. They can be headstrong, and if they attack, their jaws will lock close, and as most dogs will do, they go for the throat of the dog or person. I have seen this firsthand because many years ago one of my neighbors had a pit bull. She had found a kitten that my daughter wanted, so we adopted the cat. Our neighbor had come over to give us a can of cat food to hold us over till we got to the store, and she had her two dogs, a pit bull and a shepherd, with her. When I opened the door to get the food, my Labrador retriever ran out, and her dogs started to attack my dog. The pit bull had her by the throat, and the shepherd had her by the rear. My dog's eyes were bulging, and I just jumped into the mix, trying to pull my dog away. It was mayhem, and thank goodness her son heard the commotion and came over to pull the dogs off my dog, which wasn't an easy task because the pit bull had locked on to my dog. My girl had a small puncture but nothing serious. My other neighbor said that I was brave to jump in, but my dog needed help, so I never think in these situations, I just react.

Rottweiler's are rated the second most dangerous breed as they can be extremely territorial. German shepherds came in next. They are very intelligent and strong, and I have never had any problems with the shepherds I have cared for, except for one last year. I have now changed my thoughts on the shepherd. Huskies (fourth) and Alaskan malamutes (fifth) are two breeds I have never cared for, and they can be a tough breed for a stranger to handle. Doberman pinschers (sixth) are protective of their family, and I have a client that has certified her two Dobermans as therapy dogs. Chow chows (seventh) can be leery of strangers and a little stubborn. Presa Canario (eight) are fearless and have incredible strength. Boxers (ninth) are headstrong, and I have had hard times gaining access to the home with this breed. Dalmatian (ten), I have cared for many and have never had a problem. We have cared for Shar-Peis, and this breed could pose some possible problems. They are very strong, and the ones we care for are dog-aggressive and not to be trusted with certain individuals in an apartment building where they live. Both my daughter and I care for these tough guys, and I want my son to get acclimated to the dogs as I will not just let him go in after one meeting. There is a certain protocol we have to follow just to get out of the building, and while in the dog run, they cannot share the run with other dogs. We also must carry a drool rag to clean up any drool that they leave behind. You can check your local government to see which breeds are banned or are on the dangerous-dog list for your region. But more than anything, all information you learn will be able to help you make an informed decision on taking on any assignment, that along with your gut feeling while on a consult because we should always listen to our inner voice.

Disabled Clients

This is something that I had never thought about before when considering what services to offer. But during the last couple of years I have had new and returning clients inquire about helping with litter box cleaning or getting their dog out because they are not able to. So I have added this to the list of services I offer. Considering that sometimes these clients will be living on limited means, I will adjust my regular rate of service for a particular client, going on a case-by-case basis. Honestly, I would have never thought of this service if it weren't for my clients. These clients love the companionship their pet provides but aren't always physically capable of doing the cleaning for their pet. In my area most housecleaners will not take a job that involves cleaning of litter boxes or pet bedding. So I go in and do all the heavy-duty maintenance, leaving the client to do the lighter chores. These assignments can sometimes be time-consuming, so before you think about adding this service, give careful consideration to all that will be involved. I recently added an existing client who left their cat's area where the litter boxes were neglected due to a back injury. So what I did was set an initial price for the first cleaning and a set price for coming in a couple days a week. This price was set with the agreement that as long as I come in to maintain the boxes on a regular basis, no extra costs would be involved.

So as always, when receiving a call for a service that you do not offer, don't turn the assignment away. Instead tell the prospective client that you can set up an appointment to come and meet with them to discuss what can be done to help with their situation. I basically set my price for this on a whim but kept in mind how much work was involved and the situation of the client. I now have a basic price structure set up, and it is flexible according to the situation, and I never give a price for this type of service over the phone.

Dog Fights: What to Do

Hopefully you will never have to deal with a dog fight while out on your walks or, for that matter, between dogs that are housemates because both scenarios can happen at any time even with dogs that are familiar with each other, living together, and which normally get along well. Since the start of my business I have been involved in three dog fights on the streets while out walking dogs, and at least one that stands out in my mind was with housemates. When this happens, a very stressful situation can turn into a disaster in a matter of minutes. This is why I can't stress enough that you must keep your full attention on the dog or dogs in your charge while walking. I will never answer my cell phone when I'm out on the streets and never wear an iPod or other music device. I will always be aware of any dogs in neighboring yards or a person that looks like they might not be able to handle their dogs, always crossing over to the other side of the street to give some distance between myself and the other dog.

You might be thinking to yourself this woman is being overly cautious or is just plain wimpy. But let me assure you that until you experience a dog fight, you will never understand the stress that is associated with this situation, especially when you're out on the street and anything can happen. I have come out on top when these situations came up partly because I am always aware of my environment and the dogs in my care, focusing only on my job. I would also like to add that no one ever knows how they will handle this particular situation, which can happen in seconds. I tend to dive right in, not thinking of myself or the imminent danger that I have found myself involved in. These dog fights happen so fast that they can really catch you off guard. One moment you're walking down the street, having a beautiful walk, and the next moment you're trying to protect the dog in your care. According to the many books out on the market, I did everything wrong, but as I said, no one knows how they will react. I have been told by some trainers to let the leash go and let them fight it out. Maybe I've just been lucky four times over. But being top dog in these situations is a necessity along with a quick reaction time. Calming any fight before it escalates, in my experience, is most important.

A couple years into my pet sitting career, I had a job in an apartment building with a nice midsized dog. She was always such a pleasant dog to take for a walk, enjoying every minute we were out. So I hooked her up, and we headed out the door as we had done so many times before. We didn't get more than ten steps out the door when I noticed a man cleaning out his car with two dogs tied to the fence, one midsized dog and another very large Irish wolfhound mixed breed. Well, before I knew it, the very large dog started charging us. Obviously he wasn't tied to the fence after all. He started circling the both of us, which in the dog world is typical of pack dogs that would often circle their prey. This whole time I was yelling at the owner to get his dog. But before I knew it, this dog grabs my dog by the nape and starts shaking her. I am now trying to get her away from him, pulling on the leash, and in the process, I end up on the ground. Well, the man finally came over, and I'm sure the whole attack only lasted a few seconds, but to me it felt like an eternity. My poor girl was fine, although she did manage to pee all over herself, and I had to check and see if I did the same!

The owner of the large dog didn't even apologize; as a matter of fact, he seemed to be amused about the situation. He kept trying to come into our space, and I wanted nothing more than to distance myself from this guy and his dog. I later learned from my client that this was not the only incident with this dog and owner. She was grateful that I was the one that had her dog and that this was the reason that no harm came to her dog, at least no physical harm. But I'm positive the poor girl had some deep psychological trauma after this happened. I myself had never experienced this before, and being it was so early on in my career, it left a very deep impression on me.

My second was another unforgettable dog fight between two dogs that lived in the same house, a pit bull rescue and a boxer. I can honestly say that this entire job was a test to my pet sitting abilities from the moment I tried to enter the house. It took a good twenty minutes just to get in the front door. On the initial consult all went well. The boxer was a little distant but fine with me, and the pit bull was friendly. I was told by the client to feed one dog on one side of the kitchen and the other dog across on the other side, that they knew their places to dine. I did, and the first couple of feedings went smoothly until one feeding went horribly wrong. The pit bull finished first as the boxer was still finishing up his dinner when all of a sudden the pit bull decided to finish up the boxer's food and attacked the boxer. I managed to break them up, and before I knew it, the boxer retaliated with a vengeance that I've never seen before. Round two was on. Hearing all the stories about how the pit bull is a tough breed, I was worried for the boxer. But guess what, the boxer is another tough breed, and they were totally zoned out into their fight, not hearing a word I said. I ended up breaking up the fight with a kitchen chair. I had to use it to put between the two of them and at the same time protect myself. I felt just like a lion tamer and could never understand why they used a chair, but I'll tell you it worked really well!

After the dust settled, my nerves were frayed as I checked both the dogs, who seemed to know their place to go after all was said and done. They settled themselves into separate corners, and I checked both of them. The pit bull was unscathed, while the boxer had a small cut on his ear. I couldn't believe that after all that commotion one small cut on the ear was all that came of this fight. Needless to say, since that day I've never fed housemates together in the same room regardless what the client wants or what the dogs are accustomed to. Almost 99 percent of the time all might go well, but after what I went through on that sit, never again. I will always be cautious when feeding dogs that are housemates.

My third dog fight still affected me, although it wasn't so bad because my reaction time was extremely quick. This was a Border collie that wasn't quite a year old, a very happy and friendly dog. We had a nice walk and were just about a block away from the house when a woman walking a golden retriever came along, and I yielded to her, letting her go by, so that we could continue home. Her golden began pulling and barking uncontrollably. I saw the woman having a hard time controlling her dog, and next thing I knew she couldn't hold him anymore, and he was coming at us. He pounced on my dog, and my young Border collie wasn't going down easily. I grabbed the golden retriever's leash and managed to hold them apart while the woman came and took her dog. Whew! By this time I was getting pretty good at breaking up dog fights, but nevertheless, it was still very stressful.

My fourth dog fight, and hopefully my last as at this very moment I am servicing mostly cats and took many years to get to this point, involved a feisty twelve-year-old dog who also had a sweet little Shih Tzu housemate. I was told that the twelve-year-old mixed breed was aggressive to other dogs right from the start. So I always tried to avoid all dogs either by crossing over to the other side of the street or heading a different way altogether. On this particular day I noticed a man with his dog down our regular walking path, and he was swooning, hanging on to the fence. He was very drunk. So I decided to avoid him, knowing he would cause a possible problem. We crossed over to the other side of the street and headed down another road when I noticed three young men in their early twenties sitting on steps to a house that was being built. One of the young men had a nice-looking white pit bull sitting between his legs. At that exact moment I said to myself, "He better have a leash on that dog." And guess what, he didn't, and the pit bull came charging over to us. Now I was never one to go by stereotyping breeds, but I did know my dog was dog-aggressive to other dogs, and a problem was about to develop rather quickly.

The pit bull was not coming over to attack but to say hello, and in an instant my twelve-year-old started right in on him. Now this was a fairly young, strong pit bull; he was not about to let an older dog shame him by taking a beating. Again here I am in the middle of a dog fight, my girl is getting her butt kicked, and my poor little Shih Tzu is getting trampled in the mayhem. So what I do is grab the pit bull's collar with one hand while pulling my girl's leash to the other side of me, pulling them apart. And mind you, he gave me a look like "Hey, lady, are you nuts? Do you know who I am?" While this guy comes strolling over to get his dog, I'm furious by this point as we have a leash law in New York, and it's stupid people like this guy that will give the pit bull a bad reputation regardless of the situation, and I told him so.

There was an older woman getting into her car that witnessed the fight and came over to ask me if I was okay, and I was, but I was shaking like a leaf. My adrenaline was racing along with my heart, and I have to admit I'm getting too old for this. We cut our walk short and went back to the house to call the client and let her know what happened. I checked the dog, and she did have a broken blood vessel in her right eye, but she was fine, considering the fight. The client was angry with me for going a different way, and I went on to explain why I did go another route. She eventually came around, but here's another reason why we have great responsibility while out walking dogs. Even if we do our best in this situation, the blame could always be placed on our shoulders.

So when I tell you to be aware of the neighborhood you're walking in and not to be distracted by talking on the phone or listening to music, it's because you must be prepared for anything. Most people, including my own children who work in the business with me, sometimes say I'm overreacting or being paranoid, but that's only because they have never been involved in a dog fight. If I'm walking down a street and I see a dog going nuts by a closed screen door, there is always a possibility that the dog will jump up on the door, hit the handle, and accidently get out the door. I'm cautious of dogs in a fenced yard as there was an instance where a chow jumped the fence. Luckily for me the mailman was delivering the mail, and he was distracted by him. But it was not so lucky for the mailman, who was begging me to help him. I would have but had my dog to think of. I didn't want to have to deal with another dog fight and felt bad that I couldn't help, but at this point it's every man or woman for themselves. I still see this mailman as he delivers in one of our buildings where we walk dogs and remind him occasionally how he was crying like a baby for help. So many things can develop in the wink of an eye. Animals are unpredictable, which makes this profession so changeling at times.

I had asked my daughter, who sometimes walked the dog-aggressive twelve-year-old dog, what she would have done. Her reply was to run, which is the worst thing you can do. This will bring on a reaction from the aggressor to chase, and instinct will kick in. The aggressor will be fueled by this. As I said earlier, no one really knows how they will react in this situation. You should not show fear because, as you know, all dogs can sense this. Some people might freeze and not know what to do, letting the dogs fight it out, being fearful for their own safety, and that's okay. If this would be the case, you should yell for help. There was one time while walking a dog I saw a truck go by with two dogs in the back of the truck. Halfway through our walk I see these same two dogs coming up the hill towards us, no longer in the truck and roaming free. I knew that I was no match for two dogs, so what I did was go into someone's fenced yard and waited for them to pass. I was thinking the whole time of what I will say to the owner of the home and also praying they didn't have a dog and decide to let him out while we were in the yard. You will find you must improvise at times to avoid problems, and there will always be situations that can get out of control.

Dog Refuses to Go Back in the House

You will find that some dogs are masters of manipulation and try to get you to do what they want. I have had dogs that once outside would refuse to go back in the house, turning into more of a solid one-hundred-pound iron statue than a dog. Try to make an eighty-pound golden retriever cooperate when they become stubborn or an aloof Akita that decides to stay out in the yard for three hours on a subzero day! Thank God I haven't had too many of these assignments; although they have really taught me the virtue of patience.

My golden retriever was a very sweet boy, and our walks were pleasant until we would come to his front steps. He was also a backer, and this was in the earlier years of my business. It was a good learning experience in using psychology with my dogs. I could tell you one thing: these types of personalities will not work well with commands, for they have a mind of their own. And the more you insist they cooperate, the more they will resist. With my golden, he would plant himself down and not move. Treats worked to a degree, which is until he got one, and then down he would go again. I would basically have to wait him out each and every time we went for a walk. My client would tie him outside, so this was part of the problem as he wanted to watch his neighborhood.

My Akita, however, was the most difficult assignment I had ever had and hopefully ever will. He went outside in the backyard, and I swear the temperature was in the teens if not in the single digits. He loved it, and after a half-hour, it was time for me to leave. Well, not according to my Akita, who, each and every time I tried to hook his leash, would take off. So I decided to make a trail of cheese and have him follow it. He was definitely smarter than the average pet sitter. He would eat just enough and, when he got close to the door, turn and run away. I swear animals are psychic because he seemed to know that I was going to close the door once he was inside the house. I went through my client's fridge, looking for a tastier treat, and upgraded to some cold cuts, and sure, he loved that, but there still was no success. Two hours into this routine with this dog, I called my daughter as I had three more sits to do. She came over, picked up the keys, and, with a grin, said, "Having a hard day?" Well, I spent a total of three hours trying to get this dog inside the house again. Just like the hundred other times, I tried to hook him up, suddenly he just let me hook him up. We turned around and went into the house! Talk about jobs from hell, this was one. I couldn't leave him outside, so I had no choice but to play his game.

Another dog I had, Rocky, was the same, but I was prepared for this as the client had told me her son had to go to the groomer because Rocky wouldn't budge from his cage when it was his turn to get groomed. And after my two other dogs, I was ready for this. I always took a tasty treat—a piece of turkey, ham, whatever I could find in the fridge. I would sit on the stairs and call him to me for a treat. When he came, I would go up a few more stairs, and there were many. So before Rocky knew it, he was back in the house, and I always kept one treat for when we got in. This gave him something to look forward to. Whoever said pet sitting is easy must be out of their minds!

I really have no advice on this one because each and every dog is different. Just be prepared for waiting it out. But at least you will know if this happens, you're not the first to experience a dog that won't go in the house. This can really put a kink in your schedule and mess up your whole day.

Dogs That Destroy Client's Home

We will never know what to expect when caring for a new client. Until you walk into a home that has been destroyed by a dog, you will never believe how one dog can demolish so many things in a fairly short amount of time. Or the dog in your care can be set on destroying one particular chair or table. That is why it is important to have outlined in your contract that you cannot be held liable for any destruction of personal property due to a bad dog.

The client might be aware of the dog's chewing on various chairs or tables and clue you in before leaving. But they might not want to crate the dog for a long time. I have had my share of dogs that get bored while left alone, so what I do is close off as many rooms in the home to limit the dog's destructive behavior. This will not stop the behavior, but it will cut down on the cleanup time. I have had quite a few dogs that have destroyed the client's couch, gotten into cabinets, and pulled out all the pots and opened drawers to tear up papers. I'm amazed at some of my more talented dogs, like the one that figured out how to open the refrigerator door to get the food in the fridge. I would have loved to have a video on that one. There was a pit bull that managed to climb up on the kitchen counter and eat the sink faucet! Every time he was left alone, he destroyed something, but my client wouldn't crate him.

I worry that these dogs could get hold of cleaning products, batteries, and any number of things that a dog shouldn't chew on. Pet-proofing the home while the client is away is something I have done many times. Sometimes I bring my own baby gates to prevent access to certain cabinets or rooms where there aren't any doors to close. I will use kitchen chairs or something that will not let the dog get into closets or cabinets. I try, but sometimes these dogs are relentless to get the job done. Trying to wear the dog out by a long walk or letting it chase a ball might help alleviate the destructive behavior. Even adding an extra visit might help, but I have found with these personality types, no amount of exercise while on the visit will stop a destructive dog. I have even suggested to some of my clients that they might consider boarding their dog only to have them say they would prefer to have them stay at home. What can I say only that these clients truly love their dogs!

Dogs That Destroy Pet Sitter's Property

The longer you're in the pet sitting business, the more likely it will be, when caring for a dog, that somehow they will destroy our personal property. This can happen unexpectedly or if you leave your belongings at the client's home for an overnight stay. If this happens, it should only take one lesson on your part to remember to put your clothing or bedding out of the dog's reach. Many years ago I had two Labrador retrievers, one older and a rambunctious year-old dog. Being this younger dog was so enthusiastic on our walks, I would always take them out separately. I had brought a light jacket with me that day, but it had gotten warmer, and I didn't need it on our walk. The younger dog was always taken out first because he just couldn't wait. When I took the older dog out for his walk and we returned, the younger Lab had my jacket in his mouth. It was torn up and not in any condition to be repaired.

In my notes I let the client know what happened, and he offered to pay for the jacket. I wouldn't accept any money for the jacket. First off, I never wear good clothing when caring for the dogs, and secondly, I felt this was my fault for leaving it in the dog's reach. I learned my lesson from that point on and always made sure if I was leaving any of my belongings at the client's home, I would lock it up in an off-limits room or closet. Sometimes the dogs become bored, and other times, I believe, they become frustrated that we have left them. Our scent is left on our belongings, and this causes them to get into our stuff and tear it apart. Oddly enough, the Lab that I spoke of never chewed up any of his owner's furniture or rugs. So it's not necessarily dogs that are destructive to begin with. I would suggest being careful where you leave your belongings at a client's home, especially if you are doing overnight stays. Your sleep bag and pillow might be a thing of the past.

Cats aren't left out of this scenario either as they might soil your jacket or bedding due to a medical problem or marking your belongings as their own. I have one assignment that no matter where I leave my jacket, this cat will find it, curl up on it, and settle down for a nice nap while I'm there. She is always very interested in the scent of my belongings. Although she has never soiled my jacket, she loves to make my jacket her own.

Dogs That Slip Their Collars or Harnesses

Most people are aware that dogs can slip their collars. But some are under the impression that they can't slip a harness. This can't be further from the truth because I have had quite a few who try to slip their harness. I said try because I always watch their every move, see things coming, and react before they have a chance to make their move. This is why I won't talk on my cell phone or listen to music while on my walk. Pet care deserves our full attention because things happen so quickly out there. I remember an incident with a little Jack Russell terrier who was always trying to back out of his harness. One day near a busy road, for whatever reason, he tried his hardest to slip out and almost succeeded, but I was ready for his tricks, and this little guy had many of them. He is, in part, one of the reasons why I started using my own leads.

Then there was Chelsea, a little Shiba Inu that was a handful on most days. She also had a housemate that was aggressive to both dogs and people. So I was always on my guard with these dogs. For some reason they didn't have their chain slip collars on that day. I had switched cars for the day and didn't have my leads with me. We went out for our walk, and it was ninety-five degrees with high humidity. A kid was coming down the street with an electric scooter, and did I mention that Chelsea loved to chase anything that moved? When he went by on the scooter, I saw her starting to slip her collar, and before she managed to get out, I slipped it back on. In a flash, she did it again and was successful this time. She started chasing the scooter, so I yelled to the kid to stop, and he did. Thank God he wasn't afraid of dogs because when he stopped, she lost interest.

But we weren't done just yet; she then took off through an open field, heading over to the next street, me following behind her with her housemate and an empty collar and leash. The kid had offered to go around the other way, and I accepted his help. I tried to get her to chase me, so I started running away from her then got down to the ground and called her name. Well, neither worked. Another one of my clients lived on the street she had headed for and came out to see what all the shouting was about, and when he asked, I told him I had a loose dog. I was expecting extra help. He then replied "Oh" and turned around and went back in the house. So much for the extra help. Just then I saw the kid but didn't see Chelsea when he says, "She's right there." Thank God for his extra eyes. She was leaning in a fence, getting ready to chase a bird she had spotted. I turned her leash into a slip collar by running the lead through the loop of the handle and finally had her. Our walk was over! I wanted to give this kid a couple of dollars for helping, but he said it was okay. "Just glad I got the dog," he said.

You have to be quick when a dog is trying to slip its collar or harness, paying attention to the dog at all times. I will never talk on my cell phone while walking because this is a distraction, and just like children, dogs will wait till you're preoccupied to make their move, at least most will. If you see it coming, you will be better prepared. Chasing a dog down isn't something that most pet sitters will want to be doing but is possible if they slip their collars.

Dogs Won't Let You In or Out of the House and Cats Too

I don't know what's more difficult, getting a dog to let you in the house or signing on a client's dog that won't let you out after being happy to let you in. Some assignments might look like a piece of cake on the initial consultation. And I must admit that even after all these years of sizing up the dog on the interview, I have been fooled. After all, who would suspect a dog that was friendly when you arrived would then decide not to let you leave? But it has happened to both my daughter and me. My daughter used to have a dog named Winnie that was a friendly midsized dog, and every time she was ready to leave, she would jump up and grab her, giving her a bear hug. The more she tried to push her away, the more determined she was to hold on to my daughter. She would then try to distract her by going into another room, but wouldn't you know it, she figured out what my daughter was up to and would grab hold again. It would take her a good twenty minutes to get out of the house, usually after Winnie got tired.

I have had a couple of dogs myself that would not let me out of the house. One was a rather smart, happy big golden. When I would be ready to leave, he would take off my shoe and run through the house. And there where many days when he would slowly grab hold of my jacket and first pull one arm off, and as I was struggling to keep my jacket on, he would manage to get it off me and take off with it. He was one smart dog who knew I needed my shoes and jacket in order to leave, and if he had them, I couldn't go. I had another pit bull that would always let me in but would aggressively go after me when I went to leave. I would get all my things together and bring a treat with me, toss it down the long hallway, and haul my butt out of the house. He was quicker than anyone could imagine, and as soon as I closed the door behind me, he would pound on the shut door, acting like a Tasmanian devil. Every time I went back in, he would be thrilled to see me. It was hard to figure that dog out.

Then we had Lulu. I went through three sitters with this dog. She was food-possessive, territorial with her house, and just plain old and grouchy. I walked her for years then had one of my ICs, who also used to treat her for her aches and pains with Reiki healing, take over for a while. Being she was food-possessive, I had asked the client numerous times when we were going in to pick the food up, and we would put it down when we left, but she never did. So it was always a battle with Lulu. She would let you hook her leash on, but you would have to be fast and watch for a certain look. Once she looked at you like this, she might be inclined to bite. She actually bit my daughter, and this is when my daughter refused to go back in. Every time Lulu was on the schedule, I'd go down my list and always get a "Lulu, I don't think so" reply. She wasn't a very big dog but did have a big attitude, and when out of her environment, she was a very sweet dog. I started caring for Lulu, passed her on to two other sitters, and then I ended up being the only one to have the guts to go in. I would use an umbrella to test the mood she was in on that particular day. And if she was in a bad mood, she would work her frustrations out on the umbrella for a bit before I was able to walk in. The sound of keys seemed to perk her up, and I only found this out many years into pet care. I really don't like caring for personalities like this, but even dogs of this nature need pet care. And in this business, we never know what we are going to get.

This leads me to my most recent dog from hell. This was a new client, and I didn't see any red flags on the interview, so I took on the assignment. The client had warned me that his dog had gone after his sister, and he told me to be careful. But as I said, I saw no signs on the consult. It was Thanksgiving weekend, and I had a busy schedule. This was a Border collie, and when I went in, he started to exhibit that circling behavior I described earlier, added to the fact he became very nervous and agitated, so I took my time with him, hoping to gain his trust. I really couldn't spare extra time on this busy weekend but had no choice. Finally, I got into the house, and feeding went well, but I wasn't able to hook him up and get him out. The next visit went the same way, but I was able to get him hooked up, and he was very friendly out on the street. There's something about being out of their environment with these personalities that changes their behavior. But when we were going back in the house and we got to the front door, he turned and lunged at me and not just once but it went on for about a minute or more. I used the leash with my arms stretched out to try to keep him away, but honestly, if I wasn't bundled up with a heavy winter jacket, he would have done some damage.

I'm usually pretty good in judging dogs on the initial consultation, and in all the years I've been in business, I have turned some prospective clients down for that very reason. This was the first time in all my years of being in business that I had to terminate a contract. I called the client and let him know he would have to come back early from his trip as I could no longer go in to care for his dog.

Dogs are not the only creatures that can be tough when trying to enter a home. Cats can lead us to believe that they won't pose a threat because some are shy, most are friendly, and some are downright scary! They are more difficult to reason with and can be extremely territorial. Chances are you won't run into too many of these personality types, but there is always a chance. I've had two so far in my years of pet sitting. Dallas was one, and we used to go in to walk her housemate—a super smart Border collie who would poop and pee on command. Dallas was very territorial but was fine when her housemate was home. It was when they would go away that Dallas's true colors would come out. Now, of course, when pet sitting for a cat, one must find their hiding place. Dallas's favorite place to sleep and hide was in the attic, and she did not like to be disturbed! Picture this, a grown woman who is supposed to be good with dealing with animals, cats in particular, running down two flights of stairs from a crazed cat. She chased me all the way to the front door before I realized and said, "Hey, I'm the pet sitter, bigger than you, and I'm here to take care of you!" I found a pillow to defend myself, and she did back off once she knew I wasn't going to back down anymore. She was my first experience with an attack cat and quite mild to my second experience when I look back.

My second incident was a month-long assignment, and I should have gotten a glimpse of what was to be by her behavior on the initial consult. She was aloof, and when my client was holding her for me to get to know, she lashed out at me. But as you know, some cats are just hard to get to know at first. This is the cat that, after the owners left for their prolonged vacation, turned into the devil, I kid you not. This was the assignment that I learned how handy an umbrella came in, not only protecting me from aggressive dogs but cats as well. This assignment was horrible from the start, and I must have been dreaming when I thought that after a couple of days she would start to warm up to me. Not only did she not warm up to me but each and every time I went in, I had to corral her into the bedroom with my opened umbrella just so I could clean her litter box and prepare her food. After I did my basic chores, I would let her out and leave. I tried to make friends, but this was futile, and cats can do some real damage if given the opportunity.

Embarrassing Situations

This is bound to come up at least once in your pet siting business. I know this has for me and one time for my IC. My embarrassing moment happened innocent enough when entering a client's home. I put the key in the door and enter to see my client's husband butt naked on the couch watching TV. So he goes on to say, "She didn't call you? We had a change of plans, we're leaving tonight." The whole time I was thinking this is the longest, most awkward moment I've ever experienced and say, "OK, I'll be back tonight." What could I do, it was totally unexpected and he didn't make an effort to cover up. So I just went with the situation.

One of my IC's had a similar experience with a client's brother unexpectedly showing up overnight. She walked in to find him lying half naked on the couch asleep. She was flustered and upset; she thought this could be a burglar. Called me and refused to go back again. I had gotten in touch with the client who had admitted that she didn't know he would be stopping by. I ended up completing the assignment because my IC was so upset.

Your personality and the ability to handle the unexpected embarrassing scenarios will get you through these awkward situations. They usually come up because of a forgotten call or a miscommunication. It's the little things that make this such an interesting profession and add a little laughter to the day.

Every-Other-Day Visits

This is a subject that will more than likely come up frequently if you plan on pet sitting for cats. Most people think cats are pretty self-sufficient and every-other-day visits are all they need, that cats could care less if they have company or not, and this is so untrue. Most cats thrive on attention, at least most do, except those infamous attack cats. I can tell you from my experience that so much can go wrong over a short period when pet sitting cats. Cats have a great way of hiding their illnesses, and this would be my main concern if someone would ask for EOD visits. I will admit, when I first started my business, I did accept EOD clients, but it wasn't long before I changed my outlook on this scenario.

I think it was in my first year of sitting when I took on a client that had a young cat about a year and a half old. She was a very healthy kitty, and I thought, being she was so young, I shouldn't have any problems with this assignment. My client was going on a two-week cruise and was not reachable by phone or e-mail. But as I said, I really didn't foresee a problem with this sit. It was a week into my assignment and all was going fine when I walked into the house to see the cat lying on the floor in the kitchen next to the cabinets. She couldn't move her body but was able to move her head, and I had no idea if she had somehow injured herself jumping from the cabinet or refrigerator. Well, off to the vet we went as my client's emergency contact was her mother, but I was only able to leave a voice mail. I didn't want the vet to go overboard with tests until I spoke with my client's emergency contact, but I wanted him to do the necessary blood work and whatever else was necessary. I felt horrible for this cat. Being I was going in every other day, I wondered how long she might have been lying there. It was from this point on I vowed never to go in every other day. It turned out that this cat had a neurological problem that went undetected, and of course, it surfaced when I was caring for the cat.

Besides the fact that a cat can become very ill in a short amount of time, they can get themselves into trouble in so many ways. I did have a client many years ago that had, at first, requested EOD visits, that is until I explained to her what can happen. She then went on to tell me how right I was because one of her cats had gotten itself tangled in the blinds cord. The sad end to her story was that the cat had strangled itself. She had only gone to work that day to come home to this devastating scene. So you can bet from that point on I also warned my clients with cats to make sure the blinds cords were up and out of the way.

We all know cats are pretty independent but still require TLC. Sure, some cats might be cautious when it comes to newcomers in their home, but once they get to know you, most seem like they are downright needy for attention while their owners are away. So this is another reason that I will not do EOD visits. Then add to the fact that you will then have to clean a two-day mess in the litter box, it's not fair to the pet sitter and not fair to the cat.

I recently got an e-mail from a prospective client asking for EOD visits for their two sixteen-year-old cats. They went on to say they don't need much because they sleep most of the time. Well, I know from experience that there was no way I'd be going in EOD for two geriatric cats. My reply was that I would love to help them out but that unfortunately we do not do every-other-day visits for cats. And I asked them to call the office to discuss any concerns and told them if they had questions about the service, I'd be glad to discuss them. Their e-mail reply said they were firm in their days requested and if I changed my mind, to get back to them. So my reply was short and simple, "Sorry we couldn't help." First off, the tone of the e-mail was not very caring for their cats. Secondly, I am also firm in my policies in regard to EOD visits. I will not bend my policies when it comes to cat sitting, especially when these are two older cats. Hopefully they found someone who knew a little about cats and was more caring than their owners.

So beware when it comes to EOD visits, even if the client insists that all will be fine. Even if they sign a waiver that they will not hold you responsible, when something goes wrong, the amount of stress involved is phenomenal and not fair to the cat. They are living, breathing beings that depend on us for their care. And as I said before, it's also not fair to a pet sitter to place this extra responsibility on us just so a client can save a couple of dollars.

Euthanasia

I have never experienced having to make a decision on having to put a pet down while the client is vacationing. But do have a plan in place because I care for elderly pets. When the client is on vacation most times I will be able to contact them, but not always. And although elderly pets come to mind when the thought of euthanasia comes up, younger pets can have an illness that not even the owner is aware of until it unexpectedly shows up one day, or some unforeseen catastrophe can happen. Having a plan in place with older pets is essential and emergency contact information as well. I think in most scenarios involving euthanasia, this would not be an immediate decision, unless, of course, the pet manages to get out of the home, get hit by a car, and the vet suggests putting them to sleep. And unless I could speak with the client, I would hold off on any decision to put the pet down, even with a vet's suggestion to do so. Although I have never had to make this decision, I would assume it comes with the same sadness and stress as the pets passing while their owners are away. It's possibly even harder to deal with because this decision will then be placed on our shoulders. This is a heavy weight for a pet sitter to bear.

If the client cannot be reached, I would contact my emergency contact person and work with them on a decision. I would lean toward holding off on a decision of this magnitude if it was at all possible. If, however, there is no other possible medical solution to the pet's illness or injury, a decision must be made. Upon the vet's recommendation, a pet sitter would then have to make this monumental decision. Most vets will hold the pet after euthanasia until the client can be contacted and a decision can be made if the client wants their pet back and as to what type of urn to be used after cremation. There are also vets that will come to the home to perform euthanasia, which I believe is less stressful for the pet. I would make the decision to stay with the pet as we are the closest to family while the client is away. I had never been one to stay with my own pets as this was devastating for me. But after my divorce, I had no choice in the matter and found that the pet really needs our presence in order to make their passing a little easier. Try to make the pet comfortable and remember that animals will work off our emotions. It's not always easy to keep a stiff upper lip when our own animals must be put down, but when our client's pets must, I would think this would possibly be more difficult. I hope the heavens above will spare me from ever having to make this life-or-death decision, but I have now implemented a waiver for geriatric pets. Having a signed waiver should be included in your contract for all animals. In this waiver your client should give you specific instructions on their wishes should the pet need to be put down. Young or old, accidents and illnesses happen and are never expected.

Fears and Phobias

I have had dogs that were afraid of thunder, fireworks, and garbage bags out on trash day, and people who wear hats. I've had dogs afraid of men, dogs afraid of everything, and even one dog that was afraid every time I opened the cabinet drawer to get a spoon to feed her. The dog that was afraid of the drawer opening was in the kitchen one time when the client had pulled the drawer out too far and it fell to the floor. The dog never forgot the incident, and every time the drawer would be opened, he thought it would happen again. As far as my other dogs with fears, most were rescued or adopted later in life, so the origins of their fears were not known. But one thing for sure is that dogs have excellent memories, and I'm sure that these dogs had their reasons for being fearful.

There's really not too much that you can do with these guys except try to reassure them when their phobias appear. Or totally avoid whatever brings out their fear if at all possible. They are usually good-natured dogs, and other than being fearful in some situations, they are easy to work with.

Cats will sometimes exhibit fear in certain situations, and unless you know what has happened in the past, it's hard to pinpoint what made them fearful. One of my own cats now has a fear because one day she was lying near where I keep my pens and I accidentally dropped a pen on her head. I didn't mean to have this happen, and now my poor little kitty is fearful every time anyone tries to pet her on the top of her head. She's fine if you come from a different angle, like under her chin or from the side, but not from the top. She will never forget what happened, I fear, and I feel horrible about this, but at least I know the reason for this behavior.

The only suggestion I can give is to reassure the pet, telling them it's okay, or if they're extremely fearful of certain situations, avoid them altogether. If you're out on a walk, make sure the dog will not become so frantic as to try to slip their collar and run.

Firing Clients

Sometimes we must come to a decision to fire a client for one reason or another. They can be longtime clients or new ones, and the decision can be a difficult one, especially if you're in need of the paycheck. But after all the years I've been servicing pets, the decision isn't as easy as it sounds because we become very attached to the pets in our care. Most times the client becomes abusive or demanding of our time. I have had clients that just seemed to turn on me for no apparent reason. But one thing I have learned is that for every bad client we fire, there are sure to be two appreciative clients to take their place.

Being diplomatic when firing a client isn't always easy as well, for if the client has been demanding or abusive, it usually doesn't go very well. Just remember that in the end this is just business, and remember not to take things personally. Keeping your cool when a client isn't happy with your decision to not service their pet can be difficult as well. Keeping our clients satisfied and happy are important, but we must also make sure that we are happy in our assignments, or resentment will begin to surface. Be honest with your client for the reasons you have come to this decision. Maybe they have moved farther away from your service area and the traveling is wearing you down. It could be that they have become inconsiderate of your policies or rude and abusive when requesting service, as if they are the only client you service. It's sometimes hard to be tactful when explaining your reasons, but if you're honest, it is possible that your client might understand your reasoning.

I once had an assignment that I probably shouldn't have taken on in the first place. This dog was aloof on the consult, and the client himself had admitted that the dog had gone after his sister. This was on a holiday, and getting into the house was difficult, as was trying to befriend this dog. I have had many of these personality types in the past and honestly thought I could work through this. The dog wouldn't come near me at all on the first visit; he had showed signs of aggression by circling. On the second visit I did get him out, and he was very friendly, which I was suspicious of. I thought I had a Jekyll and Hyde personality on my hands or he was extremely territorial, being this attack took place by the doorway to the home. When I did bring him back in, he went after me, attacking my belly, which was fine because I was really bundled up. I had to pull him away from me with the leash to get him to stop and go back in the house. This was an immediate termination of the assignment. I called the client to let him know what had transpired and that he would have to return. After all these years in business, I had to terminate an ongoing assignment. Most times I would finish up the assignment and then terminate my contract.

After terminating an assignment, ask the client how they would like their key returned. Some sitters have a special key-return form ensuring that the client can't say you've never returned their key. I have only felt the need to use one on two separate occasions because of the client's attitude. And in all my years there haven't been many situations where I have had to fire a client. If you send the key back through registered mail, you will have a copy of receipt of the key for the client must sign for the mail. Reasons for terminating a client will vary but something that will come up eventually.

Fireworks, Thunder, and Pets

While pet sitting, you will no doubt run into a pet that is petrified not only of fireworks but of thunderstorms as well. Most people associate dogs with these types of fears, but cats can also suffer with anxiety from loud noises and are highly sensitive to loud noises. I have spent many a Fourth of July pet sitting, and some of my clients' pets can get very agitated from the loud noises. But an added problem with fireworks is the smell of sulfur and flashes of light that go along with the noise. So what we do is to limit the senses, and as you know, in a pet these senses are magnified. If you close all the windows and doors, leave on a fan, a radio with soft music, or the television set to a nonviolent channel. This will sometimes help to alleviate their fears. I would also suggest closing all drapes or blinds as the flash of light from fireworks can also be disturbing. This should work with both dogs and cats.

The same can be done when a violent thunderstorm comes up. Turn the radio or television on to muffle the sound from the thunder and close the drapes as this will block the flash from the lighting. One of my own dogs suffered from thunderstorms trauma. As a matter of fact, she wouldn't want to go out two days before a storm came. She would curl herself up in her corner bed and refuse to go out. I would literally have to drag her outside to do her business, and fireworks were the same for her. One of my clients had a cat that would crawl along the floor to get to her hiding spot when a storm would break out. So both dogs and cats are affected by these types of situations. Older pets that were never frightened by these noises before will sometimes become fearful later in life, mostly because they have so many other problems developing at this time. This will sometimes cause both physical and behavioral changes in an older pet. I have found that Rescue Remedy helps with both cats and dogs (all other animals as well) when it comes to easing fears arising from loud noise, new people, or visits to the vet.

Anyone caring for horses might have to take precautions as well. If the horse is left outside, make sure there are no sharp points or weak places in the fence for the horse to injure itself. If the horse is left outside, there is also a chance that they might be struck by lightning, as this happened to my cousin's horses. She was boarding them at a neighboring farm, and they were never brought in. She was devastated. Securing them in a stall is your best bet, and to make the horse feel more relaxed, you a can mix up a solution of flower essences (found at a health-food store) with water in a spray bottle and spray the stall or a dropper full of Rescue Remedy to a spray bottle full of water.

It's all about lessening the fears of the pets left in our care. Animals are intuitive by nature and will know how severe a storm will be without listening to the weather. I had a dog walk with two dogs that weren't normally afraid to go out in the rain. It was getting dark and gloomy by the time I got to the house, and one dog in particular didn't want to go, but I reassured him and told him we'll be quick. As soon as we went out, it started to rain, and by the time we were going back, this dog was getting frantic. We couldn't get back to the house quick enough for him. Well, wouldn't you know it, we had a tornado, something rare in my part of the country. But the most amazing thing this dog did was he wouldn't let me leave! He knew his crazy pet sitter would try to get across the island in this severe storm. Every time I went to the door, he would jump up on me as if to say, "Don't go." He waited for the storm to pass and then let me leave, one smart dog he was. Roads were flooded, trees were down, and I was glad he stopped me. When I got to my next assignment, there was a huge tree limb over the front door entrance and in my client's top-floor window. I might have made it but not without danger involved. Listen to your pets. They can't verbalize their fears, but they do sense danger approaching. In the case of fireworks, their fears might not be rational, but fireworks can be terrifying to the pet.

If you have an extremely terrified pet that actually tries to get out of the house or into places that they could get hurt, you will have to use your judgment on what to do, possibly staying with the pet to help ease their fears. Fear from thunder or fireworks can cause a dog to tremble or shake. It might also make the dog bark and cause prolonged stress, which, in turn, might lead to diarrhea. I would also suggest to the client that they work on desensitizing the pet with thunder, firework, siren sounds found on a CD on a low volume to accustom the pet to these sounds. This is something I would have the client do over time because changes like this will not happen overnight.

I recently had a client whose dog was afraid of thunder, and she swore by the Thunder Shirt, said it helped her little dog. He's afraid of thunder and any type of loud noises. I haven't had too much experience with this product, but the manufacturer claims it can help with all forms of anxiety, including separation, destructive behavior, excessive barking, crating, and travel anxiety.

Gaining the Trust of a Fearful Dog

Somewhere along the line you might run into a pet that is fearful. I have had a few jobs like this, and I can tell you the time invested in gaining a dog's trust can sometimes be a waste of time, especially if your client doesn't go on vacation very often. I once had a dachshund that was not aggressive but extremely fearful of strangers. I had gone over to the house a few times for her to get used to me, and she did warm up a little, but not as much as I would have liked. When the client went away, I spent additional time reassuring the dog that everything would be fine, and I would have a hard time getting her out from under the bed. During a year's time, my client went away a few times, and my little dachshund did start to warm up. But these visits took some time as I did not want to scare her and would always have to gain her trust all over again. The following years my client would only go out of town once a year, and all my work at gaining her trust had disappeared. I believe dogs of this nature were never socialized enough growing up.

We had two other dogs with this type of personality, and both were rescues that we would go in for a daily walk. One was kept in the client's bedroom and didn't have many places to hide; we would usually find him in the closet. We walked him for years, and he never really warmed up to us. This job wasn't time-consuming because he was always in the bedroom, and we would just go in and hook him up. He wasn't aggressive at all, so there wasn't too much stress involved in this job. Recently we picked up another client with a rescued, fearful dog. I used to call him Stone Dog because his body would become very tense, and he would not move at all. He too wasn't aggressive, but he did have the run of the house, so getting ahold of him was time-consuming. He was petrified of men, and we walked him in an apartment building with a doorman and lots of activity. So to make my life easier, I would just pick him up until we were far enough away from all the activity for him to feel relaxed enough to go potty. This assignment just seemed to go away on its own, and we were not too concerned as it always threw us off schedule.

So in my opinion I would prefer to stay away from these personality types. I've had other fearful dogs that after a few visits recognized us as a good thing and never had a problem with them even if the client only went away occasionally. So my advice is to not to waste too much time on these personality types as they might do better with a family member as gaining their trust is sometimes a monumental feat.

Getting a Client to Call
When They Return

Good luck with this one. I can't help but think of the many sitters I've heard complaining that their client doesn't call upon returning from a vacation. That includes myself, and in the beginning of my business, I found myself spending so much time tracking clients down. So what I have done is to put this in my policy that the client is responsible for calling upon returning. I go over dates and times with the client, confirming before they head out of town, so that we're both on the same page. I also make it clear to them that they are responsible for notifying us of any changes. In my opinion you would need a secretary to make all these calls once your business picks up. And would you have a secretary work late nights, waiting for a call from a client, and then get in touch with a sitter to go over to the client's house if you get no answer? It doesn't make for good business sense no matter how much we care for our client's pets. I found that I was beginning to be resentful of clients who didn't call.

When I first started out, I would have to check my schedule and then call the client who rarely picked up the phone. With no answer, I'd head over to the house to find suitcases when I go in. Sometimes the client would be sound asleep in their bed, something that I would have liked to be doing, and I'd get back in my car to head back home. Even charging for a visit didn't make me feel any better. When you're out all day and you have a certain amount of stops scheduled and get back home or to the office to find no message from the client, it's very frustrating. You then have to go back out again, and even if you charge the client for this visit, it is a tremendous inconvenience! I also had complaints from any independent contractors that helped me out if they had to go back out. Sometimes clients will be getting in very late and don't need the visit, so being up front with their sitter is very important. Always ask for the estimated time they will be getting home because when traveling, luggage can be lost and flights missed.

Some of my clients call regularly, usually on their way back from the airport, but not many. These are my special clients; they are considerate and lower my anxiety level. So by adding this to my contract and the client fails to call upon return, I place the responsibility on them. The longer you're in business, the more clients you will have to keep track of, and I think this is very unfair to the sitters. I make it clear to the client that if they are delayed and need additional visits for any reason, they must give sufficient notice by calling or e-mailing. I also let them know that we have other pets in our care and might not be able to get to their pet if they don't give sufficient notice. It's all about consideration and respect. If the client cares about their pet, they won't take it for granted that we are mind readers and call us when they return from their trip.

Of course you can put in your contract or policies that you will visit the home if they fail to call and charge for the extra visit; this might work with some clients. You will soon find yourself running around needlessly and begin to feel burnt-out. When my business started running full throttle, I found my independent contractors and myself starting to suffer from burnout and frustration from uncaring clients. Once we're home from a long day on the road, who wants to go out again? Make your client responsible for their schedule. Since I have taken up this policy, my stress level has been reduced considerably. As long as you go over your schedule with the client and double-check before they leave, there should be no mistakes with the visits requested. When they are delayed due to extreme weather or other mishap and call for an additional visit, it is an inconvenience, but at least I know that the client will not be returning on time and adjust my schedule. This has worked for me for the last eighteen years.

Giving and Receiving Gifts

Gifts aren't necessary but always nice to get. My clients have always treated me well, whether it was a small token to say "thank-you", holiday "bonus", or they knew it was my birthday; they have always been generous with gifts. It could be money, perfume, gift card, dinner gift certificate, and they have all been appreciated. This also shows a pet sitter that our clients really care and appreciate the extra effort we give at times. My clients are extremely generous around the holidays as well.

This brings me to giving our clients gifts. I make a decent living but cannot afford to give for birthdays and special events but will leave a card if I'm aware about their birthday. The holidays are the only time I will go all out for my clients and their pets. I try to find inexpensive gifts for the pets as there are many. Toys and treats can be gotten on sale throughout the year. For my clients, I will give a nice picture frame with a picture of their pet, a pet Christmas ornament with their breed, breed-saying posters, a new leash or collar, a nice pet bowl for the home, and anything pet related to give my client. One year I made breed cookies for my clients. I had found cookie cutters in almost every breed and cat shapes as well, put them in a small cellophane bag, and tied it with a colorful bow. If you use your imagination, you can find thoughtful little gifts for your clients, and by doing this once a year, it shows you appreciate their business. If you're on a limited budget, cards will be fine, and if you're talented, you can make your own to add a personal touch. Taking a picture of the pet and putting it on the card adds that personal touch.

Giving Advice

As a pet care professional, we might encounter situations where we are either asked for advice or feel the need to give advice to our clients. When this applies to a medical problem and I see some type of problem, I will definitely mention this to my client. I might also suggest that they should run this by their vet. I try to educate the owners but will not talk down to them, always being tactful in my advice. When giving advice, we cannot push our opinions on our clients. The best we can do is to plant some seeds of advice and hope they grow. Sometimes just by mentioning you noticed a change in their pet's appearance will get them to actually take a good look at their pet and hopefully take your advice. Sometimes we might think we know what's best for someone else's pet, and if you're a good pet sitter, you probably do. Don't be too critical and condescending though as some of your clients might take offense to this. And you would have then shot yourself in the foot, defeating the purpose of offering advice.

When asked for advice, I try to follow these same rules. Being in the pet care industry for a number of years, I'm constantly asked by my clients for advice. It might seem like an easy task, and at times it is. Other times, when the pet is ailing and they want to know what the right thing to do is, it is hard. I've had a difficult time when faced with my own decisions, let alone another's, like when the client wants to know how you do know it's time to let them go and they have to be put to sleep. My response to this question would of course depend on the circumstances. Most times I leave it at "It's really a difficult decision, and when the pet's quality of life goes downhill rather quickly, I would say its time." I add that we tend to keep them here for ourselves as we humans are selfish and how it's not fair to have them suffer like that. This would be a pet that I know is having a difficult time and have had them for years and years. I personally can't see those sad eyes asking for help when all treatments have failed and they're shivering in pain.

Sometimes the client will not want to admit that their pet is in pain, living in self-denial as, I'm sure, many of us have done at times, refusing to give up on their pet. This is when being very tactful will help all involved get through a difficult decision. One alternative would be to have them seek the advice of a holistic vet that might be able to provide alternative treatments. I have had clients who actually felt like their whole world was caving in and couldn't bear the pain of watching their pet suffer. In these instances, we become more of a therapist or grief counselor than a pet sitter. Always taking the time to talk with your clients, even when you're pressed for time, shows that you truly care. Most of us have gone through some type of illness with our own pets that we can relate to. Remembering with your client all the great times and distinctive personality traits that the pet has and the wonderful care the client has given might help ease the anxiety. Let the client know they are wonderful parents and caregivers.

If in doubt about what advice to give, I would just tell your client that they should speak with their veterinarian, that their vet would be able to help them. I never give advice on things I know little or nothing about, always knowing my limits and being honest about them. This is an area that can be tricky. If your advice is not wise, you might begin to raise doubts in your client and cause damage to your reputation. If you are going to give advice on something, then make sure you have done your research or have learned through experience what the right path to take would be.

Handicapped Pets

If you plan on caring for handicapped or elderly pets, keep in mind that they will require more time and worry. I'm always concerned about their health and will usually drill the client for signs of illness or what is normal for the pet considering the circumstances. For instance, you will not want to become overly concerned if the client tells you that a dog that is having difficulty with its hind quarters refuses to get up at times. Don't start to panic as this is sometimes the case because the pet itself will have to help with the process. You can't lift an immobile object no matter how hard you try. Then there will be other times as soon as you come through the door the dogs will be attempting to get up before you can take the key out of the door.

Handicapped pets can be an amputee, a dog with severe hip dysphasia, a dog suffering from Cushing's disease, or have any number of problems that make it difficult for the pet to get up and around or hold its bladder. I tend to place elderly pets in with the handicapped pets because by this point in their life, they are suffering from problems such as arthritis, incontinence, problems with hind quarters, and so on. I can go on, but I'm sure you get the idea. The client will usually clue me in on how they do things, and every assignment is unique. Being that I have been in business for years, most of my clients' pets have grown old along with me. So I have dedicated a section to the care of older pets in this section.

Another type of handicapped pet you might encounter is a deaf dog; they will need special attention but aren't so hard to care for. The owner will have to show you sign language to help in communicating with the dog. Yes, I have been taught sign language for deaf dogs and welcomed the opportunity from the client to learn this. I just wish I would have had this knowledge when caring for the three others I had; this would have made it easier for the owners as well. They can also feel vibrations, so when caring for them, walk a little harder, slam the door a little when coming in. This will let them know you are there and won't startle them. Other than the fact that they can scare easily if they're not watching you, they are pretty easy.

I have been specializing in the care of handicapped pets for most of my time in business, and although it is very rewarding, it can be very sad at the same time. We usually do not have these pets for very long as there will come a day to end their suffering. So I let them live to the fullest, and whatever they want to do, we do. These pets are sometimes anxious because they are uncomfortable or in pain. Just work with them and help to ease their fears. On these assignments I've found I've had to improvise quite a bit; what works for the owner will not always be the case when we go in.

If you are new to caring for disabled pets, on the interview, go over with the client how to hook up their dog wheelchair, walking wheels, or other aid. These can seem complicated to the novice. But more than learning how to hook up the chair, you need to know how the owner goes about this process. If they have a hard time getting the dog to cooperate, you can bet you will have an even more difficult time with this. If the dog has been using the chair for some time, they are eager to get going on their walk. Every situation is very different.

For the most part it takes some time, but you will get the hang of caring for handicapped pets if you feel inclined to do this. As I said earlier, it is very rewarding. Not too many tools are required by a pet sitter, but I do carry a few with me in case I can't find what the owner uses. One is a plain old beach towel as these are long but not bulky. If a dog has hind problems and can't get itself up, place the towel right in front of the back legs just in front of the chest cavity in the form of a sling. Encourage the dog to get up, and when the dog makes an effort to get up, gently lift the towel by holding both ends of the towel, making a rocking motion. I always tell the dogs, "Okay, 1, 2, 3, up." Of course, it's not as easy as that, but after a few tries, we're good to go. If you feel the dog is starting to stress because they can't get up, sit with them, give reassuring words, and, after a few minutes, give another try. You might have to do this several times depending on the severity of the dog's handicap.

Another tool I use is the bottoms-up leash; it works well once the dog is up and helps support the dog's hind legs while walking. As I said, the dog must be up already, and the leash has two loops (they look like leash handles) that the dog's back legs will go in. This leash will aid the dog on its walk if they become weak or if they seem like they might go down. This is something I try to avoid as getting them back up is a chore. Having support on the torso and not the neck will be safer and more effective helping the dog regain balance.

Sometime back I purchased a firewood carrier; this is my most handy aid of all as I like the support it gives the dog and has two handles. It is made out of leather and will serve me for many years to come. I had purchased this for my own dog, and it wasn't cheap. They do sell canvas carriers that are considerably cheaper. Although the towel serves it purpose, the firewood carrier gives added support to a handicapped pet. Handles are easier to grip than an end of a towel. You can find these in any home-improvement store or online. Make sure the carrier has open sides as one of my clients had bought the kind that was more of a bag. She then had to cut the sides out, and it wasn't as useful as the open-sided carriers.

I have only declined one handicapped pet in all these years for a few reasons. One was because the owner could not get the dog to cooperate at all. The dog refused to go down the stairs. It happened to be a German shepherd. It was not the largest I've ever seen but big enough. The second reason was the stairs leading to the apartment. I counted twenty steps just to the front door and an additional six to get to their apartment. No wonder why this poor dog was giving his owner a hard time. It would be like climbing a mountain to get back up. Remember what I said earlier about knowing what you can handle. The owner was quite upset with me, and I did feel bad that I could not help in this situation. But these disabled dogs can't handle the amount of energy required to get up and down the stairs even with assistance. We must be mindful of our own bodies when we're helping the dog up and down the stairs, being careful not to injure ourselves in the process.

I knew this job was very difficult and could not risk injury to myself or the dog.

Not too many pet sitters will want to take on assignments like these, but I really enjoy being able to comfort a handicapped pet while their owners are out of town. This will be something to consider when deciding on what services to offer.

Helping Your Client Deal with Loss of Pet

This is a topic that will come up many times in a pet sitter's line of work. Pet Sitters are usually the first to hear of the loss of a client's pet. Most of my clients will either call me or stop by my home shortly after making the painful decision of euthanasia or sudden death. Pet sitters create strong bonds between the pets in our care and our clients, becoming an extended part of the family. So it will become necessary to help our clients through this process. You might find that some of your clients begin to feel guilty about not doing enough for their pet that they should have taken better care of them, which couldn't be further from the truth. Guilt and grief go hand in hand, and because the pet cannot tell us they are sick, we sometimes punish ourselves by saying it's our fault because we should have taken them to the vet sooner. Being powerless to help our pet is a real fear that is disguised as guilt. By saying we could have done something more helps to ease our fears that we were unable to keep our pet alive.

Others will be having a hard time making a decision to euthanize their pet. Reminding the client that the quality of life is just as important for pets as it is for people might help to ease their fears of making the wrong decision. Some of my clients often regret not staying with the pet, and some people, including myself, find it very difficult to stay with the pet during this emotional moment. Although I have stayed during euthanasia, I wondered if this was wise as animals work off our emotions, and with me sitting there in tears, how could I be comforting the pet? This can be overwhelming to most people, and saying farewell is always difficult. Most of our clients will see their pets as their children who give unconditional love, making this a debilitating time.

We, as pet sitters, can help our clients by offering our support and kind words. Remembering the cute little nuances of their pet will make them smile, if only for a moment. What I like to do while pet sitting / dog walking is to take lots of pictures of my clients' pets. Sometimes these are some of the most current pictures that the client will have. I try to capture the personality of the pet. For example, I used to have a Doberman that loved to carry around his blanket always. I snapped a shot of him doing this and gave a copy to my client in a nice frame. Another client that I just recently lost was an eighteen-year-old Yorkie client that had almost no teeth. A few years back I snapped a picture of him with his tongue hanging out to the side; he was famous for this because of missing teeth. I made an eight-by-ten copy for my client. She didn't have a picture taken since he was a pup and said this captured his true self. I also will send out a sympathy card and include a copy of "Rainbow Bridge" or some other memorial poem that brings a tear to the eye.

Other options to help memorialize your client's pet are to create a scrapbook, make a collage of different stages in the pet's life, plant a tree, or donate money to a charity for animals in the pet's name. If you're talented, you might also consider writing a poem or letter for the pet, dedicating this to the client in the pet's name.

Everyone needs to grieve, but we do not all grieve in the same way. Some clients will grieve deeply for the loss of their pet, while others seem to grieve silently. Just reassure your client that this is a normal process, and it will take time to heal from such a loss. There might be a support group or grief counselor in your area that could help your client cope, and being aware of any in your area will be helpful to your client. I would also like to make mention of a local pet bereavement support group that I had found many years ago when one of my clients' pets had passed. This is a great resource to pet sitters as well as anyone who is having a difficult time dealing with the loss of a pet. Paw to Heart Pet Bereavement Support Group located in Massapequa, New York, offers support groups and chat rooms free of charge. You can find them on the web at www.pawtoheart.org.

They have a great education packet on animal loss available upon request, a needed tool for pet sitters helping their clients cope. I strongly suggest you request an education packet. Even if you're just starting out, you will find that this will be valuable to you in the future. They offer lectures and workshops for your facility or event with qualified speakers and universal grief to grieve the loss and suffering of all animals abused, neglected, hunted, and trapped.

There are books you can read to understand this process more clearly, and you should also recommend these books to your clients. Here is a brief list of recommended reading:

1. *Death: The Final Stage of Growth* by Kübler-Ross, E.

2. *Talking About Death: A Dialogue between Parent and Child* by Grollman, E.

3. *Coping with Sorrow on the Loss of Your Pet* by Anderson, M.

4. *Absent Friend* by Lee, L. and Lee, M.

5. *The Loss of a Pet* by Sife, W.

6. *Oh, Where Has My Pet Gone?: A Pet Loss Memory Book, Ages 3–103* by Sibbitt, S.

7. *Surviving the Heartbreak of Choosing Death for Your Pet: Your Personal Guide for Dealing with Pet Euthanasia* by Peterson, L.

8. *Pets Living with Cancer: A Pet Owner's Resource* by Downing, R.

9. *A Final Act of Caring* by Montgomery, H. and Montgomery, M.

10. *Good-bye, My Friend* by Montgomery, H. and Montgomery, M. (good for children)

I always have sympathy cards on hand for the passing of my clients' pets, and I usually have a card with all types of animals on the front with a saying of how sorry we are for their loss. I also have another card that sympathizes with the client's decision in putting their pet to sleep. The two sources where I purchase my cards are the following:

It Takes Two—They have a nice selection of pet-bereavement cards and are located at www.ittakestwo.com.

Sharper—They have bereavement cards and many other products for pet care professionals and are located at www.e-sharper.com.

I have a few poems that I enclose with my card that always bring a tear to the eyes. I believe in having a good cry; it is therapeutic and a natural phase for our clients mourning their pet. I can't tell you how many times after leaving off a gift or card where the client calls to say, "Thank you, you really made me have a good cry." I have also found small pet stones with a paw print and heartwarming sayings such as "If tears could build a stairway and thoughts a memory lane, I'd walk right up to heaven and bring you home again." I have also given pet-sympathy kits, which include a small candle and a nice bag for the client to place the collar, tags, and the like. I have given a picture of their pet in a nice frame, paw print memory stone (these can be done ahead of time if you are aware of the pet's health and time with us). There are many things you can do for your client and keep their pet's memory alive. Donating to a local rescue in honor of their pet is another option and needed for other pets to find a forever home. It's very sad for the client, but it also affects the person who has cared for the pet, sometimes for many years. This is a very difficult aspect of the pet sitting business.

Hotel Pet Sitting

Pet sitting in hotels is another scenario that I didn't consider when starting up. But there have been a few occasions where I have had requests for this type of service. Most times these are one-time clients who have to attend some type of event in my area and want to take their dog along. Being I've never considered this scenario, I really didn't have a price for this type of service. So I charged what I would for an overnight being this covers an eight-hour time frame. I would have one of my ICs do the assignment, and they loved it. I always outsource these assignments because I have a full schedule, and I tend to get restless staying for a prolonged time in any one place. The assignment consisted of taking the dog out every couple of hours, playtime, TLC, and nap time. If the client is generous, they might tell the sitter to order food for the stay and charge to their room. I had instructed the sitters to not take advantage of this extra benefit, and one of my ICs declined to do this altogether and brought her own food in a small cooler. One thing to consider when pet sitting in hotels is the time involved. If you have no backup or ICs and have a request of this sort, it will be difficult to take on pet sitting in hotels. Scheduling will become important, and if you have other pet sits, there will be a conflict. I never advertise for this service, but if I get a call, I will give them a quote, and if they want to book, they must pay a month prior to the date of service. This ensures payment with no problems involved. I have had clients that used my service call to request more dates in other boroughs but declined service even when they agreed to pay for transportation fees on top of service fees. In cases like this, I usually refer them to sitters in the area they are staying. Pet sitting in hotels can be enjoyable for the sitter, but extra help is usually required.

Household Problems

Leaks

Although they don't happen all that often, when a leak occurs in a client's home, it must be attended to. What I usually do is contact the client first; I never hesitate to call if the client can be reached. If I can't speak with the client, I then call my emergency contact telephone. I work on the fact that two heads are better than one. Sometimes it's a small leak from a pipe in the sink or toilet. Other times it can be a major leak involving the hot water heater, so these situations are judgment calls. Sometimes just putting a bowl under the leaking pipe in the kitchen would be enough, depending on the length of time until the client returns home.

Other major leaks will require calling a plumber and coordinating a time to meet at your client's home to have the problem resolved. Imagine having a full schedule and then having to squeeze in meeting up with a plumber, not to mention the additional time spent at your client's home. I had both situations come up. The small leak was easy to handle, and the client was due back in a day, so they would take care of it. I did, however, have to spend extra time waiting at a client's home for a plumber to come fix a leaking radiator with a client that was unreachable, and the leak was causing damage to the floor.

Recently one of my client's toilets sprang a leak. The hose that fills the tank had come off completely. Luckily I was in the kitchen, cleaning the cat's dishes, and when I turned the water off, I still heard water. I followed the sound to the bathroom to see the hose spraying all over the bathroom. The super lives across the hall from my client and thankfully he was home. In a matter of minutes the bathroom floor was soaked, water started to go into the living room and by his quick response not too much damage was done. She lived on the first floor, but could you imagine the damage that might have occurred if I was not there and if she lived on the second floor? It would have been a nightmare for sure. I cleaned up the mess, and I had to empty water out of everything, but it could have been much worse. These things can happen, and we are responsible while the client is away.

Furnace and Air-Conditioning

Most of my clients will leave a relative's telephone number when they suspect they might have a problem with their heating or cooling system, taking the responsibility off my shoulders. I started to encourage this after my house leak. In the event the client has no family close, I suggest a friend. I will always contact the client first, and if it is necessary, I will then have to wait for the repair man. If the central air breaks down when they are away and the temperature outside is very high, you could have a problem with the pet and heatstroke. The same will hold true for the heating system, and sometimes there seems to never be a dull moment while pet sitting.

Leaking Roofs

Leaking roofs can sometimes be a surprise. I had a client who had had some roof damage from Hurricane Irene and told me that she had set up some buckets in case it rained while she was away and that I might have to empty the buckets. So we had a heavy rainstorm, and when I went in, I thought all I would have to do is empty the buckets. Well, the roof sprouted a new leak, and when I went in for the morning visit, I was shocked on the condition of the kitchen. There was water all over, the area rugs were wet, and added to the cat care, I now had to clean up a leaking-roof mess. I placed a call to the client, and she opted to let it be until she returned as this was on her list of things to do when she got home. Being a pet sitter is so much more than just caring for pets.

Lock Malfunction

Being we go into so many homes, some new and other older homes, we will more than likely run into a problem with a lock. What I usually do is carry a can of WD-40 lubricant. Most times this will work on a sticky lock. The key will go in but will not turn the lock to open; this should be your first option before calling a locksmith. Another trick is to use graphite by rubbing a pencil on the edges of the key. This should work to open the lock, and I have used this technique in the past. Make sure you don't use too much force trying to open the lock if it's not working. You might break the key in the door. If all else fails, you'll be waiting on a locksmith. This is a good reason to have a clause in your contract outlining who will pay. My clause holds the clients responsible.

Appliances

I try not to worry about this happening. In all my years of pet sitting, I had one appliance start to malfunction. This happened to be the refrigerator, and it slowly began to go down in temperature. The client was unreachable, and being it wasn't such a major breakdown, I let it go till the client came home. She had told me after the repairman came in to look at the fridge it was determined she needed a new refrigerator. I place some household problems low on the need for immediate attention, and this is one. Again this will be on a case-by-case basis.

Alarms

Most of my clients have their alarms in excellent working condition, reason being that my area will fine the homeowners after three false alarms. Most times when a client goes on vacation a common problem that might come up is when the battery gets low. This can be more of an annoyance than a problem because of the constant beeping, alerting the client of the low battery. And to call the alarm company for something as minor as this isn't necessary. On the other hand, an alarm that is going off at all hours will need attention. I will touch base with my client and ask what they would like to do and go from there. Sometimes it's not even a malfunction, but most of my clients have motion detectors that cause the problem. When the sensor detects motion from the pet, it will go off, a cat jumping off a counter or a dog barking can cause this. I have recently learned that a solution to this problem is to set the alarm on stay. It works like a charm. The house is still protected, but the sensor is set to think someone is home.

I'd like to add that you might want to question your client as to how many seconds you have to enter the home. I have been greeted by some very happy dogs, cats too, that make it difficult to get in and shut the alarm off. Most are set to go off after a minute or so, but I have had a few that were set to thirty seconds. This is not much time to get into a home with pets, in my opinion, so I always ask. Some clients will assign my own code; it makes them feel more secure. It is also important to get their password in case of the alarm going off. There have been quite a few times that I have either punched in the wrong code or have not gotten to the keypad in time. My clients always notify the alarm company that I will be coming in, so I never have a problem in that regard. If your client is skeptical of giving you their password, they can either disarm their alarm while they are away or ask their alarm company if you can have your own personal password. I require their password to protect the client from unnecessary false alarms. The alarm company will call, and I usually identify myself and give the password with no problems.

Break-Ins

I have only had to deal with one break-in during all the years my pet sitting business has been in operation. I found this to be a very stressful situation, and I'm very thankful that this was a daily walk because the client was not out of town. If you suspect a problem, exit the home immediately. Go to a nearby neighbor's house; contact the police and client. Never attempt to investigate the home on your own as the intruder could still be in the home. If the client is vacationing, you will need to contact the client's emergency contact because these things will take some time. If you have a full schedule, you will need to attend to your other clients. A police report will need to be filled out, and the client's emergency contact can take care of this. If any information is required from you, they can call. It's very important to have all your emergency contact telephone numbers up to date, so have this as one of your questions before the client goes on vacation.

Dog Barking Complaints

Unfortunately this might come up from time to time, and it is something that is out of our control. Some dogs can start to feel lonely or be very good watch dogs, and we never know how understanding our client's neighbors will be. I have had to sweet talk a couple of my client's neighbors, hoping to alleviate any hostility that might be developing, and I believe our attitude in a situation like this can bring positive or negative reactions. I will always have a friendly attitude to all surrounding neighbors as I feel this will give them the opportunity to approach me if they have any concerns. If they do complain, I usually tell them I will put the television on to make them feel like they are not alone or try to find some other solution, maybe even adding an extra visit. This has worked for me in the past, and I know my clients will hear about this when they return. But if you have a good attitude in this situation, it can, more than likely, make the neighbor just a little more understanding, hopefully. If, however, all the neighbors come out at once to complain about the dog barking, a call to your client might be necessary, and some other arrangements might have to be made. You might also want to suggest to your client they purchase a Barker Breaker, which is a humane way to stop dogs from barking. But I wouldn't take this upon myself while the client is away as all pets differ, and there is no need to bring unexpected results in case the dog acts in a negative manner. Some of my clients have used shock collars for their dogs. I'm not very happy about having to use these collars, but it can be necessary at times when all else fails. Another option would be to use a citrus spray collar; this will spray a citrus scent every time the dog barks. I have had a client whose dog was so determined to bark that this collar wasn't successful, and I had to resort to the shock collar. Once the dog is conditioned to get a shock every time they bark, it can be left on the dog but not turned on. The dog will associate the collar with the shock and not bark while wearing it. This will only work after some months of use.

Nosey Neighbors

Ah, the nosey neighbor, every neighborhood has one, so you're sure to encounter one on your assignment. I love the ones that seem to be waiting for you just to get some information as we're getting out of the car. What I do is try to be as vague as possible. If they want to know when they are coming home, I say, "Tonight, I think, wait, maybe it's tomorrow. I'll have to check my schedule." It's really none of their business, but I'll never say that. I never let them know what's going on, where they went, how long they're gone for. Whatever they ask, I say I'm not sure. If my client wanted to tell the neighbor, they would not be asking me all these questions. Be nice, but don't divulge any information about your client. Another situation that you may encounter is not a nosey neighbor but a neighbor who has a complaint related to your client. I dislike this situation because this proves to be awkward for the sitter. It is similar to the barking dog complaint, but it could relate to anything about your client that their neighbor is not happy with. Personally this is none of my business; it's between the neighbor and my client. I'll give you an example: I went to visit one of my cat clients who also requests that I feed the outdoor cats. I never charge extra for this because the cats need to eat, and every neighborhood has a person who takes on this mission. I was greeted by their next-door neighbor, who asked if I charged for feeding the outside cats. Then she went on to explain that cats are dirty. "Why doesn't she take them in if she cares about them?" she asked. The list of complaints went on and on. She then went on to tell me it was against the law to feed outside cats! What? I looked this up both on the ASPCA and mayor's website. This is not true.

They encourage people to feed the strays but to also trap and neuter them, which I have asked my client if she wanted help with this as I could provide a trap and assist her. She declined. I told her neighbor, "I'm not the pet police and could only plant a seed for my client. What she does with it is her business." I don't feel the need to justify my business or my client's personal outlook on life. So I then proceeded to come out in front of the neighbor and feed the outside cats. She really got under my skin, and that's usually hard to do, but these cats need to eat as well as all nature's creatures do. And despite what the neighbor thinks, cats will keep down the mice and rat population, not bring them closer to civilization. So be prepared to come up against some nasty, nosey neighbors at times and try not to take it personally; although that is sometimes hard to do when they are attacking your client and taking it out on you.

Power Outages

They can happen during a bad storm or in the summer months, when outages are a common occurrence. Most times they are short-lived and no real problems come of them. However, some can be long term, say a day or so, and can create more problems. Food in the refrigerator can go bad. Alarms won't be working. I have even had to visit homes in the dark, and just navigating around the home is an adventure. My cell phone has come in handy for times when the power went out while

I was in the home, helping me get to the car for my flashlight. Going from home to home in a power outage can be a bit frightening as all those scary movies that were watched seem to come rushing in. It's just something that we have to work through, and if you have visits scheduled, you have to go, power or not. I told you this job is an adventure! If you have any assignments in larger buildings where an elevator is used, you might find yourself walking up eight flights of stairs. This has happened to us several times, and going up is always tougher than going down, not once but twice if you're going in to care for a dog—to get the dog and then going for a walk.

Unexpected Guests

This can be scary, awkward, and downright aggravating. This situation is out of our control, and although our clients are aware, we have to know who might have access to the home. There have been times when even the client did not know that a relative would be stopping by. I have been in homes where I'm doing my chores and hear a door open, start to get really nervous, and out pops the client's mother, who happened to be just as scared as I was. She didn't know they were going away and saw the light on. She lived right next door. One of my ICs was also startled on a morning visit to see a man sleeping half-naked on the living room couch. This happened to be the client's brother, and they didn't know he was coming. My IC refused to go back to the job, so I took over the rest of the visits.

Sometimes the visiting guest will try to talk you into not coming because they are there. This is not possible for my service unless I hear directly from the client. I will also inform my client that they will still be charged whether I go in or not, so most times they continue service.

Clogged or Nonworking Toilets or Drains

When we're working on assignments, it will become necessary to use the bathroom. There have been two recurring problems with toilets that I have run into. One is the mechanism in the tank will get hung up, and after you flush the toilet, it keeps running. So my suggestion after using the toilet, stay until it stops running and the bowl is full of water. What I will do if the chain or flapper gets hung up is I will take the cover off the tank and fix it manually. The other problem is the toilet isn't working; most of my clients will point out a toilet that I can use or one that isn't working. But on occasion, I have used the toilet and gone to flush it and it was broken. Luckily it wasn't a leaking toilet, but the mechanism was broken. So here again I was able to flush it by taking the tank lid off and doing this manually. Drains can pose another problem; sometimes the drain is somewhat clogged. The water goes down slowly. Here's where being a bit of a handyman helps. I have gone searching the house for a plunger and worked at the clog. Sometimes this helps; other times it's enough to get you through the assignment. You must be careful that the faucet is turned off completely because a constant drip will build up while you are not there, and you might come back to a flood. Anything major will have to be looked at by a professional after contacting the client. Most of the time my clients will send a friend or relative over to take care of the problem.

How to Keep Stray Dogs Away

In New York State we have a leash law, and all dogs are required to be on a leash while walking. Only in a dog park are they allowed off the leash, but that doesn't stop some owners from letting their dogs roam free. Avoiding a possible threat to the dog you're walking can make life a lot easier. I have been able to ward off some dogs by taking a firm stand and by making my voice sound like a growl with a "Grrrr," telling them to go home or a firm no. In dog language, a growl means stop or "I'm not liking what you're doing, stay away." Usually a dog will approach me while I have my hands full with two or three dogs from the same household.

One instance of warding off a dog happened while I was walking three beagles. Two boys who were loud and obnoxious all by themselves and a sweet female made up this pack. Controlling these guys when another dog walked by was a handful, and the sweet female would turn on her housemates, starting a fight with the boys. One day we weren't out but a minute or two, and a couple had their dog loose. This particular assignment was on an old army base with government employees living on the land with availability for sightseers to view the old fort. So the couple was wrong for letting their dog loose. My guys started to go nuts, and what I would do when I saw this coming is plant my feet firmly and get a tight grip on the leads and prepare for all hell to break loose. And wouldn't you know, the couple sees this, their dog is heading straight for us, and they say, "He's a puppy." My reply is "These dogs want to tear into him, and they mean it." They still didn't do a thing, so I had to use a strong tone and chase him back to his owners, all the time holding on to my beasts, who were going wild and fighting amongst themselves.

So whether the dog is loose on its own or with their brainless owners, you will need to be prepared to chase them away. Be firm and gruff in your tone; being the alpha should keep them away. This type of scenario has happened at other times with various dogs in my care, and I've always used this method. Most times it works. But like anything while walking dogs, seeing it coming and a quick reaction time will prevent it from escalating into a dog fight.

How to Protect Yourself from Cat or Dog Attacks

I will rarely care for aggressive dogs, but sometimes we don't know what we're dealing with until the client has left for vacation. After all these years, I am usually pretty intuitive when it comes to ascertaining a client's pet. I took on a new client during Thanksgiving weekend. I didn't see any aggression from the dog on the initial consultation, although my new client had told me that the dog had gone after his sister. This should have put a red flag up for me. I took the job anyway and regretted every moment of it. This was actually the first assignment I ever had to terminate due to the dog's aggression. He was fine on his walk, very friendly, but when we were going back in the house, out of nowhere, he attacked me. If it wasn't for all the heavy winter clothing I was wearing and my quick reaction time, he would have done some damage. Had I been prepared for this sudden aggression, things might have turned out differently, but I wasn't prepared for this as it came out of nowhere.

Most dogs will warm up to a sitter after a visit or two; if not, it is possible to work through these assignments until the client returns. Many years ago a dog trainer had told me about a simple technique—to fill an empty soda can with a dozen pennies, put tape over the opening so the pennies stay in the can. So I started to carry a can of pennies with me in my pet sitter's sack. When a dog is showing aggressive behavior, you would shake the can and take a firm stand with your dog, either telling them no or give a command to lie down, to make an aggressive dog submissive. Of course, there might be instances where this will not work, and then you will need to shield yourself from the dog, and this is where an umbrella comes in. If they are going to munch on something, better the umbrella than your leg. The can of pennies works well by startling the dog, and this is great for any inappropriate behavior.

Believe it or not, the can of pennies works great with attack cats as well. As you know, due to their sensitivity, cats don't like loud sounds, and I would never deliberately antagonize a cat. But when faced with an attack cat, there is sometimes no other choice. This will stop them in their tracks, and hopefully they will retreat into another room. Cats can be very territorial, and although they aren't many of them, believe me, they do exist. An opened umbrella is another option in protecting yourself from an attack cat but rarely makes them back down.

I would also like to add to be cautious when feeding dogs. I always give the dog their distance when they are eating because many years ago I found out that not all dogs like it when you're near their food dish. Wait till they are finished and away from the dish before picking it up to clean as this can bring out aggression in an otherwise gentle dog. It is always better to be cautious. Even if you've cared for a dog for many years, you must remember that they are still animals and unpredictable.

Improvising on the Job

Whether it's going against your client's instructions on caring for their pet or having to use a piece of cardboard with a paper towel to sweep up messes because your client doesn't have the necessary tools, there will be many times when you will have to improvise while performing your assignments. Sometimes what works well for the client but will not always work for the pet sitter.

Take for example the time I had to care for a fun-loving, sweet golden retriever. My client's instructions were that after he went potty in the yard, I would give him half a bagel, but only in the morning. This client requested three visits per day, and it wasn't long before my lovable golden took charge of the situation by refusing to come back into the house until I brought him a piece of bagel to entice him back in. He would come so far and then plant himself by the neighbor's fence and wait for me to bring him a piece of his bagel, or he would refuse to come back in. This was the only thing that seemed to work, and he left me no choice but to let him get his way. Well, wouldn't you know it, the neighbor told my client that I left the dog in the yard all by himself. And this was partially true because I would always end up going back to get a piece of bagel for my manipulating puppy. My client had already known about my changing of her routine by my note that I had left and had to explain to her neighbor. I really couldn't understand why she would even have to explain what had gone on, but I never question my clients. Her dog was very ingenious and cute, waiting for me to come bring his bagel to him, waiting patiently by the fence, always in the same spot.

There have been many other situations where I have had to change the pet's routine. Medicating the pet can sometimes be an adventure, and what will work for the client will not always work for us. Sometimes it could take a number of tries before I can find way to get my pet to cooperate with me. We will have to be a jack of all trades, knowing how to fix a broken lock to a gate by using some duct tape or wire so the dog will not escape. Knowing how to temporally fix a toilet comes in handy while the client is away as it's not always an emergency to call a plumber, especially if you know your client is handy with minor repairs. Improvising on the job will come up frequently, and as long as our judgment is sound, these temporary fixes and adjustments will become necessary from time to time. When I first started my business, I would always stick to what my client had requested, but after some time, I found out that I would have to improvise in order to make my assignment run smoothly. I always let my client know that I had a problem while they were away and how I managed to get through the situation. Most times the client understands, and if they don't, then I probably won't have them as my client for very long. These situations are few and far between, but still keep in mind some clients will not be happy with changes, however necessary they might be.

Invisible Fences

I have only had one client that has used an invisible fence, and I wasn't happy about that situation at all. As a matter of fact, I wasn't even aware of this until arriving at the client's home to see the dog roaming around in the yard. I was beside myself and called the client immediately thinking that the dog had somehow gotten out of the house. The client reassured me, saying that they had an invisible fence. When I questioned the security of the fence, he said she wouldn't try to get out because when they first installed it, she got a good shock and wouldn't do it again. Well, there was no way I would be able to feel comfortable leaving the dog out in the yard all day without worrying something could go wrong. So I went against my client's wishes and left her in the house. She wasn't a bad dog, and I never understood their reasoning. I just wouldn't be able to relax knowing there could be a chance the dog could get out and I would then have to spend time looking for her or she could get injured.

Dogs have been known to get so excited or agitated. Like my client's dog, they would risk the shock from the collar and get lost or, worse, get hit by a car. Another problem that can happen, if a dog would risk the shock to get out after another dog or animal, they would not be able to get back into their yard for fear of being shocked again.

We all know that mechanical devices can malfunction. Not only that, but an invisible fence does not prevent other animals from entering the yard, leaving the dog vulnerable to harm. With the decline of our economy, it has been documented recently that thieves have been stealing dogs with hopes of collecting a reward. And an invisible fence won't be able to keep intruders off a client's property. Although I cannot remember where I read the report, I do remember it stated it was mostly smaller dogs, and I wouldn't want to take the chance with any size dog.

Jekyll and Hyde Personalities

Have you ever watched the movie *Dr. Jekyll and Mr. Hyde*? Be prepared to enter your own horror movie; this time you'll be dealing with a beast that has hidden aggression. These personalities can be either a dog or cat, and I have experienced both. They can be extremely loving and affectionate at times and then, out of the blue, turn aggressive on you. This is totally unexpected, and since I have experienced this in the past, I have learned to be cautious until I know who I'm dealing with. Most times the client is aware of their pet's personality and will let you know; other times this will be totally unexpected. Sometimes this is caused by behavior issues or medical problems. I have often wondered if animals can suffer from some of the same psychological problems as humans, due to a chemical imbalance, mood or personality disorders. And I have cared for pets that are on medication to help with these disorders. I think most times trainers are called in to correct these problems, but I think there is more than correcting behavior to help these pets. Yes, sometimes these pets have medical issues that can cause these reactions, and I believe that if you are close to the pet, they might associate that you are the cause.

Some animal behaviorist may call this type of personality idiopathic aggression when animals appear normal then out of nowhere they growl, snap, bite without any warning. If you approach their food dish, try to take away an object or toy, they will get aggressive. But I have had cats that I believe get overstimulated when petting and turn aggressive when they are normally friendly. This is the same with dogs.

I have had dogs that have a mind of their own, and if you insist on hooking them up to their leash to go for a walk, they turn aggressive. Most dogs love to go for walks, and I'm not sure if there is some fear associated with a sitter wanting to take the dog out. Maybe in their minds they are thinking we will not bring them back. Now mind you, these dogs can run up to you when you enter the home, thrilled to see you, then get aggressive for whatever reason. These personalities will definitely keep you on your toes, never knowing what to expect, and you might find yourself improvising on these assignments.

Job Sharing

If you want to protect your business from any liability issues, I suggest you do not job share with any friends or family members of your client. As the pet sitter, you will be the one who is blamed not only for theft but this also goes for cats getting out of the house, dogs being allowed to enter rooms that are off-limits, and any number of things that can arise. Unless you are in a good relationship with a long-standing client, I would be wary of taking on job sharing. Don't get me wrong, there have been occasions where I will accept these assignments, but even then I'm not happy with the interference from others coming into the homes. I know some clients might be wary of letting a stranger into the home, and most times this is the reason they have friends and family check in to see if you are indeed coming in, that things are in order.

I find that they are more of a nuisance than help. As a matter of fact, I recently had a client who said his friend might come in to visit with the dog, and he ended up locking a lock I did not have a key for. This happened to be on the storm door, and I was able to get my hand in through the screen section by slipping my fingers under the frame from the screen and unlocking the handle. Now mind you, this took me about fifteen minutes to do, and I ended up mangling one of my fingers in the process. As a pet sitter you will have to be very resourceful, and if I haven't said it already, this job is definitely an adventure. You could put a clause in your contract that states you cannot be held liable for circumstances arising from a second party coming in, if you agree to this. I have done job sharing on occasion and always have added it to my notes section and have the client sign, date it. On one occasion I had a client have two of her friends come in on different days. I was instructed to water the few plants they had, and I noticed close to the end of the assignment that the plant was dying because every one of us coming in was watering the plant! No big deal really, as opposed to screwing with pet care. I left the client a note and explained that this is one of the reasons why I wasn't thrilled about job sharing.

The same scenario can happen in regard to pet care, and this is what really bothers me. Workers being in the home is another situation I'd prefer to avoid. Both dogs and cats can escape with the workers coming in and out. This has happened on a daily dog walk I had, a Jack Russell. When I first came in, I saw the workers, and my first thought was *Nice, no one called to let me know.* They had the garage door and inside door to the home opened as well. The next thing I heard was "Get the dog!" And not one of the workers made an effort to catch this little bugger. I ran out and saw him heading to the neighbor's yard and was able to corner him somewhat, but more importantly, I gave him a look and command that said, "Don't you dare!" I grabbed him and brought him back in the house. Then one of the workers said, "Last time that happened, we chased him for an hour." They thought it was quite amusing. I was furious, and needless to say, I no longer service this client.

Another instance is cleaning people coming in; they also tend to interfere with pet care. Although I have found some to be responsible, who do their job and let me do mine. Others have locked cats in closets, allowed access to off-limit rooms, hid my reports, and, in general, interfered in my routine. Maybe I'm a control freak, but I do have a problem with others coming in as they always seem to create problems. So in my experience, I've had more problems than not when job sharing, and I really wouldn't recommend it.

I have had a few assignments that have turned out very well when it came to job sharing. One recent assignment was when I was called to take over for another pet sitter, who really wasn't a pet sitter but rather a hairdresser looking to make a couple extra bucks. She didn't know what signs to look for, and the cat became very ill. A client I had had years ago had suggested to the owners of this cat to call me. So both my old client and I were nursing this cat back to health. I was in charge of medication, cleaning, and feeding. And she spent time at night with him, also encouraging him to eat. This client was not coming back for another three weeks. Both my old client who I was sharing the assignment with and I were starting to feel confident the cat was improving. My old client would go in between ten and eleven at night, and I came in the morning and evening. One morning going in, I saw the cat as soon as I came in lying lifeless on the floor. It was very upsetting. This old client of mine came over immediately and helped with getting in touch with the client, and I took care of crematory arrangements. So she was the extra help that was truly needed and never interfered with my job. So it can work, but I will only job share on a case-by-case basis.

Jury Duty

In the event you are called to jury duty, you will need to make arrangement for a backup sitter to help with your assignments. For many years in New York, if you were a business owner and wrote a letter of excuse giving reasons why you could not serve for jury duty, they would excuse you. But you cannot anymore as the laws have changed. I recently had to serve and found it quite boring. My daughter and son filled in for the daytime sits, and I resumed the nighttime sits. This was only for two days, and then I was sent home. But what happens if it runs into a longer time frame and you end up losing out on some nice assignments if you have no help. Even if you get help for the day and you have to go finish up the nights, it makes for a long day. You will have to check with your local region's laws pertaining to jury duty and if it's possible to get excused. You will have ample time to find help and rearrange the schedule before your time to serve, and it's possible to get a postponement if you call and request one. Originally my jury duty was scheduled when my daughter was taking her vacation in August, which is usually a busy time for pet sitters. So they rescheduled my time to serve for February, and this worked out nicely. It's our obligation to fulfill our duties both to our clients and to our state, so this is something that can be worked through.

Keeping Clients Satisfied

I'd like to tell you what works best for my business when it comes to keeping a client happy and satisfied with the service provided. I started my business in 1994, and believe it or not, I still have many of my original clients. Even after they lose a pet, they return to start up service again, so I must be doing something right. I've always told my children to give 100 percent in whatever they do. Whether you're flipping burgers in McDonald's or performing brain surgery, you must give your all. This is how I perform my job, and being my children also work for me, I expect the same. My daughter started working with me as soon as she got her driver's license, and we had many "discussions" about what was expected from our clients. She would often say in the beginning that it didn't matter, and my reply would always be the same—everything matters. Our clients shouldn't be able to tell who came in to care for their pets, whether she went in or I went in. I expect perfection or a close comparison. Keeping our clients happy has always been top priority for my business.

I may not always get back to my clients immediately, but my clients also realize that I am running a mobile business and always out of the office. I do set certain times for call backs and bookings; most of my clients have my cell phone number for emergencies. But they are also aware that I will not take reservations while on the road. I do have some that call to ask about availability, but constant interruptions will affect the quality of care your pets will receive. Being my office is also in my home, I can't tell you how many times I've sat down to dinner when my business phone will ring. What I do is let it go to voice mail. I love my clients, but I cannot be at their beck and call. After a hectic schedule with all sorts of problems coming our way during the course of a day, I have to shut down for a while. I gobble down enough lunches and dinners with more than my fair share of interruptions.

My answering machine message will let my clients know that I will get back to them as soon as possible.

I will always make time to squeeze in a last-minute booking for established clients. As a matter of fact, I actually spoil my clients by making someone available for pet sits, if at all possible. I believe they truly appreciate this for they treat us well with extra tips, presents, and the like. And in the rare event that we cannot come in, most are understanding and will change their plans to work around our schedule. Most of my business is repeat clients, which speaks volumes for my service. With so many newer pet sitters and day care facilities that have opened in my area, if I was not able to satisfy my clients, they now have many other options available for their pets.

I respect my clients' privacy and base my service on honesty and trustworthiness along with keeping the home spotless while the client is away. I always take the added time needed, whether cleaning up a mess left by the pet or if the client is less caring about the condition of the pet's dishes, litter boxes, or bedding. They will certainly notice the difference upon returning home. We will always rinse the pet food cans before placing them in the recycle can. I believe my clients like the fact that we take the extra effort in caring for their pets and home.

Let's face it, this is not a perfect world, and it's virtually impossible to keep everyone happy. Some of these reasons are totally out of our control, but most times we are the ones that get the brunt of the criticism or abuse from an unhappy client. I'll give you an example of a longtime client that went away on a weeklong vacation. She requested three visits a day because her girls both required various medicines at different times during the day. Originally on the day of the last visit she wanted three visits, and then at the last minute she changed it to only two, morning and afternoon. But I never made the correction in my schedule, so I went for the night visit, and when I was finished and ready to leave, she knocked on the door. She was so happy I was there because she had forgotten her key, and I had the only other key. She did question why I was there, and I said that I thought I was to come in, but she was still happy because she had a horrible time while away, and this ended on a positive note. She didn't have to medicate her dogs and was able to get in her home with no problem.

A few days later I dropped off her invoice with the additional visit added. I had been paid for all the original dates except the one visit she had canceled on. Well, she called later in the day and was furious for charging tax. She said I never did, and this couldn't be further from the truth. Another complaint was that I came for the nighttime visit when she didn't need one, never mind the fact that her dogs received excellent care with no mistakes on giving medications and that she had no problem getting into her home after a not-so-great vacation. So what I did was concede to her complaints and told her to forget about the extra visit as this was my mistake. I did let her know that she was always charged tax on her invoice as I am required to do so. I was upset for doing a great job, and because she had a horrible vacation, I had to be abused. Honestly I considered dropping her as a client, but I love her dogs. So two months later, she calls for service, just a weekend sit, and I gave her a total for a check to be left. Well, she ended up leaving extra for the visit after all. People never cease to amaze me!

I'm flexible when dealing with my clients but will not always stand for certain behavior. You will have to make certain judgment calls when dealing with your clients. There's an old saying that the customer is always right. Well, this is true to an extent. You will have to strike a balance between keeping your client happy and making sure you're not being taken advantage of. This will be a personal choice for you, and please keep in mind not to take it personally. After all, it's just business. I know sometimes clients will know all the right buttons to press in order to push our threshold of patience, but if you keep your cool, most situations will work themselves out. This is possibly the toughest part of the job as I bite my tongue often because we all say things in anger that we later regret. I often remember the old *Honeymooners* episode (my age might be showing right now) where Ralph Kramden would recite "Pins and needles, needles and pins, it's a happy man that grins" right before he explodes in anger. This alone makes me laugh at times.

So if you want to keep your clients for the long term, you will have to provide excellent service. Going above and beyond will always be appreciated. Be reliable, available, competent, confident, caring, and honest for all your clients. Cope with difficult clients and situations. They will pass, and your integrity will shine through. I would also never recommend offering a satisfaction guarantee as some clients are never satisfied, and this will give some the opportunity to try to get out of paying for your services. If they ever ask if you give some type of guarantee, just tell them that your reputation and references are your guarantee!

But to ensure that your clients are satisfied, you could send out a questionnaire to help your business improve on service. This will give your clients a voice to express their opinions, and who better than to make suggestions. I have direct questions that the client can rate the level of service provided. This will also serve as a way to lean how your clients heard about your service, the reason they chose your business, and this will give the client the opportunity to suggest services or how to improve. I recently added a section for the client to give names and addresses of family and friends that might benefit from using my service. This helps build up a mailing list. Even if the client's friends and family won't use the service at the time of mailing, if a coupon or other incentive is mailed, they might be inclined to use my service in the future.

So be there for your loyal clients. Be available for them, sometimes at a moment's notice. Always take the time to talk to them, no matter how pressed for time you might be. They will appreciate your thoughtfulness when their pet is having problems either physically or behaviorally. Here is a sample of my satisfaction survey:

It was a privilege to care for your pets while you were on vacation. Please, if you would take a moment to complete and return this questionnaire, you can be assured this information will be helpful in assisting our continuing efforts to improve service. Your candid comments will be appreciated. Thank you for your cooperation in filling out this short survey.

Please check the appropriate answer.

1. How did you first learn about Soft Paws?

( ) Mail

( ) Newspaper

( ) Friend or relative

( ) Car signage

( ) Vet ______________________________________

( ) Other______________________________________

2. What was the main reason you chose Soft Paws Pet Sitting Service?

( ) Price

( ) Peace of mind

( ) Referral

( ) Website

( ) Other______________________________________

3. On the initial consultation:

( ) Yes ( ) No **Were soft Paws policies explained clearly?**

( ) Yes ( ) No **Were Soft Paws fees clearly outlined?**

( ) Yes ( ) No **Given helpful information?**

Comments:______________________________________

____

____

Please circle the number that corresponds to your level of satisfaction with Soft Paws Representative:

How satisfied were you with: Excellent ------------- Poor (please circle one)
1. **Pet Sitters honesty and helpfulness?** 5 4 3 2 1
2. **Pet Sitters ability to answer all your questions?** 5 4 3 2 1
3. **Pet Sitters professionalism andcourtesy?** 5 4 3 2 1
4. **Pet sitter ability to accommodate special requests?** 5 4 3 2 1
5. **Overall presentation pet sitter made on consultation?** 5 4 3 2 1
6. **The convenience of appointment time to fit your schedule?** 5 4 3 2 1
7. **The ease with which you got through by telephone?** 5 4 3 2 1
8. **Pet Sitters explanation of services and pricing?** 5 4 3 2 1

(Back of Survey)

Please make a check mark next to the appropriate answer:

For our records, are there any services that you would like Soft Paws to add, such as:

( ) Dog Training
( ) Errand Service
( ) Grooming
( ) Other _______________________________________

Please list below any friend or relative who would be interested in Soft Paws services.

Name/Address

____

Name/Address

____

Name/Address

____

Last-Minute Bookings

I think I might be the queen of last-minute bookings! If I can fit my client into my schedule, I have no problem with this. Most of my clients are long-term clients, and after all, they are the reason my business is still flourishing. I will admit some are chronic last-minute bookers, but they treat me well with gifts, tips, and appreciation for accommodating their requests. I will make them aware that I might not be able to get there at their requested time and ask if it would be better to go earlier or later than their request. Take for example this week. I have a client that lives two blocks from me. Her dog was injured and is recovering from a spinal injury. My schedule was mostly cats, and I had the luxury of sleeping in, something that rarely happens. This client shows up at my door about five minutes after I woke up. I hadn't even halfway finished my first cup of coffee. She had just gotten back from the vet and needed help getting her Doberman pinscher into the house because no one was around. She is literally two minutes from my house, so I told her I'd meet her at the house in five minutes. This only took me five minutes, and she paid me for a full visit. This happened twice this week, but it wasn't like I had to drive across the island. This same client had called last minute on my birthday, and I went in to care for the dogs before we had my birthday cake. When she got home, she stopped by to give me an extra $50 for my birthday, so as I said, I'm always taken care of. This same client will sometimes call last minute and not leave any money out for me for the visit and say, "You know where the money is. Go in and pay yourself." Talk about trust, but there would be no reason for me to jeopardize my relationship with this client.

If there is a new client and they call last minute, providing I am able to accommodate their request, what I do is charge a late booking fee of $25. I look at this fee as an inconvenience fee, but to the client it is a late-booking fee. This goes on top of what their total would be for the booking. I mark this on my invoice as a late-booking fee. I have to admit that I do lose some prospective clients when I tell them this. But I got really tired of people calling late to book (anything less than four days' notice), so I decided to make it worth my effort in rearranging my schedule to meet with them. I also have many that don't mind paying this fee because they realize they waited to the last minute and are actually happy that I can do the job. I have taken on some last-minute clients that actually expected me to come right over to care for their pet. After explaining how my service works, these clients turned out to be some of the best clients I have had. So I'm not quick to judge these clients for waiting till the last minute. As with anything in your business, you could charge what you want. I find what I charge is reasonable for myself or my ICs.

I will also ask some pointed questions of the prospective client on the phone interview to feel them out. Some of the questions I ask are as follows:

- Why did you wait so long to make arrangements for someone to care for your pet?

(If they say the person they were going to use backed out at the last minute, which will put some red flags up for me, I will then ask why.)

- Did you ever use a pet sitter before?

(If they answer yes, I question why the other pet sitter won't be coming in this time, and depending on their response, this might send up another red flag.)

- Have you ever left your pet at home before?

- Who came in to care for your pet (friend, relative, etc.)?

- How did they react to a new person coming in?

- How does your spouse/partner feel about having a pet sitter coming in?

(If they're not comfortable with the situation, give another red flag. But I still might go to the consult to meet the spouse/partner.)

You can then base your decision on what you have gotten out of the phone interview. If they're demanding and arrogant about needing service immediately, I wouldn't take them on as a client anyway. You see, it's not only the client that has a choice in the matter; we also have the right to decline an assignment as well. If they call prior to a major holiday, even though I have a late-booking fee, I will more than likely turn them away, referring them to another sitter or boarding facility. I like to leave last-minute bookings around the holidays for my loyal clients or enjoy a little downtime to spend with my family. I will also not take on any new clients as last-minute bookings if I'm planning a vacation. I prefer to get to know my new client and their pets so I can feel confident that no problems will creep in while I'm away. This lowers my stress level, and I can relax while vacationing.

Leaving Key on Last Visit

During the course of my pet sitting career, I have had a few clients who requested that I leave the key on the last visit. In the beginning I would oblige the client, being more of a pet sitting genie, saying, "Your wish is my command." But after a few incidents where the client was delayed, as I closed the door, I remembered my glasses were on the kitchen table or I forgot to take the trash with me. I decided that even when the client requests this be done, I strongly recommend against this. The number one reason is that if they are delayed, I wouldn't be able to get back in. I charge for a key return, and some clients might be hesitant paying for a key return. So what I tell them is to air on the side of caution that I will bring the key back when I have an assignment in their neighborhood or close-by and not charge for this. Or if they want, they can drop by to pick the key up. Although most of my clients have me hold on to the key, I still have some that feel more comfortable when their key is returned for one reason or another.

I will no longer leave the key on the last visit as this might be convenient for all involved. It can lead to problems if the client doesn't return on schedule. I wouldn't recommend leaving the key on the last visit.

Messy Homes

I have never had a problem when it comes to messy homes; although sometimes the mess can be excessive. Most times I tolerate the mess and just work around it. My job is to care for the pets, so I will concentrate on the pet's bedding, dishes, and of course, I will make sure any messes made by the pet while in my care are attended to. If the pet's area is neglected, it's not my job to judge my client. But I will certainly make sure that while I'm caring for the pet, I will go the extra mile and thoroughly clean all dishes and bedding. After all, this is what I'm being paid for. When I first started my business, when a client would leave a mountain of dishes in the sink, I would wash them. But I came to realize that that really wasn't a part of my job description, so now I will work around the mess to clean the pet's dishes. If I was to continue to clean the client's messes, this would take away from the actual time spent with the pet and would then change my job description from pet care to housekeeper.

If the home is a danger to both the pet sitter and pet due to hoarding or certain doors are not accessible, we have the right to decline the assignment. So this would be a judgment call on the consult. I have only declined one assignment in my many years of pet sitting; the smell from urine was so strong it was hard to tolerate. But even in an instance like this, you could wear a mask or handkerchief to protect you from the stench. The main reason I declined this assignment was due to a roach infestation; they were out in the daylight, mature roaches along with tons of babies. This is where I draw the line, and we all have our limitations.

Missed Visits

This is a subject that most pet sitters prefer not to talk about, but at some point, this might just happen. In all the years I've been pet sitting, this has happened twice to me in two separate incidences, and both occurred when my mother fell ill. One was a weekend sit, only two visits, and I knew I had the assignment lined up, but my mother fell ill to congestive heart failure. So with all the last-minute decisions that I had to make regarding my mother, I didn't even think about calling my daughter or my IC. I felt horrible after this and told the client what had happened. To make up for my not coming in, the next time I gave her a free visit.

The second was the same scenario a few years later when we were having a heat wave like I've never experienced before. With my mother's heart condition, she has difficulty breathing in the heat. I totally blew off my once-a-week evening walk, forgetting to call the client, who is home when I go in. This is a walk that I do prior to the client leaving for vacation. This gives her dog time to get used to me coming in. So basically I missed the visit, but no harm done because the client is home.

Years ago I was lying in bed when I suddenly got this sinking feeling that I forgot something. I sometimes do this and just get up to double-check my schedule, thinking I didn't get keys ready for assignments for the following day. When I looked at my schedule, I had an assignment that started that night. This was a last-minute booking from an old friend who only lived a few blocks from my house. So I get up and head over to her house at midnight to let the dog out. This was a near miss.

I did have an independent contractor a few years back that was notorious for missing her assignments. I always request that the independent contractor call and let me know everything went well. She was also famous for not doing this. I would usually have to track her down to see if everything was fine. I was preoccupied with my own work and didn't notice the time when I got a call from one of my clients asking if my dog walker was in to see her dogs because her boyfriend was at the house and the dogs' treats were still on the table. I had to admit that I hadn't spoken to her and told her I would get back to her. I called my IC, and when I asked, she said she totally forgot. So a missed visit can happen, and hopefully they won't happen too frequently. The main thing is to be honest with your client and offer them some type of compensation to make up for the missed visit.

Multipet Households

Multipet households can be a bit challenging. I have cared for up to six dogs in one household, and I have another client that has four floors of cats with cats in every room. When I have these types of assignments, being I charge per pet, I offer a multi-pet discount. It's only a couple of dollars, so I still get compensated for the time involved. These jobs can take up to an hour or more, so remember to pay yourself a decent salary. When I have these larger jobs, what I like to do in the morning is give a thorough cleaning. It seems that overnight, the pets can really make a mess and this involves extra clean up time in the morning.

I will not walk the dogs in a multi-pet household because I would have to take out two sets of dogs. It would either be three at once and then the two. If each required a twenty-minute walk, the time involved in this alone would be forty minutes. Add in the cleaning and feeding and this would run about an hour and a half, so all the dogs go out together in the yard. Most dog owners with this many dogs have fenced-in yards anyway. If not, then I would have to charge extra for my time.

And of course, stay with them in the yard, as six dogs can cause quite a ruckus, and we don't want to alienate the neighbors. I have never had problems with dog fights among housemates in these households, but I do take precautions by feeding dogs separately. Even if the client doesn't do things this way, I can't handle the stress that's involved in a dog fight.

My multi-cat, multi-floor cat job is a tremendous job, and she uses my services about four times a year. Did I forget to mention she also has quite a few outdoor cats as well? This client is great for laying out all the cans of food with labels for that day and for cats, both indoors and outdoors. So this makes it easier when trying to remember who gets what food. She also has a sweet cat that needs thyroid medicine twice a day, but she is well behaved, and I've never had a problem with this. So I work methodically, starting with the outside cats then to the lower level and other three floors. Whew, I'm tired just thinking about it. I use a tray for new food and to carry out old food and dirty dishes. I carry my trash bag with dustpan from room to room. Every couple of days I have to clean the self-waterers, and I will break this down over a couple of days, doing a few in the morning and a couple at night. It seems like every time she calls she has added another cat to her home, and she's not a hoarder, but she rescues them, gets them to the vet. But as we all know, sometimes finding the right home is difficult. Her home is very clean, and personally, I don't know how she does this on a daily basis. I only do a week or two at a time. She also has a lot of plants, so they also need tending to every couple of days.

This client has been with me for years, and I had tried to keep her price reasonable. I had gotten a call for her one day saying, "Geri, I'd like to give you a raise because I realize that there's an awful lot of work involved." So I told her what I would normally charge, and we settled at five dollars less. I was originally only going to charge an extra ten dollars and call it even; she was the one who wanted to pay more. So in this case I really feel appreciated by the client. I actually got a call the other day and took on an assignment that the client has twenty-nine cats. I know what you're thinking—this woman is a hoarder. But she has worked with the rescue, and it isn't my place to judge. The woman was going into surgery and would not be home for a week. Even after she returned, we went in for a few days to help out while she recuperated. This assignment took about two hours as she has multilevels of feeding and watering stations. She had ten litter boxes to clean and scoop, and I really had to keep moving to get everything accomplished in those two hours. Both my son and daughter came in to help a couple of the days and cut my time down to a little over an hour. The assignment paid well but was exhausting, and I was happy when our services were not required anymore. I had mentioned to the woman that I didn't know how she did this on a daily basis. She said she has all day and takes her time; she really loves her cats. I charged her a price per cat without my initial base fee, and this worked well. Her daughter came in at night just to scoop and feed the cats when we did all the heavy work during the day. The daughter was very happy as she had done this on her own the last time her mother was in the hospital and mentioned how easy it was that I was coming in.

Now when trying to figure out as what to charge, I would suggest always setting the price higher with multiple pet households if you're not going to charge per pet because you're sure to run over your time in regard to pricing. The longer you do the assignment, the easier it will become, if that's possible. What I mean is that you will get into a groove, your way of doing things, a routine. I like to eliminate extra trips up and down the stairs if I can. Multipet households are exhausting but pay well. When I went on vacation, my daughter took over one of the multiple-cat assignments and couldn't believe the amount of work involved. Now mind you, she does mostly dog walking, so she got to see the world from my point on the mountain. But she also got paid very well, and after the job was completed, she was able to relax again.

Older Clients and the Terminally Ill: The Need for Pet Guardianship

I have some clients that are terminally ill and a few clients that are older and live by themselves, and most times it's a topic we would rather not speak about. But the need for pet guardianship has come up on occasion. I will always ask if they have guardianship for their pets. I do have one client that already has hers in place. We can't force the client to do or think about something, but if you suggest to them more from a concern for their pets, they might be more willing to consider having guardianship set up. So I have started to include a pet guardian form in with my new client paperwork—one detailed guardianship for the client to place with their will and a shorter version that will enable my service to hand over care of both the pet and home to an assigned individual.

If they don't know who might be the best choice to place their pets with in the event of their illness or death, you might want to suggest that they assign a temporary guardian until a permanent caregiver could be found. Assigning a temporary caregiver is also a good idea in case a long-term guardian cannot take the pet immediately. Your client might also need some time to ask family members and friends who would be willing to adopt their pet. When a client is ill and worrying about their pets, this can be a very stressful time. And we don't necessarily have to be old or terminally ill because when traveling, many things can happen, and if in the event the client becomes incapacitated, the pet will still need to be cared for. Just remember 9/11, and if your client is traveling by car, accidents happen all the time.

If your client has a pet guardianship in place, you should remind them to be sure to include instruction for the pet in their will. The client's executor would ensure that the person named in the will should be the caregiver after they pass and to include a portion of the estate to go towards care of the pet. Advise your client that by doing this, their pet will be indirectly still under their care. This should help to alleviate some of the stress your client has been having up to this point and give comfort to your client. Recently I received a call from a young man whose aunt had gone into the hospital and requested my service. We had made arrangements to meet the following day as they lived in New Jersey and were temporally caring for the cats. The next day he called to say the aunt had passed and wouldn't need our services. By the afternoon his mother called back and said they would be needing service until they could find a home for the cats. This woman was only in her early sixties and had no will in place.

So I agreed to go in every other day, which is against my policies but I made an exception. They then asked for advice on how to place these cats and asked if I could also help. The response from many of the rescues was to put the cats to sleep as they were all around ten years old. The woman did offer a generous donation to anyone who would adopt, and she had also asked if I could take them in. I am at my limit of six cats but did find one rescue who promised to not put them down. I went to meet the woman from the rescue and helped get the cats into carriers, and as of now they are still waiting to be adopted. We never know when our time is up. This woman's illness came on suddenly and went downhill rather quickly. I highly suggest you encourage your older or terminally ill clients to have care for their pets in their will. These particular clients whose aunt had passed were devastated at their loss and, on top of that, had to secure plans for the cats. The guardianship that I have included in this book is in case of an emergency due to illness or death of the client. My business would be authorized to release both the pet and home over to an assigned individual.

Pet Guardianship

In the event of an emergency that I become incapacitated by severe illness or death, I authorize Soft Paws to turn care of my pets and home over to:

Name:

Address:

Home Phone:

Cell Phone:

Work Phone:

Relationship:

Client Name:

Client Signature: Date:

Soft Paws Representative: Date:

Older Pets: Special Needs

This is another part of my business that seemed to develop on its own. I tend to keep my clients and, in turn, grow old along with the pets in my care; I never saw this coming when I first started up. So between my own dogs and all my clients' pets, I have learned so much from caring for all of them. All pets need TLC, but older pets will need additional TLC and visits. Dogs tend to become incontinent with old age along with being anxious because they themselves can't do what they used to. Cats are no different with the exception that they have a litter box. I always suggest to my clients to have me in at least two times a day for a geriatric cat. I have to laugh when I get calls or e-mails from prospective clients who say they have an elder cat and there's not much to do because they sleep a lot, so they only need me to come in every other day. I won't even do this with a young cat as cats need that attention when their owners are away.

I have had owners go away leaving me with their senior dog who didn't see that the dog had no traction on a tile or wood floor. I would then proceed to move every area rug they had in the house into the tiled room to make it easier for the dog to get up and around. I would leave them there with a note explaining why I had done this and that they should get some inexpensive runners for the dog. I was always worried about dogs with stairs while I was not there because the dog may still try to get up or down the stairs and possibly injure themselves in the process. I have spare baby gates that I used for this very reason. I had an old Labrador retriever that I had cared for since he was one year old who was always determined to do what he wanted. And one of his favorite things to do was to steal the cat's food. Now the cat's food was down stairs in the finished basement. I couldn't close the door because the cats needed access to the basement for the litter box. My baby gate worked for the most part, until one morning when I went in and he was on the landing halfway down the stairs. By this time in his life he was pretty crippled with arthritis, and I'm not sure how long he was on the landing. So I started looking for something to get him up the stairs. I did find a nice plastic sled just his size but a bit large for maneuvering around the corner. This was before I bought a portable cloth stretcher. He was about ninety pounds, and with dead body weight, it made it difficult to get him up the stairs. Every time I started to pull him up, he started to slide off. Now I'm off to look for something to tie him down with, and it had to be soft and long. I rummaged through their linen closet and found that a sheet would do the trick. But Yogi started to get nervous going up the stairs, and I really could use some help, someone to hold him down and comfort him while another person pulled him up. I didn't want to chance him trying to get up while I was pulling him up the stairs, possibly injuring himself in the process.

I decided to call my daughter, who has rescued me on several occasions. Yogi and I had to wait it out, and I sat with him to help relieve his stress. Once my daughter arrived, we got him up the stairs, and I then barricaded the stairs with the baby gate again along with a few chairs. The cats could still get down, but Yogi would have to really work at this now. Older dogs will become restless even when their owners are home, and with a pet sitter coming in and out, even with additional visits, they will, no doubt, find themselves in a predicament they can't get out of. So always look for danger. As the dog ages, things that were normally common in the house can become obstacles for the dog. If you read the section on handicapped pets, some of the tools I use for them are a big help with elderly dogs. The most common problems of older dogs that I've cared for are as follows:

A. Arthritis is common in many older dogs, causing problems climbing stairs, stiffness after sleep, and irritability due to increased pain of the joints.

B. Cancer seems to be high on the list of many dogs in my area. Any sore that does not heal, weight loss, bumps and swellings that continue to grow, loss of stamina, and difficulty eating are the more common signs.

C. Cataracts are common in older dogs, causing loss of vision and cloudy eyes, and can make the dog's stress level increase. Be careful when walking these dogs as well because they cannot see branches or bushes and can walk into them and possibly get hurt. They cannot judge distance and depth as well, so be their extra eyes.

D. Heart failure is also quite common for older dogs with coughing as the most obvious sign. This will be brought on by exercise and excitement. The dogs will also exhibit less energy, weight loss, and loss of appetite.

E. Seizures are another common ailment for older dogs (younger dogs as well) with muscle contractions and sometimes loss of bladder or bowel control.

F. Incontinence for the older dog is very common as the dog will sometimes lose control while getting up or when sleeping.

I would also like to add that when walking older dogs, they shouldn't be walked too far from home. The older pets might still have the will to go on a long walk, but just like an elderly person they will tire easily and could cause more harm than good. If the client insists you take them for long walks, explain to them that an older dog needs frequent stops along the way and doesn't have the stamina they used to have. What I usually do is take them so far, and if it's a nice day, we will sit and enjoy the beautiful weather. Sometimes the client doesn't see the pet aging and might even be annoyed by you pointing this out to them. If you have a dog that is really arthritic, moving is good for the dog. But you still don't want to overdo this. Getting so far from home and then having the dog collapse on the way back is going to be difficult to deal with. I once had a dog that this happened to. I had to have a neighbor help with this big Lab, and we only went down the block about five houses. Watch their breathing for any signs of them tiring. If their legs are wobbly, they are getting tired and having a hard time.

During the last few years I have switched to mostly cats, and with this change came a whole new array of problems. I also advertise that I specialize in the care of older pets, so I have picked up additional older cat clients. Any cat over the age of ten is considered elderly, and cats over the age of fifteen are considered geriatric. Most people think cats are easier to care for than dogs; this is not the case at all. The only thing easy about cats is you're not walking in the blaring sun or frigid temperatures. A dog will let on sooner with an illness than a cat because cats instinctively mask their pain or illness when they go into a survival mode. In the wild, if a cat lets on that they are weak or ill, their larger predators will take advantage of this. So even though the cat has been domesticated for years, the instinct is still there. Cats can have liver or kidney failure for years before any detrimental signs appear. Your client goes on vacation, you ask all the right questions about the cat's health, and before you know it, you have a very sick cat on your hands. Some of the more common signs that I have noticed with the older cats I care for are as follows:

A. A normally friendly cat suddenly starts to hide and doesn't want any attention; this is the most obvious sign with a friendly cat. When you have a cat that hides, this could present a big problem. But on the flip side, a cat that normally hides might even be out and really doesn't seem to mind you being there because they will be in a weakened state as their heath may be failing.

B. Hyperthyroidism, kidney and liver problems with weight loss are one of the signs of failing health. Being we don't go in as often to see the cats, only while the client is vacationing, we will notice this more often than not before the client does.

C. A cat that is becoming more vocal could be in pain and have anxiety related to this.

D. Grooming is a sign of an unhealthy cat as cats are usually fastidious about their appearance. A failing kidney or liver may be the culprit if the fur shows the appearance of being neglected by the cat.

E. When an older cat starts to miss the litter box, there can be a problem developing. Cats tend to associate pain with urination and the litter box. Also, some cats, as they age, will suffer from constipation, which can be an underlying sign of a more serious illness, making it difficult when using the litter box.

F. Geriatric cats that suffer from diabetes or any other health issues can become sick rather quickly.

G. Older cats can get infections due to a breakdown in the immune system. So while caring for older cats, keep a keen eye for problems that might develop.

As a precaution, when I care for older cats and cannot monitor their water intake, when I give them their wet food, I will always add lots of warm water to make it more of a soup. If the water is cold and the cat has a dental problem, it might make mealtime less appealing. Older cats can get dehydrated fairly quickly, so I like to make sure they get the extra water. Again, dehydration can be a sign of a hidden illness. If you pull up on the cat's skin and it does not bounce back to its original position but rather stays in the pulled-up position, the cat is dehydrated.

Outside Dogs

These are my least favorite of assignments because I find the stress level from caring for these pets is sometimes overwhelming for me. Even if they are only out during the day to be let in at night, I will worry if an impending storm is coming. If it's too hot or cold outside, will the dog get out of the yard somehow? If it's on a tie out, I worry that they might get hung up on something. So many things can happen. And although the client might do this, I feel uncomfortable doing so.

I've only had a total of three of these assignments during my time in business, and I will sometimes go against what the client wants if there is a threat of bad weather or I don't feel the yard is secure enough to let the dog roam free. I even had an older dog that the client would let stay out on the deck during the day, and I thanked God it rained most of the week. We had one sunny day, and I did leave her out but made sure the stairs down into the yard were well barricaded. I was a nervous wreck all day, worrying that she might get hurt somehow, and all went well. But a few days after the client came home, I returned the key. She had told me that she had left the dog out as she usually did, and she couldn't make it up the stairs, and the neighbor had to bring her up when no one was home. The choice is yours whether to care for outside dogs or not.

Overnights and Sleepovers

If you're planning on offering sleepovers to your clients, you will have to determine what is acceptable or what you feel comfortable with. Most clients will be very hospitable and appreciate your being there for their pet. I did feel a little awkward when I first started doing sleepovers, but after a few assignments, I adjusted. Most of my clients will let me know that I am free to use their Internet, shower, and have an assigned space to sleep. I don't like using my client's computer; the reason being, if any issues with their computer come up, I don't want to be the one blamed for a crash or other complaint. So what I do is bring my laptop and just use their access to the Internet. Most of my clients will even bake up a nice dish or some other goody for me to enjoy, trying to make my stay over as pleasant as possible.

I have also never showered at my client's home, for I would shower before going over and just start my morning stops after leaving their home. But if you feel comfortable with this, I would go ahead and shower at the client's home. Remember, it's all about what you're comfortable with. I will bring my own blankets and must have my own pillow to feel comfortable while staying over. I recently bought myself a sleep sack, which is basically a thin sleeping bag, and what I like about this bag is that it rolls up to a compact size. In the winter months I sometimes bring my favorite blanket and use this along with the sleep sack if I'm doing an extended stay. I bring my own toiletries, and the only must-have for me is coffee in the morning. Most clients will have a coffee maker, and I just ask quick directions for operating. I have also found individual coffee bags like tea bags and this works well for me.

The one thing I will suggest is to note the location of the telephone in case of an emergency. Now some clients don't have a landline, so be sure to write down the address of the home you're staying at and keep it next to your phone because in an emergency, your mind might go blank, that is, if you're anything like me. You will also have to determine how long will you stay over. I base my fee on an eight-hour stay. I usually get to my sleepover around 10:00 p.m. and finish up by about 6:00 a.m. This way I have plenty of time for my nighttime stops and have ample time to get out for my morning rounds. Of course, if you feel like spending more time at your client's home, that would be entirely up to you and how you want to structure your business. But I can tell you from experience, my eight-hour time frame works really well, so you might want to consider this because if you're doing sleepovers and have a full-day schedule, you will appreciate any time you will be able to spend in your own home and with your pets. I try not to do too many sleepovers because I really begin to miss my bed and start to feel guilty about neglecting my own animals. So sleepovers might not be for everyone, and as a business owner, you will be able to decide what works best for you. You might be able to find someone who will thrive on sleepovers, so this could be another option.

Packages, Mail, and Newspapers

Most times I will ask the client what they would like me to do with mail while they are on vacation, where they would like me to place the mail and newspapers. Some of my clients have a special box where I place the mail, and what I like to do is separate the mail from the magazines, and the magazines will always be placed on the bottom of the pile. When I take in the newspapers, I will always take the rubber bands off and make sure the pet cannot get access to them. Eating the rubber bands can cause a danger to the pet. I will open the papers and place them in date order in the case the client wants to catch up on the news when they return. If the client is going to be away for an extended period, they might stop mail delivery altogether. Keep in mind that I have had dogs that will destroy the client's mail and cats that will pee on the mail or newspapers. So if the client designates a certain spot for the mail and newspapers, you might have to move it to a cabinet or closet to keep it safe.

Packages can sometimes be a bit more difficult to manage, especially if your client has many arrive while they are away. If a tag is left for a signature, I usually sign for it and bring the package in on my next visit. Most tags have an area where you can tell them where to leave the package. Sometimes these packages are large and fairly heavy, so what I will do is bring them in and leave them by the front door. Some of my clients seem to get an extraordinary amount of packages, and I find it hard to keep up with the number of tags left to be signed. I have never had a problem with packages disappearing when signing for them and having the delivery person leave them. I have always signed for packages because they will only make two attempts to deliver before your client will have to go pick them up personally. So I just want to make it easier for my clients when they return from their vacation. If you're not comfortable with having this extra responsibility, you might want to discuss this with your client and have a neighbor bring them in. In some instances the client themselves has arrangements with the delivery person to leave the packages, so in these instances you will have no choice but to bring the packages in.

Pets That Refuse to Eat

Occasionally when we are pet sitting, we might have a pet that will refuse to eat. Your client might clue you in that their baby is finicky with their food or that they might need encouragement while eating. Other times you might have a client that hand-feeds their babies in order to get them to eat. There will also be other times when a pet is missing their pet parents, and they will lose their appetite. This might happen when the client is on an extended vacation and you might begin to notice that the pet is becoming depressed. Animals have emotions just as humans do, but the only difference is that they cannot verbalize their feelings. So you will have to watch for signs if you see that the pet in your care is becoming depressed. This mostly happens when one member of the family is usually home all day, so when the family goes on vacation, the pet's routine is mixed up. Although being at home is the best alternative for the pet, they will begin to miss their owners.

Most people associate that a pet's loss of appetite is due to an illness, which it can be. Also if a cat does not eat for an extended period, this can lead to future illnesses. So being professionals, we must determine if the pet is not eating due to missing their owners or if there is an illness going on. The most obvious sign of depression in dogs is that they don't want to go on their walk. I once walked three pit bulls, and one of the younger pits had died suddenly. The oldest pit started to suffer from depression, missing the younger dog. Her appetite had decreased, she was shaking, and the last sign was she refused to go for a walk not only for me but her owners as well. These dogs happened to be a daily assignment. Although shaking in a pet can be a sign of pain, depression is a different type of pain. Cats can also suffer from depression as one of my own cats had this at one point. Again it started due to a death of another one of my cats, and these two were the best of buddies. We had brought Tarzan to the vet, and he never came home. For months our Angel would sit by the window, looking for Tarzan; it was very sad. I would tell him, "He's not coming home," but it did no good. His appetite wasn't what it used to be, and he seemed to be annoyed with my other cats. Eventually he came around to his old self.

Encouragement usually helps with getting a pet to eat. I had a little Yorkie that always needed fresh people food to eat while the owner was away. For the first day or so he was fine with eating, and as the week would go on, he would decide he wanted no part of his dinner. I would rummage through the fridge, looking for something to entice him by adding it to his food. If I brought breakfast or dinner with me, I would add a little of my food in tiny pieces to his food. Remember that this dog would only eat human food to begin with. So with other pets, you must make sure that they have no food allergies or sensitive stomachs before you give them something different. Another thing that seemed to encourage a lot of my pets to eat, both dogs and cats, is to sprinkle a little Parmesan cheese over the food. Sometimes talking to them will help; I usually tell them how good it smells and looks. I'll call them over and pet them to help stimulate their appetite. When we have a pet that refuses to eat, this can become a worry. As long as they eat something, they should be fine. I once had a dog that lived on treats most of the time the owner was away, and you know when they go for their treat but refuse their food, they're just playing with you.

Pet Sitting in Extreme Weather

Well, I never said this job was easy, and when you couple this with extreme weather conditions, it becomes a downright adventure. Traveling in extreme weather, unfortunately, is part of the job. So if you're scared of driving in the rain or snow, you might consider another profession. And it seems, as the years have gone by, the weather has really gotten unpredictable. Through my many years of pet sitting, I have experienced hailstorms, blizzards, tornados, and flash floods.

No matter what the conditions, sooner or later you will have to go out in the elements. And of course your safety should always come first, but if you're a die-hard pet sitter, as I am, you're more concerned about the animals. If you're aware of a potential storm or other weather condition, it will give you time to prepare by leaving extra water and food out because you are sure to be late. You should also be prepared to do some extra visits as your clients will also be delayed, flights will be cancelled, transportation to and from the airport will be cancelled. Clients having trips scheduled to go on vacation will more than likely cancel as well. Your whole pet sitting world will be turned upside down. It is also important to have a backup plan in case it could be days until you can get around, neighbors or family close to your client for example should be on your list of emergency contact numbers.

Many years ago we had a drought and then a very bad rainstorm that caused a flash flood. Our sewer system couldn't handle the amount of rain that had fallen in an hour's time. Being the ground was so dry and we have a lot of hills, the rain just rolled off the hills, settling in the lower areas. I had an SUV at the time, and my path of travel was stopped by a sudden one-block flood. Cars and vans were stuck in water that had seemed to rise out of nowhere. Police and emergency vehicles had to rescue some drivers. I was stuck, and my engine seized. I was there for about an hour, and a group of men pushed me to the side of the road to wait for a tow, and all worked stopped. The tow came for my car; my daughter came for me to finish up my pet sits. So I not only got delayed by the rains and flood, but my car was now out of commission. Did I forget to mention how much of an adventure this job is at times?

Usually these weather conditions are few and far between, but in September 2010 we had a tornado. We don't get tornados in Staten Island, New York; of course, I was out working at the time. It came on very quickly, was looking a little gray when I got to my 5:30 p.m. dog walk. One of the dogs was acting very skittish; he really didn't want to go out at all. We were only out about five minutes out when it started raining very heavy and strong winds came up; it was whiteout from the heavy rains. I waited with the dogs in the house because the dog that was scared wouldn't let me leave. When it finally calmed down a little, I was able to leave and could not believe the destruction that the storm had left. As I was driving down to my next sit, there were trees downed on cars and detours all the way because some streets were underwater or blocked by fallen trees. I finally arrive at my stop to see trees down all around my client's home, one going through the front window, making it hard to get into the house, and I had to crawl under a downed tree to get in the house. After checking on the dogs, I went out to see half their fence down, large branches down, and trees down, a disaster for sure. The only good thing about this was that my client wasn't on vacation but working, so I called, and they came home as soon as possible. I started to realize that my previous sit, the one where the dog wouldn't let me leave, had more than likely prevented me from getting injured or stranded during the storm. I've learned that animals have more sense than me most times. This was not predicted by the weather man and only lasted about fifteen minutes.

Another weather event that took us by surprise was the blizzard on December 26, 2010, and this storm lasted till the December 27. Knowing I would wake up to a lot of snow, I didn't expect to see snow halfway up my front door. Now I've been through quite a few winter storms, and there was one year when we had at least fifteen winter storms, but they were an accumulation of snow after a time. This was not so on December 2010; we had two and a half feet in a twenty-four-hour time frame. I was booked for the holidays with fifteen sits a day for over a week. I woke up at 7:00 a.m., looked outside, and started crying. I knew it would be a good couple of hours till I shoveled my car out, if I was to get out at all. And coincidently New York's sanitation department was protesting our mayor's recent cutbacks and had a slow down with some streets not getting plowed out for up to three days. But I have to say that I live next to some of the greatest neighbors ever. They shoveled the wife out, then their daughter, and when I came in to take a break, they finished shoveling my car out, not to mention they also shoveled the whole street to the main road. The sanitation did manage to plow the main routes, and that's the way I went. I picked up my daughter, who lived down by my first few stops, because I knew there would be no parking, and just in case I got stuck in the snow, I would have help. We packed my grandchildren in the backseat with their games and off we went into the winter wonderland. Our adventure had begun. My grandson actually said, "This is way too much snow!" And I had to agree.

Now most of you might be thinking I had an SUV or some all-terrain vehicle, but you will be surprised to know that by this time in my pet sitting, I had traded my SUV in for a more gas-efficient vehicle. I now own a Toyota Yaris, the best little car I have ever owned, and it handled great in the snow. We only got stuck one time, and that was at the end of the day on a road that was not yet plowed. I made all but two of my stops. One was a two-times-a-day cat job (was only able to make one of those stops), and the other was on a hill where we were stuck behind a row of cars that couldn't get up the hill. My client had actually come home and tapped on my window to let me know she was home; we were on our way to the house. She had parked in the dentist parking lot on the bottom of the hill and was walking home when she saw my car. So where there's a will, there's a way. Despite how long it took to get all these pets cared for, we did it! This profession is like an adventure. Among the pets and not knowing what to expect and Mother Nature with all her little jokes, you will definitely need all your will and perseverance to pull through these extremes in weather.

Now some of you will also have to contend with extremes in weather such as earthquakes, tornadoes, and hurricanes. Along with your typical rain, snow, sleet, and freezing rain, some regions will also experience intense heat with fires involving all sorts of problems for your business. Disaster planning will be necessary in some regions, so learn to be prepared for the unexpected. I worked through 9/11, so having a good disaster plan in place with backup neighbors or relatives that are close-by should be included. This might become necessary for extremes in weather or devastation of any kind. Always leave extra water and dry food if possible just in case things get a little crazy. Lately Mother Nature has been surprising us with unexpected weather, so this has become a rule in my book. I have also had clients that had to cancel their flights due to the weather, this would require additional visits to their home. The extremes in weather can play havoc with scheduling, and you will find that being flexible to changes is a necessity.

Special Requests

Special requests can be something not within the realm of your regular services. Although I'm not one to dismiss special requests, there are some that either are excessive in my opinion or something I'm not comfortable with. And each individual will more than likely have their limits when handling special requests. Whether they include getting to the clients home at 5:00 a.m. or dressing the dog with layers of sweaters in a certain order, special requests will surely come into play at some point. I have had many other strange requests in my many years of service. Although I did think some were ridiculous, I complied with the client's requests. An example is getting to a client's home at 6:00 a.m. for a cat because they are used to being fed at that time. As we know, cats are usually a little more flexible when it comes to visits because of their litter box, but I agreed.

I am currently servicing a client who is allergic to perfumes and certain shampoos. I cared for this particular client for vacation care, but currently I am cleaning their litter boxes while they are home. This is done three times a week, and we have worked out an agreement. I can't afford to go out and buy all hypoallergenic shampoos or personal hygiene products, and my morning regimen includes putting on my favorite perfume. So three days a week I call earlier on in the day and give an approximate time of my arrival, and they make arrangements to leave while I come in and clean the litter boxes.

There have been other special requests including wiping the dog's bum with a baby wipe after he goes poo. I had another request that required me to dress an elderly dog with four sweaters in a certain order then a jacket, a hat, and boots; I spent more time dressing and undressing this dog. I had one where I would have to wash the dog's feet off after our walk with a special solution the owner had mixed then dry his feet with a hair dryer. I had another one where I could not give the dog any water after I fed them for exactly fifteen minutes and would have to use the timer for this. On one assignment I was instructed to let the dogs out in the yard in a certain order or they would fight, and the same held true for bringing them back in the house. I had others; some I have done while others I felt were unreasonable and would not do. This would be a judgment call for many sitters as we are all different, and some can handle certain situations while others cannot, but special requests are bound to come up at some point.

The Need for a Locksmith

I must admit that I have had to call a locksmith on at least three separate occasions that were my fault. This was long before I required two sets of keys for my assignments. Both times I left the key in the house and, as I closed the door, remembered that I forgot the key. And one was on Father's Day, on a Sunday at night, which I paid big time for dragging the locksmith out. Another time I did the same thing, but this was on a weekday in the afternoon, so I was charged a regular fee. The reason I had to call a locksmith on these occasions was that both my emergency key contacts were not reachable. So even though I asked for extra key contact, I came to realize that this isn't also a solution to the problem. And if you have a busy schedule, it is possible to make this mistake. I know for myself. I double-check to make sure all water sources are shut off, all doors and windows are secure, plants are watered, and notes are made, then I grab my car keys and out the door I go. But considering I've been in business for all these years, I guess it's not so bad. There was another time where I closed the sliding glass door while taking the dog out in the yard, and it locked behind me. I mention this in "When We Do Stupid Things" section when I had to call a locksmith. That falls under this category as well.

Now when calling the locksmith, I usually identify myself as the pet sitter and I'm caring for Mr. Brown's dog. They give me an approximate time they will be there, and I either wait it out or, if it will be some time waiting, head off to my next assignment. When the locksmith arrives, you will need identification, and I also show him the contract. They do their thing, make a bill, and I pay them. I have wanted to kick myself when this has happened for it eats into the profits of the assignment.

Now this has also happened one time when a steady client had to leave unexpectedly and left the key in the backyard hidden. But he left the wrong key, and I couldn't get in. He had no family nearby and had friends in the area, but no one had an extra set of keys. In this instance the client had to pay for the locksmith for it was his mistake. Nevertheless, I still had to call the locksmith and go through all the hassle involved. So it's best to never have to call a locksmith, but we're all human and make the occasional mistake of leaving the key inside the home. Now if you ever lose a key and can't get an extra set from your emergency key contact, don't panic because a locksmith can make you a key for the lock. It's not a cheap mistake to make but one that can be fixed.

Transporting Pets

Whether you plan on offering transportation as part of your services or if you walk in on a sick pet, making sure the pet is well secured and comfortable on the ride is very important. I had offered transportation at one point but now only offer this service to my existing clients. And I have found that this type of service in my area is not in demand. Most day cares and grooming facilities as well have vehicles for transporting.

So most of my transports are clients' pets that need to get to the vet due to illness, and most are cats. When transporting cats, make sure to have a well-made, preferably airline-approved pet carrier and make sure the door is secured well. To ease the stress that can accompany a cat being transported, it is best to cover the crate with a blanket or towel, limiting their vision. This seems to calm the cat somewhat. I have pet carriers made by Petmate, both for the cats and larger crates for dogs. Although I have never transported dogs to the vet, I have some clients who use my service for daily walks, but when they go on vacation, they board their dog. What they do is have me pick up the dog from the kennel and bring the pet back home to alleviate some of the hassle when they return. I have a hatchback car and put a blanket in the back and secure the dogs' leashes, so when I open the door, they cannot jump out until they are released.

Now if you plan on operating a transportation service for pets, you must find out what is required by your region in regard to rules and regulations for animal transportation. Your government or local council should be able to guide you in making sure your transportation service is set up correctly. In the United States, according to the USDA website, under Licensing and Regulations under the Animal Welfare Act, Guidelines for Dealers, Exhibitors, and Researchers, it states that you are required to be licensed as a carrier or intermediate handler.

> Carriers—any enterprise transporting regulated animals for hire as a common carrier must be registered as a carrier. This includes airlines, railroads, motor carriers, shipping lines, and other enterprises. As a carrier, all your facilities where animals are kept or held are regulated, including terminals and freight storage. You are responsible for enforcing all restrictions on animals that can be legally shipped by your customers. You also are responsible for proper crating, whether the shipper or receiver is a private pet owner, a business, an institution, or a government agency. Pets transported by their owners as carry-on baggage are not subject to these restrictions.
>
> This would include any transportation from state to state if your client moves and requests that

you drive, fly, or the like to accompany their pet to another location.

Intermediate handlers—anyone taking custody of regulated animals in connection with transporting them on public carriers must be registered as an intermediate handler. This requirement covers boarding kennels that take responsibility for shipping animals or receiving them after or during shipment as well as freight forwarders and freight handlers.

This would include picking up pets at the airport or various means of transportation. Both carriers and intermediate handlers can license by contacting the USDA website.

On the other hand, if you plan on transporting locally, the website states you are exempt if you will only offer animal taxis. Animal taxis are individuals who transport private pets to and from the veterinarian, groomer, and the like.

If you are setting up business in Canada, United Kingdom, or Australia, you will have to check your local region's laws that may apply to transporting pets. Your government agencies should be able to help you find the right resources to assist in obtaining information on transporting pets. As I was researching this information, I found on the Canada.gc.ca website that you can find info on this subject under the section titled Animal Welfare and Transportation of Animals and also under Transportation Safety Board of Canada.

In the UK visit Defra.gov.uk website, under Environment, Food and Rural Affairs, for policies and regulations for a licensed animal transporter. In Australia you would have to search the Australia.gov.au website under Animal Welfare Standards and Guidelines for information.

Liability issues are another aspect to consider, so making sure you have the proper insurance coverage is essential. You can search your government resources. These are the same government agencies that would help start a business or expand on an existing business. Also keep in mind that a functional working vehicle is needed if you plan to do more than just an occasional visit to the vet or groomer. This vehicle should be climate controlled so the pet will not overheat in the summer months or freeze in the winter months. This will all depend on how much money you plan to invest in your business. You might want to consider testing the water before investing too much money in this part of your business. If you feel it start to take off, then the money you will invest should be worth it.

Turning Down Jobs

Being we are in business for ourselves, we usually don't welcome the opportunity to say no to incoming business. But sometimes due to the condition of the home or temperament of the pet, we have no other choice. I haven't had to turn down too many assignments because I find I can put up with messy homes, difficult pets, and clients too. But some very uncomfortable situations have forced me to rethink taking on some clients. Take for example the time I had gone to a consult with a man who had three dogs. It's been so long ago I can't even remember what type of dogs he had. But I do remember that two were very sweet, and the third I saw signs of aggression in. So I had told the client I would care for the two, but he would have to board the aggressive dog, which he agreed to do. The second problem I had with this assignment was that the home was a complete mess. It was horrible smelling, and I thought I could work past that. I never judge my clients on housekeeping or anything else, for that matter. But after we were speaking for a few minutes in the hallway, in the middle of our conversation the man started hitting various spots on the wall. At first I wasn't sure what he was doing, but then I realized the house was infested with roaches! So even after he agreed to all my terms, I had no choice but to turn down the job.

Just today I went to a consult for a woman who has twenty-nine cats, mostly feral, with eleven litter boxes. I almost forgot to mention the dog. He would be no problem. I just had to let him in the yard and feed him. The woman told me it takes her three hours to clean and feed, but she is a bit older than me. I charge per pet with an initial set fee for the first cat and three dollars for each additional cat. Well, I waived the initial fee and just totaled up for the twenty-nine cats. This assignment will take up a considerable amount of time to do a good job on cleaning and taking a head count. I plan on taking help with me to split the work and, in turn, the pay as well. The woman wasn't sure I would want to take on the assignment, and I almost cringed when I gave her the price, but there is a lot of work involved. She initially wanted two visits a day and asked if that was for both times, which it is not. So her daughter might help with the second visit, and I told her I could charge for just cleaning the litter boxes, which is five dollars per box. And her daughter could do the feeding, so I gave her time to think about what she wants and get back to me. Remember never to undercut your prices; this job is a strain both physically and mentally at times. If I had set a low price for all the work involved, I would have begun to feel resentful, and then I might have not even taken on the assignment.

Another time many years ago, I went for a consult for a small dog, and this was a referral from another client. When I get to the house, the prospective client lets me in, and I notice signs in her dog that I should have listened to. Instead I listened to the client saying, "It's okay, come in." That was a bad decision; the dog proceeded to bite both my legs from ankle to thigh. I had shorts on. And guess what, the owner didn't say a word to stop her dog. So what I did was to take my foot and put it in the dog's mouth. I had sneakers on and thought it better he chomped on my sneakers rather than my leg. Well, it was when I did that the owner decided to step in and stop the dog. I abruptly took my paperwork and left the home, getting a call from the client on the road asking me to come back. I told her that was a deal breaker, and I would not be caring for her dog. Although the dog did not break the skin, he left black and blues up and down my legs, which I took pictures of just in case the client wanted to make a stink on how I ruined her vacation plans by not caring for her dog.

I would say the key to being a successful pet sitter is know when to turn down an assignment because some assignments can bring more grief than the money you're compensated for, especially if you're just starting out and eager to get clients. Know your limits on what you can handle. When I first started out, I wouldn't consider giving injections, but with time I gained confidence and experience. I also stayed away from very sick animals but realized that they too need special attention, and it's better they are in their own environment. I recently ran into a couple that was asking about my service, and they remarked what a tremendous responsibility this was, and I had to agree. But by this time in my career, I have cared for so many pets with so many problems it has become second nature to me. I care for disabled pets and had a prospective client that had a dog who was very crippled. They had something like twenty-four stairs to get into the first door and an additional six steps to get into their apartment. I couldn't chance injuring myself by carrying this smaller shepherd up this many stairs if he couldn't make it. By knowing your limits, you can avoid any pitfalls along the way.

TVs and Those Darn Remotes

This might seem like a simple task, but I can't tell you how many different types of remote controls and television setups there are out there. As a matter of fact, this has become a part of my consultation questions. If you're doing a two-week assignment and can't figure out how that darned remote or, sometimes, three remotes work, you'll spend time trying to figure out which remote turns the TV on, and I really don't even know why someone would have that many remotes in the first place. I have one client that has a computerized remote with different locations for watching TV, for sound, and for recorded shows. I do mostly weekend sits for this couple and always had a difficult time trying to watch some TV. Well, one weekend I finally figured out how to watch TV with the sound on by going to a different screen. These clients went away for two weeks, and I would be sharing the assignment with the husband's office help for he has a business that he runs out of his home. I did the mornings and nighttime visits, and the workers would let the dogs out during the day and keep them company. The TV was working fine for the first two days, and then I couldn't get the TV on. One of the workers must have fooled around with the remote, and I ended up doing the rest of the assignment watching recorded wrestling matches—not my choice but at least it was something.

Luckily, in the age of computers you can bring your laptop with you on overnights to watch a movie or do some work to fill up the time. I've never been one to be tech savvy, so I must admit I sometimes feel a bit lost when I try to do a simple thing like watch TV at a client's house. Maybe you will be more talented than me when it comes to figuring out which controller works what device.

Unaltered Pets

Personally I'm not a fan of caring for unaltered (not spayed or neutered) pets because they can pose problems on walks and in households. First off, an unaltered, pet male or female, dog or cat, will mark their territory. Of course, in multiple households, spraying can occur with neutered cats, but they will not be as aggressive. Female cats in heat will spray as well. Male dogs and cats that aren't neutered are aggressive when it comes to protecting their territory, so this should give you a clue on what to expect.

Female cats in heat are affectionate to everything from kids' toys, other cats, furniture, and humans. Cats can be very annoying, and I can't see why someone wouldn't neuter their cat. But if you ever sit for a female who keeps putting her butt up in the air, rubbing everything in sight, rolling around on the floor and yowling, don't get alarmed because more than likely the cat you're sitting for is in heat, and cats can go into heat as early as four months. Be careful the cat doesn't escape out the door because when they are in heat, they will be eager to get out of the house.

We can't dictate to our clients what to do with their pets, and some of my clients refuse to spay or neuter. And I have experience with dealing with households with this scenario. I have been toying with the idea of letting prospective clients know that I will not care for unaltered pets but haven't come to a decision on this yet. If you have a female dog in heat and she is bleeding, although she will not be ready to let a male dog mount her, the males will be attracted to the female during this stage. It will be very hard to distract a male dog if you're out walking when he has one thing on his mind. Another thing is that after the female stops bleeding, she will then be ready to mate. The length of this cycle varies greatly, anywhere between four to twenty days. And the males will come crawling out of the woodwork looking for a female. I once had a sit where a beautiful black Newfoundland male had planted himself on my client's porch, waiting for his moment. I wasn't even aware that this female was in heat because she was not bleeding, but I knew something was up. I couldn't chase him away and decided it was better to let her in the yard to go potty, never leaving her for a second.

Another time I had a houseful of five female pugs. This was a new client, and she had told me that the youngest was in heat. They didn't have a chance to spay her and wanted me to take them for walks. I told them I will not walk any females during their heat cycle for obvious reasons. Females in heat will act extremely affectionate to people and male dogs but very aggressive to other female dogs. And let me tell you, this household was in complete mayhem with these little pugs fighting amongst themselves. The client left a spray bottle for the dogs, but this really doesn't work when dogs are fighting. So I brought my can of pennies and straightened out this household right away.

Unaltered males can be a handful on walks, so be careful not to let them socialize with other dogs known or unknown to you. And unaltered females can draw unwanted attention on your walks if you're not aware of their heat cycles. Pets in heat can be very determined to procreate, so be on your toes for odd behavior from any pet in your care in case your client happens to forget to clue you in. Adding this question to your contract will give you a heads-up on strange behavior from the pet and what to expect.

Uncooperative Pets: What to Do

If you have children, you might have an idea as to what to do if you have a pet that will not cooperate. Patience, patience, patience are the three key ingredients in making this situation work for you. I have always believed that children and pets are on the same wavelength, and if the pet you're caring for is not cooperating, you will not get anywhere trying to force the situation. You can try fooling the pet, and bribing works well, or you can just wait it out and hope that the pet decides to do things your way.

These assignments will sometimes throw you off your schedule as well. I have spent time trying to get a shy dog out from under the bed to go for a walk and extra time waiting for a dog to go back in the house. I've tried throwing treats in front of a dog to get him to walk down the street to go potty. I've spent time chasing a dog that has stolen my shoe or jacket around the house. I've tried looking for cats that seem to become invisible because they don't want to take their medicine. I've had to take the cat to the vet, and he took off running when he saw the carrier. There are so many pets that won't cooperate. And you know what, most times they pull this when you're running late on your schedule with little time to spare. I have noticed that when I ignore this behavior, they seem to come around a little sooner. I sometimes forget all about my uncooperative pet and sit myself down on the couch to watch a little television. Most times they will come up to me, and I ask them if they're ready now because they also know that sooner or later things are going to be done my way after all is said and done. But all this will teach you the meaning of patience.

Being every pet is different, you will have to figure out what will work with this particular pet. Honestly, this is not something that can be taught from any book. You will have hands-on learning when it comes to getting a pet to cooperate, and as I look back, it can be very amusing and challenging, which makes this profession so much fun to be involved in.

Unfair Competition

When starting out pet sitting, I guess I was a little naïve to the business world. I was honest and thought others were as well. Well, I found out pretty quickly how ruthless some people can be when it comes to business. But I've always gone by the rule that I will not lower myself to the tactless antics of others. A friend of mine would always say, "You have to know what your competitors are doing." And my reply to her would be, "I don't care what they are up to. I put my blinders on and follow my path." Those of you who have horses should get it; basically blinders keep a horse focused on what's in front of him, blocking out distraction and becoming fearful. This has worked really well for me.

Despite what might occur, I suggest you do the same when dealing with unfair competition. Put your blinders on. Don't worry about your competition; let them worry about you. You have no control over your competition, but you do have control on how you run your own business. Run your race without looking at your competition. I refuse to waste my energy worrying about what the competition is doing. Instead I focus on my goals and long-term plans.

You might be thinking, *Well, what could the competition do?* I will tell you a couple of short stories of what happened to me during my years of pet sitting. Now remember I live in New York, and hopefully, in your part of the world, you won't have to deal with some of these problems that I had to contend with, but people are people, and it takes all kinds to make the world go round.

A couple years into my business, after my daughter started working with me, we both started to get a traffic ticket every couple of weeks. Now we're not that bad at driving, and we were both close to losing our licenses because every ticket in New York adds up points. When you hit a certain amount of points, your license will be suspended, no more driving, and to a pet sitter it will be the death of a business. I had said that "I bet there are cops out there doing pet sitting, and they want us out." Everyone said, "Oh no, they wouldn't do that." Well, some tickets were issued by the same police officers, and at times it was like they were sitting there waiting for us. I know what you're thinking—that's what they do, sit around waiting for the someone to blow a stop sign or run a red light, whatever the offense. But did I tell you this was within a couple of months' time frame? Never in my whole life did I get that many tickets in such a short time, and it wasn't only me. My daughter was getting them also. I was very suspicious about the whole situation, and although we didn't lose our licenses, we came very close. Our insurance was sky high and made things just a little tougher.

Well, a year went by, and I got a call from someone who needed a pet sitter. I went on the interview. He happens to be a detective with the New York police department. During the interview he tells me that there are a couple of cops doing pet sitting and then proceeds to turn to his wife and says, "I wouldn't let them into my house, let alone take care of the cats." Did you ever have an *aha moment*? Well, this was mine! My suspicions were correct.

A few years after that, another one of my clients and I were talking, and this subject came up. She then told me I should have reported this to internal affairs for investigation. It had never occurred to me, and I thought, how could I actually prove this? But they could have checked this out through records of the cop who issued the ticket and the volume to same offenders, namely me and my daughter. Whether you believe this or not is up to you, but to this day I'm convinced that this was the case. It was rather ruthless, if you ask me.

I'll give you another instance involving a city agency. The difference was this was when I had opened a pet store and continued to run the pet sitting through the store. This increased business with my pet sitting, and the pet store was just about making it. There was a lot of overhead eating up the profits. Now here's where it gets interesting. Every store in the area had signs out to advertise their business. But in New York, as you know, there are all sorts of laws and regulations that govern our state. Okay, rules are rules and must be obeyed, right? But I was the only retailer in the area getting harassed by the local sanitation official; they give tickets for unsanitary conditions, check rubbish removal stickers, and are in charge of signage! Well, I got a ticket for having a sign for a sale on pet food and pet sitting not being allowed on the huge sidewalk. When I asked about why the other stores could have signs out and why he was harassing me, I got no answer. He was totally abusive and demanded my license, no, not for the store, but my driver's license. What? I'm a law-abiding citizen, and I obey. I filed a complaint with the sanitation department for this official's abusive behavior.

After the dust settled and I thought I was done with this whole mess, I got a call from my daughter saying he (my sanitation official) was sitting on top of my street. I also have surveillance cameras on my home and saw him on the camera from time to time. I was now being harassed at home, being he had my home address from the license; he was upset that I filed a complaint against him and was going to get even. Well, his behavior was dismissed. I paid the ticket, and from this point on, you may not believe the story as it gets very weird. On my street there was an old house across from me; it was almost falling down. One afternoon I was home from my pet sits, and I got a knock on the door. A man was standing there, and he showed a badge, and I thought, after all that's been going on, what now? He showed me an order to condemn my home! I couldn't believe this. He said he was here earlier in the day, and no one was home, so he wanted to stop back on his way home because he knew something wasn't right. He asked if my house number was always on the mailbox, and it was, so he couldn't understand what was going on. He also said he was glad that he stopped back, went the extra mile, because he could have lost his job, and I would have been able to sue the city—but not after all the aggravation. Imagine coming home to a boarded-up house with your pets inside. I swear I felt like I was living in the twilight zone, and I was furious. So I called 311 (a New York information hotline) and started my own investigation. I didn't get a name of who had filed the complaint about the house across the street and put my address on it, but I did find out that it was an organization that had filed it. Can you guess who? Possibly the sanitation department and my friendly neighborhood sanitation official?

Well, that whole time was very stressful for me, but thankfully, it all faded away. He disappeared, and I never saw him again. They must have given him a desk job or something. My store closed down, but I still delivered pet food, kitty litter, and the like. I spoke with one of my delivery guys, and he told me a little story about a sanitation worker who had opened five pet stores on the island, had a lot of money, blah, blah, blah. Talk about another aha moment. He had one of his buddies do his dirty work, like I was really going to take over the pet store industry with my one little store.

It seems I've had my fair share of the bullies playing hard ball, and I guess they think, *Ah, she's just a woman. It will be easy to make her buckle under the pressure.* But guess what, I'm a pet sitter, one of the hardest jobs I've ever known, and I've had many. We're a tough bunch, we are. Someone once said to me that people mistake kindness for weakness. Maybe that's true in their minds, but not in reality.

I also experienced someone stealing my business cards to put theirs up in my place, continuing to put my cards back and leaving theirs. I used to just let it go, but not anymore, not after all these other things I had to put up with. If and when it happens again, I will politely call them up and ask why they keep taking my cards down. Knowing they will deny it, I just want to let them know there's plenty of work to go around, and I'm aware of what they're doing. They have just as much of a right to have their cards left out as I do. Little do they know that I'm inspired by competition. It fuels my fire, and I never worry about what they're doing because I have my blinders on. In all walks of life, from childhood through adult life, we will find people who will try to get ahead no matter what the cost, and unfortunately, pet sitting is no different. If we want to ensure a professional tone is represented in pet sitting, we must remember to play fair and not get wrapped up in the competitors who fail to play by the rules. So try to keep calm when confronted with these situations. Keep your focus on your business, and time will tell who will withstand the test of time, and I've seen many pet sitting businesses come and go. No one will ever put me out of business. When the time comes and I decide to sell, it will be my decision and no one else's.

Walking in on Sick Pets

If your business is going along smoothly, there is nothing like walking in on a sick pet for a wake-up call and realizing what a tremendous responsibility we have. It can happen at any time; even a young pet isn't immune from getting sick. And these scenarios are the very ones that can catch us off guard. That's why it is so important to educate yourself on recognizing signs of illness. Cats are the worst at hiding their illness, while dogs, I've found, love the attention that they will get from even a mild upset stomach. Although some dogs are great at disguising their illness, every pet is unique just as every assignment is. After you've done a certain job for some time, this will become easier because you will become familiar with what is normal for the pet in your care. This is why it's very important to get as much information on your initial consult in regard to the health of the pet.

And I can honestly say that the cats will bring you the most visits to the vet. Getting them to the vet quickly can sometimes be the difference between life and death. Come to think of it, there has not been one single incident involving a dog in my care that had to make an emergency visit to the vet due to an illness until recently, where one of my clients' dog that suffers from a heart condition had to be rushed to the vet due to a blue tongue. It was News Year's weekend, and on my first visit, when I was administering his oral medicine, I noticed his tongue was blue. Their vet saw the dog immediately, and thank goodness, my client's son was on hand to help. He had to be taken to an emergency vet in New Jersey, and the son spent seven hours there. It was determined that this dog had the beginnings of Cushing's. The vet said the blue tongue is also a sign that the pet has Cushing's along with a distended belly that was tender to the touch. I have had many with existing illnesses taking medications, but their owners were on top of their health and aware of problems. And if this is not the case, it's up to the pet sitter to notice these signs of illnesses. As long as you administer these medications properly, hopefully, no problems should arise.

The first thing to do when you walk in on a sick pet is to try to keep your cool. Assess the situation and the severity of the illness, and then before you make any calls to the owner, get in touch with their vet. I say this because time is of the essence, and most times when you have a sick pet, you will find that your client's vet doesn't have hours coinciding with your pet's illness. If you're on top of your game, you will have backup veterinarians' telephone numbers in your pet first aid kit, and you will have to make alternate arrangements. Once you have spoken to the vet's office and have made arrangements to bring the pet in, you can then place a quick call to the client to let them know what is going on. I always feel so much better once the pet is at the vet. I can then breathe again and continue with my schedule. Most times my client will then take over long-distance with payment and instructions to the vet, taking that weight off my shoulders. If that is not the case, then the decision-making is left to me and my emergency contact.

Sometimes if you have a large dog that is unable to get up on its own and need additional help, you can reach out to a neighbor. Or if your emergency contact is able to come over and help, this makes things so much easier. Once at the vet office, you will be able to get help from the technicians to get the dog in. I have used sleds and large blankets acting as a makeshift gurney for my own dogs. Sometimes when at a client's home, we have to scavenge around to find something to get the dog out into the car. A good alternative would be a lawn chair or a piece of plywood, and blankets are usually readily available as are children's sleds. I have a couple of vets that will come to the home and one in particular that I can reach out to. But this isn't always possible because the vet has a schedule as well, and an emergency clinic is the best bet.

I can tell you from experience that walking in on a sick pet can be very stressful and make for a hectic day. Keeping your wits about you along with having a backup vet for emergencies and a backup plan in place for all situations will make walking in on a sick pet just a little easier. It's not easy when this happens to our own pets let alone a client's pet.

Washing a Pet

Unless you plan on offering grooming along with your pet sitting assignments, this scenario will not come up too often. But there will be occasions where you will have no choice if the pet is suffering from diarrhea, especially dogs and long-haired cats. It won't even matter if the dog is crated or not because I have walked in on some really big messes from dogs that are allowed to roam free. These dogs still managed to get poo all over the rear end and legs. If the weather is nice and this happens to be a larger dog, it is easier to take them outside to clean them off. Always make sure the dog is dry before bringing them back in, especially if the air conditioner is running. If I can find their shampoo, I will use this, but there have been times where I have had to use the client's shampoo, and this really doesn't matter as long as the pet gets cleaned up. I once had a smaller dog that had gotten a bout of diarrhea, and not only did he manage to get poo all over himself but he also made a mess on the client's couch. I placed a call to the client asking if he would be receptive to a bath and then asked what I should clean the couch with. The dog was easy, but the couch was a different story. I always will clean up whatever mess because letting it sit will make this much harder to clean. And the client truly appreciates the extra effort when they come home to a clean home.

The colder months will make this much more difficult because you won't have the option of cleaning the pet outside, and besides cleaning the dog, you will also have to clean up the bathroom. But in my opinion it must be done so the dog does not develop a rash and not to mention the smell. Cats are not free from becoming messy due to diarrhea, and we know how most cats love to get a bath. So with the cats, I will not clean the whole cat, just the messy end, and I usually do this in the kitchen sink. Always make sure both cats and dogs are dry before leaving, making sure they don't get a chill. I have never charged extra for this but will include this in my notes so the client is aware of the problem when they return. Most times they tip me generously, so I am compensated for my time. Remember, this is your business, and if you feel the need to charge extra for bathing a pet, I wouldn't see why your client would be upset for this extra charge. I'm grateful that this doesn't have to be done all that often because it will make me run over in my time at the client's home, and there would go my well-thought-out schedule.

When a Client Accuses You of Stealing

This is a topic that we really wouldn't like to have happen, especially if we know we have done no wrong. But unfortunately this subject may rear its ugly head at some point, and it actually has happened to me many years back. I found this to be rather upsetting for I never even like to go into clients' drawers to look for can openers or spoons for feeding let alone steal. For I take great pride in my business and promote it as being the most trustworthy pet sitting business on the island.

My story begins innocent enough as I was caring for a private investigator client of mine who had a lovely basset hound. This basset loved to eat coins and shiny objects as I had noticed this in her stool from time to time. Nickels and dimes seemed to be her favorite and would be eliminated in her business. On a weeklong assignment all went well with the exception of the dog getting into the mail and chewing apart a box that had come in the mail earlier that week. I had gathered all the pieces of the box along with what had come inside the box and placed them in a bag with a note to the client, letting her know what happened. Upon my client's return, I get a call asking me where the necklace was. Well, I never saw the necklace and told her all I had found was placed in the bag, and I was then accused of taking the necklace! So my response was (just like back in the school days) maybe the dog ate it. It was strange to say and, more than likely, stranger to hear. But I knew I didn't take the necklace. But knowing the history of the dog liking to eat shiny objects, I honestly thought she might have done just that. I then told her to look where the dog had chewed up the box and that maybe I missed the small jewelry box the necklace would have been in. Well, sure enough, the small box was pushed under the couch with a few bite marks in it but was undamaged. She did call me to tell me she had found the necklace under the couch but never apologized for accusing me of taking it, which hurt a little. I know if I unjustly accused someone of something like that, I'd be apologizing up and down. Maybe her phone call was her way of apologizing, but still, it would have been nice to hear those words.

The moral of the story is be prepared for anything in this business, which brings to mind the reason we should not share jobs with friends or family of clients as we would then be held liable for any disappearance of valuables even if we know in our hearts we did nothing wrong. Always conduct yourself in an appropriate manner, being totally honest with the client, even if this means sometimes getting slapped in the face for no reason whatsoever, and to keep your liability insurance up to date just in case. Keep in mind also that some clients have security cameras and could also be watching from a distance. Most of the new security cameras have Internet access and can be viewed from anywhere. Most times I might just add to my notes that I had to search for the can opener, dustpan, paper towels, and the like. Respect your client's privacy; don't go into drawers unless it's absolutely necessary. I suggest on my initial consult that they could leave necessary supplies on the counter or label cabinets with sticky notes for food, treats, cleaning supplies, plastic bags, and so on. This limits my need to go searching for things; most of my clients abide by these rules. But I do have some that never seem to remember to leave things out or have the necessary supplies to begin with.

This is even harder to do when you take on employees or ICs as there is then a third party involved, and doubts might begin to surface when faced with a situation of this magnitude. In this instance it is essential to carry a bond for your business and always to perform background checks on your help. Remembering that, as a business owner, you are responsible for your business and the help you will employ. I would never consider taking on someone without performing a background check, and I was told by the private detective that took care of my background checks, even then something could be missed. But your basic groundwork was taken care of, and you really wouldn't want to take an IC or employee on if you knew he was not a trustworthy individual. On the other hand, if there is no trust on a client's part, they themselves might have some issues. But it does little to console the person being accused of stealing—a sad situation to say the least.

When a Pet Escapes

I thank my lucky stars that I haven't had to deal with this situation except on two occasions. One was out on a daily walk when a dog slipped her collar; I chased her around the neighborhood for about ten minutes before I got hold of her. The second was due to workers in the home letting the dog escape and it becoming my responsibility to get him back in. So both these situations turned out nicely, but what if they hadn't? What if they just kept running and I didn't get them back? I don't even want to think about the stress involved in a situation like this.

This is why having pictures of the pets in your care becomes very important. I would say about 75 percent of my clients leave pictures of their pets for me. This helps me identify them in a multiple household. It tells me who needs medication and is especially helpful if the pet ever escapes. If no pictures are left for me, I will take my own with my digital camera. This is another reason to have in your contract a Permission to Photograph Pet section that the client will sign. Time is of the essence in a situation like this, especially with a dog. When the dog is still in your sight, if you turn and run back to the house, calling the dog in a happy voice, most times the dog will run back with you. I said most but not all the time. If the dog is faster than your feet can run, I would suggest you get into your car and scout the neighborhood immediately. Added help is great, so if any neighbors are home, you might ask for their assistance.

If the cat gets out of the house, they usually don't travel very far, and most times they stay within a two-block radius to the home because they like to protect their territory. However, an unaltered cat will travel far to find a mate, and it's hard to determine how far they might go if they get out. If the cat you're caring for is natured/spayed, they might be hiding under some bushes or in a neighbor's yard. And they can be little devils to get back in once they get out. Or they could get scared and be too afraid to come back right away. If the latter is the case, you could try to entice them with some tuna or sardines while calling the cat in a soft voice. If the cat does come out to get a bite to eat, don't pounce on him right away, but go over slowly, talking in a calm, low voice, and start to pet the cat. Once they are relaxed enough for you to get a hold of them, continue to talk in a low voice so as not to spook them and definitely have a good hold on them because they can get squirmy to free themselves. Then you would have to start the whole process over again. Cats will teach you the meaning of patience for sure.

Hopefully you will never have the pet become so elusive that you will have to go to great lengths to get them back. But in the event that you lose a pet, there are several things that can be done to get the word out about the lost pet. The first thing that should be done is to make a poster that is easy to read at a distance. The print should be large and done in dark bold letters, listing the type of breed/pet, whether it is a male or female, young or older pet, and a telephone number where someone can be reached at all times. And of course, offer a reward to get people interested in finding the pet. Here's a sample of a poster ad, and while out posting your lost-pet flyers, make sure to read any other postings in case someone has already found the lost pet.

~$100 REWARD~

LOST DOG ~ OLDER ~ MALE

LABRADOR RETRIEVER

NAME ~ DUSTY

TEL# 123-456-7890

(PICTURE OF PET)

The next step should be to contact your local newspaper and see if they have a free lost-pet section. If not, you should place an ad yourself. This ad should contain more information than your poster, like the pet has a scar on its left ear, is neutered, and is black with a white spot on the chest. Make sure to add that a reward is being offered. This might increase your incoming calls, but it will also motivate anyone who has seen the pet to call. Again, look at current ads running in the section in case someone has found your pet.

You can also check online for any lost-and-found organizations and place your information; most times these services are free. Petfinders is one organization that you can post a missing pet report. They have a national database, and you might be surprised as to how far a pet can travel if they are frightened. The USDA's Missing Pet Network can be found online, and you can leave a report free of charge.

It is for all types of animals, including horses. The Bird Hotline is a place to list for birds and is an international lost-and-found listing site.

Place calls to the local shelters (Animal Care and Control) every day because they will only hold the pet for a few days. Call your local radio stations; sometimes they will announce lost pets for free. Post a flyer in all pet-related businesses, including the local vet offices, groomers, and pet stores. This flyer should include more information, including picture of the pet, personality traits, scars, and if the pet is altered or not, than your poster for roadside posting. Try to be diligent when entering and exiting your client's home, never talking on your cell phone because this is a distraction. As with anything when dealing with pets, being on your toes should prevent any mishaps. Some of the creatures we care for can be very crafty and determined if they want, so consider yourself forewarned.

When a Client Doesn't Leave the Air Conditioner or Heat On

When a client goes away and tries to save money by not leaving the air or heat on, it is very frustrating for me. I have taken responsibility for raising the heat or putting the air on and disregarded whatever the client has wanted, even with my most difficult clients. We are left to care for the pet. How can we possibly care for the pet if it is left in a sweltering apartment or home? If the temperature outside is in the single digits and the pet is left in a cold home, this might be a better scenario, but the pet will still feel the cold. My clients won't actually turn the heat off in the winter but keep it at a very low temperature. Some short-haired breeds are really affected by the cold, and it's not fair to the sitter either.

I have never lost a client by going against what they left the thermostat on. And the first thing I do is explain to them when they get home that I was worried about the health of their pet. I take full responsibility, and before they get a chance to complain, I'm the one complaining about how hot or cold the home was.

I did have a new client many years ago, and right before they left, they said the air was not working. This happened to be a sleepover, and the temperature was extremely high. She had a house full of five pugs and only left a few fans to cool the dogs off. I was very worried about the pugs because they cannot tolerate very hot temperatures. I tried my best to make it pleasant for the dogs and myself by sleeping outside with the dogs on the enclosed deck. The mosquitoes were terrible, but it was better than the hot house. When I left in the morning, I put ice cubes in their water and a bowl of ice cubes in front of the fan to try to cool the air. I had already committed myself to the job, and I'm not one to back out of my commitments. They only used my service that one time for they were moving.

Keeping the pets in our care comfortable, healthy, and secure should be our top priority, and we shouldn't be afraid to use our better judgment. Sometimes we have to go with the flow, and other times we have to swim against the tide.

When a Client Won't Let Go

Here again we have another tough topic. I have had many clients who don't want to face the fact that their pet's health is declining and the quality of life for their pet is suffering. I myself have been guilty of this situation and didn't want to face the fact that it was time to put my baby down. But when we are on the outside looking in, it's a little bit easier for us to see what should be done.

Suggesting euthanasia to your client is a very delicate situation as some may become angry with you for even thinking such a thing. They will make excuses, saying that their pet still has an appetite, even though the pet is in noticeable pain and is having a hard time getting up and around. Losing control of their bladder and lying in their own urine isn't really a nice way to live their golden years. What I try to do is to drop little hints in a subtle manner on how much the pet is suffering and say that we usually want to keep them here with us forever because they give us unconditional love. I'd say how we are selfish and want to spend as much time as possible with our little angels and that if I was a pet, I would want to go peaceably in my sleep with my family holding me, that it's cruel to make them suffer if no other options are available and that natural death will take some time.

I'm sure not one of us wants to have to make that decision, but in actuality, it's something that all pet owners must face at one time or another. Some clients need a little advice as they know in their hearts it's time. I also suggest to them to think about it, that it doesn't have to be put down immediately and, in the meantime, to give their pet steaks for dinner and make them as comfortable as possible, maybe even sleep with them even if their bedding is on the floor. I tell them to spend as much time with them telling them how much they are loved and will be missed greatly. I ask them to try to stay calm and relaxed as they tend to work off our energy, and if they sense we're anxious and nervous, they will also be. Some people think I'm nuts, but the truth is that animals are highly intuitive and sense our emotions. We all know this is not the easiest thing to do, and your client will appreciate your compassion and understanding in the end.

When a Client Turns on You

If you think pets are unpredictable, then you should also be aware that our clients can be just as unpredictable at times. Sometimes they are longtime clients, and other times they are new to the service. Remember when I spoke about keeping clients satisfied and I spoke about clients taking things out on the first available person? Well, this is more than likely why the client would turn on you. I've had three completely different situations happen in my years of pet sitting. And at the time these problems came up, I was very upset at the attitude of the client, knowing I had done a superb job. Human nature tends to make people take their own frustrations out on someone or put some type of blame for even the tiniest reason, and who better than a pet sitter for a lousy vacation? Even a bad time in their life or having a hard time coping with their own situations can make even a longtime client act irrational.

I'll first tell you about my longtime client. During the fifteen years of caring for their cats, I was aware of the tension in their relationship, but it really was none of my business. They had gone away for a week, left payment as usual, and all went well. There were no problems with the house or pets. But I did have a problem with my cell phone; I had dropped it and needed to check my messages. Figuring they were such good longtime clients, I used their landline to check my messages. I honestly thought nothing of it. Was I wrong? The client was furious that there was a $2.50 charge on her bill! So I told her I could refund her the amount or deduct it off their next trip. Well, I was fired.

About six months later I get a call from the client, who was nice as pie, requesting service. My first thought was to say I was booked but reconsidered and decided to take her back but raised her rate. I like to think of it as abusive-behavior compensation. When I went in, I did a head count and couldn't find their beautiful Ocicat. So I called the client frantically. She then told me that a friend had cared for the cats the last time they went away and didn't know what signs to look for in a sick cat, and he died. I felt horrible that I had ever used her phone because if I was to have cared for the cats, this would have never happened. And I'm sure the client regretted the decision to fire me as well. After all, I serviced this client for fifteen years with no problems. It was a hard lesson to learn.

Another client I had for about five years had to go away on short notice due to her father's death. I never had a problem with this client and loved her Labs. Being it was short notice and I was booked, I shared the job with my daughter. My daughter had told me on one of her visits that there were two young women in the house, and they said they were checking on the dogs. This client would sometimes have a friend come in and check the dogs, but this was her boyfriend. So I called the client but got no answer and let it go. This client then requested two extra days of visits, and again, I accommodated her request. Now I'm very particular about laying out newspapers and mail always in a neat pile; papers are opened and placed in date order. Her dogs were drinking a considerable amount of water, and every time we went in, their water bowls were empty. So she returned and blasted that there was no water in the bowls. She didn't like what she saw, and when I questioned her about what she saw, she wouldn't answer. She wanted her key back immediately! So I told her she was indigent and abusive on the phone, and I tried to understand that she had just lost her father, but it was no reason for her to act in this manner. I also told her she wasn't getting her key back until we were paid, so she made a check out for me, and I handed her key back. We were done.

The funny thing about this whole scenario is that she had recommended my service to a friend of hers who I have to this day. And this friend of hers has referred a couple of clients to me as well. I love working with animals; it's people I can't stand at times.

My third incident was with a client I had for about two years who had a cute dog but a bad little boy. This little dog would pull everything off the table, including the tablecloth, every time I went in. He was pooping on the floor and very hyper in general. The wife would always book, and they always managed to come home early, always sending me away, saying they were home and all was fine. If I travel to the home, I charge for my visit. If they had called before I went over, I might consider crediting the account, if I felt so inclined. My contract reads that the client agrees to pay for contracted visits. Well, one day they came home early. I had called the wife from my cell phone, she's very happy, their home and thank you. Now I had driven down to their home and was being followed by a storm, so by the time I got to the house, it was raining. As I'm getting ready to pull out of the driveway, the husband comes running out of the house with the leash in his hands and asks if he was being charged for the visit. My reply was yes, so he demanded I walk the dog, and by this time it was pouring out. He wanted to know why I came when it was raining, like I can really control Mother Nature to work with my schedule. He questioned me if I came at all. I'm telling you the tension in that house could be felt for miles. So I walked the dog in the pouring rain, and then he went on to complain that the dog was soaked. Now if they had not come home early, I would have waited till the rain let up a little, and we would not have had a tension-filled walk.

So if this ever happens, try not to take it personally because I believe that we get abused at times because the client themselves are miserable. I've often said to my friend that the pet sitter gets blamed for everything, and it's not fair, but neither is life at times.

When Disaster Strikes

Every region will differ in regard to what type of disaster that a pet sitter might be faced with. Whether it's some type of natural disaster such as a tornado, hurricane, or a "national" disaster such as 9/11, working through these types of pet sitting situations can be extremely difficult. We recently had to contend with Hurricane Irene in my area and had a mandatory evacuation for certain areas that were by the beach. Hurricane Irene was such a massive storm I felt that Mother Nature could take any path she chose and no one knew where it was safe to go. With this storm there was a warning, so first thing was to make a plan for my family and my own pets. Both my home and my mother's home were in the mandatory evacuation area as we live directly across from the beach. My mother went to my daughter's house; my son, who is living in the basement apartment at my mother's, stayed upstairs at her house and weathered the storm out. The Friday before the hurricane hit, I got a call from my client that I was caring for their three greyhounds. She had offered her home for me to stay over, and at the time I declined. But I reconsidered because I had these same clients in the blizzard of 2010 and wasn't able to get to their home till 12:00 p.m., after shoveling out. Being the majority of my other pet sitting assignments were in the same area, I decided to stay over with the dogs. I slept downstairs with the dogs because I was afraid of the large trees that might come down, both in front of the home and in the back. I was also worried about my pets; my dog went along with my mother down to my daughter's house. The skies were ominous that day, and I have to admit I was a little frightened. I have six cats, and two are hard to get ahold of because they were rescued and never really tamed up. I couldn't take all six of my cats with me to the greyhounds' house. So I made a decision to leave them on the second floor with plenty of water and food along with their litter boxes. This was a hard decision to make.

Before the worst of the storm hit on Saturday, August 27, 2011, I was able to get out and do a scheduled visit starting in the afternoon for a golden retriever. Luckily my client decided to turn around and come back home, so my other visits extending into the morning of the twenty-eighth were cancelled. It was a stressed-filled, restless night for all, I'm sure. I decided to get out early as I couldn't sleep, worrying about my own home and animals. The worst of the storm was to hit at 8:00 a.m., and I wanted to get to my morning stops and get them out of the way. This hurricane happened on the weekend, so luckily I had no daily visits on my schedule. By the time it had reached New York, it was downgraded from a hurricane to a tropical storm but still managed to do major flooding and damage.

As I emerged from my client's home on their tree lined street, two houses down was a huge tree that has toppled into two homes. I was grateful that this tree did not come down on my client's home as I looked around in amazement. The streets were a mess with downed branches, leaves, and debris. The streets were desolate, and although it was still raining on Sunday, the twenty-eighth, it was nothing compared to what I had driven in the night before.

I was eager to get to my home and shortened my morning visits. Things could have been a lot worse if the storm hadn't lost some of its strength. I first checked my mother's home and was most concerned for downed trees, but there weren't any.

But we did have two feet of water in the basement apartment, something common in low-lying areas like mine, so I was relieved. Then I was off to my home to check the damage. I also had two feet of water surrounding my home; imagine coming home to slush through all this water just to get in the front door. This is an actual picture of my home with the water surrounding it.

I was thankful that no trees came down, and unlike my mother's home, I have no basement. My kitties weathered the storm well, and the only other problem was no electric power. I have several clients in my neighborhood who were also concerned about their homes, so I had gotten calls to check their damage when I had a chance, which I did and did not charge for. I live in the same area and could understand their concern as they left when it became a mandatory evacuation.

I was one of those people who wouldn't fall for all the hype but decided to take precautions just in case. Living down the beach all my life, I think I became accustomed to the threat of floods. So several days before, I started to get supplies together; this included breaking out the camping gear. If you're ever faced with having to evacuate for any natural disaster, it is important to be prepared. Although I had most of my supplies together, I visited the www.noaa.gov website and realized I hadn't included all the supplies needed, just in case.

- Water supply—1 gallon per person up to 7 days
- Flashlights/batteries
- Battery-operated radio
- Propane lantern
- Propane camping grill
- Small camping utensils—pots, pans, paper plates, knives, forks, spoons, cups, manual can opener
- Nonperishable packaged foods, canned foods, juices, snack foods up to 7 day supply
- Sleeping bags, blankets, pillows
- Toiletries, hygiene products, baby wipes
- Clothing, rain gear/boots
- First aid kit/medicines
- Important documents in waterproof plastic bag—insurance, medical records, SS card, bank account numbers
- Cash/credit cards
- Full tank of gas for your vehicles
- Pet's ID tags, medical records, muzzle, harness leash, blanket, food and treats up to 7 days

When I sent my dog to my daughter's, she asked why I brought so much, and my reply was, "Just in case." The media was relentless as to be prepared, which sent some people into a panic mode. The day of the hurricane, gas stations were out of fuel, the shelves were empty in the food stores, and it was days before they were able to restock due to some roads being washed away, and the delivery trucks weren't able to get through. All this and we still have to carry through with our scheduled assignments.

As I'm typing this, it is the day before the tenth anniversary of 9/11, and they are playing reenactments of survivors making it out of the buildings and actual footage of the planes hitting the buildings. It was a day that I worked through that was surreal, looking back. And as time goes by, I remember exactly what I was doing—getting ready to go on my runs. I didn't have any clients on vacation at that time as the majority of my assignments were daily walks. I had a regular client that would call to let me know when she was leaving and when the dogs would need to go out. But this day I called her as I was watching the morning news and heard all the bridges were being shut down. I let her know she might not want to head over to New Jersey because she might not be able to get back home. But all my other clients were already gone for the day. Most worked on the island, and we were shut down from the rest of the city. I traveled on the expressway with only a few other cars, FBI and police vehicles, speeding by. How I managed that day, I don't know. I reached one of my stops, which was by the water and right across from New York. This is a building I work in till this day, and when I arrived at the building, the doorman, workers, and residents were all standing outside, watching the tower burn. The first tower had already come down, and the second tower was still burning but standing. I go in to get my dog, and by the time I came out, the second tower had fallen. It was unbelievable.

I walked dogs watching the fighter jets flying by, mayhem all around me, and I continued with my walks listening to updates on the radio as I drive to my assignments. Had I been a dog walker in New York instead of one of the suburbs, I'm sure my memories of 9/11 would be quite different. As pet sitters, we must continue with our routine for the sake of the animals. Working through these situations is tough, but what can be done? There used to be a creed that the United States Postal Service would use, "We are mothers and fathers and sons and daughters who every day go about our lives with duty, honor, and pride. And neither snow nor rain nor heat nor gloom of night nor winds of change nor a nation challenged will stay us from the swift completion of our appointed rounds—ever," I think that we as pet sitters should have this as our motto, for I have been out when the postal service has closed down due to snow or inclement weather. With Hurricane Irene, the bus service was shut down for a day, something that in my lifetime was unheard of. If anyone deserves this as their motto, it's definitely a pet sitter.

Being prepared in a disaster situation is a plus, but what if this disaster is unexpected? Sometimes a fire, tornado, hurricane, floods, or even an attack on our country can cause a disaster situation. These situations happen quickly and sometimes without notice. Below are some websites that can give some insight into disaster preparedness:

- Alley Cat Allies—www.alleycat.org
- American Red Cross—www.redcross.org
- American Veterinary Medical Association (AVMA)—www. avma.org
- Code 3 Associates—www.code3associates.org (They offer free services and how to prepare for a disaster.)
- My Horse Matters (American Association of Equine Practitioners)—www.myhorsematters.com

So in reality, when disaster strikes, we must remember that we are only human, and we will do everything humanly possible to make sure our clients' pets are safe and secure. We cannot put ourselves into a dangerous situation. We must wait it out, and when the worst is over, we then can check on our clients' pets and homes. On an average week I can have anywhere from ten to fifteen stops a day. When I'm aware of bad situation developing, I will go out as early as 3:00 p.m. to do my nighttime stops, making sure all pets in my care have sufficient food and water for an extended period. If they mess the floor, this would be the least of my problems. If we are injured, we will be of no help to anyone, and at times I push my limits as to how far I will go, but even I know when to batten down the hatches.

When We Break Something

Honesty is always the best policy when it comes to breaking something in a client's home. It is never done purposely, and accidents will happen. So if something gets broken, let the client know what happened and offer to pay for it. There has been two occasions where I broke something at a client's home. One time I was parking in the driveway and accidently hit the planter that they had by the garage and cracked a piece off the pot. I told the client what had happened and offered to buy them a new one, and they were very forgiving and said it was okay and not to worry about it.

Another time a client had a shelf above the litter box with a collection of cups that I had hit with my head while getting up. Some of the cups came crashing down, hit me in the head, and I saw stars. I spent some time cleaning up the mess I had made, salvaged what I could, and left a note explaining what happened. They called when they got home and actually said they were sorry for having the shelf there and that it was a bad place for it. I thought the cups had more of a sentimental value and was upset about breaking them. But it seems it didn't make a difference to my client. So be truthful, and you will find your clients will be very understanding.

This is also why we carry insurance, in case we break something of real value. If I had broken an expensive vase that cost $2,000, this would hurt a little if I had to take the money out of my pocket. Although I have never had to file a claim with my insurance company, I will always carry my insurance for any situation that might come up.

When We Do Stupid Things

Well, I have been guilty of doing stupid things quite a few times during my years of pet sitting. You will find that these stupid things can make you feel mentally impaired at times, wondering how you could have done that. The most common would probably be closing the client's front door and realizing that the keys to the client's home are inside the house. I'll never forget the time I did this when I had taken the dog for his walk. This happened on Father's Day, at night, no less. So here we are, my dog and I, waiting an hour and a half for a locksmith because I did a brainless thing. Not only that, I ended up paying top price for having the locksmith come out at night on Father's Day. This is why requesting two sets of keys is mandatory for my business these days as we never know when the brain will decide to quit.

Another incident I can remember was sitting for a nice dog that only had to go in the yard. It was an easy job, and after going in, I would open the sliding glass door and close it behind me because they also had a cat. I would do this to make sure the cat wouldn't get out when we were in the yard. One morning I did the same as I always did, and when I went to go back in the house, the sliding glass door was locked! From the outside I could see my cell phone sitting on the kitchen counter, so I had no way of calling anyone for help. This client had a six-foot chain-link fence with a gate but had a combination lock on the gate. I ended up having to climb the fence and knock on a neighbor's house to call a locksmith. Thank God this happened early on in my career because I'm not sure how a woman of my age would look climbing a six-foot fence. She was a nice young woman, and it was about eight o'clock in the morning, and I could tell I had gotten her out of bed. She was kind enough to let me wait for the locksmith in her home, and I didn't have to wait too long for the locksmith to show up. He let me in, and I was back on schedule. But for the life of me, I couldn't figure out how this had happened. I must have closed this door ten times, this time making sure I was on the inside, and it never happened again. So from this point on, when I have a sliding glass door, I never close it all the way, leaving just enough of the door open so a cat couldn't get out but ensuring I wouldn't have a problem getting back in. Some might be saying I should have brought my keys with me, but honestly, who would think by going in the backyard you would have to bring your keys?

Then there were times I got my keys together for the assignment and locked my car, not even realizing that my car keys were still inside the car. I finished up the job and started looking for my car keys, retraced my steps, looked in the car, and there they were. Now I've done this more than I'd like to admit, and a few times my kids were called to the rescue. On the rare occasion when I didn't lock my hatchback, I ended up crawling through the car to get the car keys. I have traveled across the island only realizing a block away from my assignment that I left the keys for the assignment on the front table. One of my clients once called me the absentminded professor, for I could go on an interview and conduct myself as a professional only to come knocking back on the client's door looking for my day planner. Now most times these things happen as business is booming. And this could be a reason why as I am all over the place, thinking about what has to be done next even before I completed my last task.

I have let myself into clients' homes thinking I have used the remote for the alarm only to find out that it was my car alarm that I had used. This, of course, was before my second cup of coffee, and I could go on, but I'm sure you get the idea. Many years ago I had a client who felt uncomfortable letting me into the main section of the house and had a separate area downstairs for the dogs. Well, this door was never locked; as a matter of fact, they didn't have a key for this door. The door was locked on my first visit, but it did have a doggie door. You guessed it; I ended up crawling through the doggie door! It must have been a sight to see, and the dogs were delighted that I came in through their door. The only thing that was stupid on my part was not insisting on having a key to the main section of the house, and after this incident, I did. My daughter isn't free of doing stupid things either. On one assignment she went into the client's garage only to have the door shut behind her and get locked in the garage for an hour. Luckily she had her cell phone with her. She called me, and in turn, I called the client, who told me where she had a spare key in the garage. She has also gone to her assignment realizing she left her keys home, like her mother, I think.

I'm sure that some of my clients have gotten a kick out of a happy dance with the dogs or singing to them (a little off-key) on occasions. For many of my clients have cameras and I sometimes forget I'm not really there alone. So if any of you are thinking it couldn't happen to you, remember the old saying "Never say never" because, after all, we're all human.

When We Get Injured

I have been lucky in this respect but not free of getting hurt on the job. I would say it was about five years into my business when I used to walk three pit bulls. The neighborhood had a local dog run but only for paying neighbors, and this was an old school yard that the church was renting out. There was a very large set of stairs down to the old school yard, and these guys were always eager to be loose and run off their excess energy. One day, going down the stairs, they pulled a little too hard, and I lost my footing, and down on my butt I went. Well, the pain was so intense that I lost my breath for a minute. What had happened was I fractured my tailbone, and you cannot believe the pain that it caused. But did I stop working? Not a day. It did take longer to get in and out of the car and to walk in general. This was before my daughter started working for me, and I had no choice. There was nothing that could be done, and I really should have taken some time off, but when you're a sole proprietor and breadwinner, this isn't even an option.

Another time I was walking a Labrador retriever. When we were coming out of the house, she was ahead of me. We went around a pole. I heard a pop, and my thumb started throbbing. I thought I broke it, but the X-ray showed no break or fracture. What the technician failed to report was that it was dislocated. So they wrapped it, thinking I had a sprain, which wasn't a good thing because the whole time it was still dislocated. My youngest was about three years old, and he had bounced back on my hand, and at that moment I felt a horrible pain. What he had done was put it back into the socket. It was extremely painful at the moment, but it was back where it belonged, something that should have been done in the emergency room.

When working with animals, especially dogs, it's easy to injure yourself. There have been many other times where I was pulled down the stairs, dragged across grassy lawns, and body-slammed by overly enthusiastic dogs. But I was never really hurt, maybe bruised, but nothing serious. I once had a Rottweiler that was a very big, strong boy. It had snowed and then rained on top of the snow. It was very slippery walking, let alone walking with Bruno. When we went out for our walk, Bruno saw a cat, and I knew I was going down. Not only did I go down but Bruno dragged me three car lengths down the street to where the cat had run under a parked car. By this time we had really picked up speed, and I was about to kiss a car. So what I did was put my arm out, and I grabbed the door handle of the car to stop. I had just been dragged across a cold, wet surface and still had five walks to do in wet clothes. In nasty weather, when you're working with dogs, it's a good idea to have a dry, clean set of clothes in the car just in case.

If I had been seriously injured, it would have been easy to cancel daily dog walks. But other arrangements would have had to be made if I had vacation assignments lined up. So it's always a good idea to have another sitter in your area that could help in a situation like this. But whoever you have to fill in for you should be familiar with dogs because, as you can see, dogs can be brutal at times.

When You Go on Vacation

This is something that must be done from time to time or you will start to feel the effects of burnout. I'm always nervous when I go on vacation, delegating assignments and getting shifts in order. My daughter usually does the bulk of the assignments with my son doing a few dallies and my IC helping out with morning visits. I stay in touch long distance for a day or so until everyone gets into the groove of things, and they usually have a couple of questions about the assignment. After that, they're on their own, and I can finally relax.

Having a good, professional relationship with other sitters in your area will help when you need a backup sitter when you plan a vacation. You shouldn't have to worry that you will lose a client to your competitor as this can become a big help to both parties involved. Of course, to really make this work well, it would be best to have at least two backup sitters as these sitters will have their own business. Coordinating schedules with other sitters before leaving can sometimes be complicated until all is worked out. But it's definitely worth it if it means you get a much needed vacation.

If you have no backup, you can opt to make your clients aware that you will be taking a vacation and will not be servicing clients during this time. You can let them know via e-mail or send out a postcard. Give your client ample time, at least two to three months, to make other arrangements if their planed vacation coincides with yours. As pet sitters, we tend to neglect our own need to take a much needed and deserved vacation, so scheduling time off for a week should be mandatory. Even if you aren't able to take a week off, a weekend can be just what the doctor ordered. Only recently did I realize the benefits of taking some time off. Your clients will be there when you come back, and you will be rejuvenated, ready to handle all those high-energy pets.

When You Lock Yourself Out

Never say never when it comes to getting locked out of a client's home. I am sure we all have had that moment as the door is closing behind us, we remember leaving the key inside. I don't try to do this often, but occasionally it will happen. I have used several types of key chains throughout my career. One was the coil key chain for the wrist, which works well, but if you take it off when doing chores, it can be forgotten. I had used a large round split key chain where all my keys would be placed on but found out after some time that it became too cumbersome. There has been two times where I have let the dog out in the yard to go potty and couldn't get back in. I normally wear my key on a lanyard around my neck, but sometimes while performing my duties in the home, I will take this off because it tends to hang down. I have dragged it through the pet's food, in litter boxes, you get the idea. So if I take it off and get distracted by the pet, it can be left behind. One time I did this early on in my career, and I thank the man above this was when I still had youth on my side. I had to climb a locked six-foot fence to get to a neighbor's home because my phone was also left inside, so I had no choice. Another time I thought I had checked to make sure the door wasn't locked, just in case, and the wind had blown it closed. This time I was lucky enough to have my license on me and was able to get the lock open by using my license to get back into my client's home.

I have left a home after making sure all was in place, garbage in hand, all water shut off, and all pets accounted for, to forget the keys on the counter of my client's home. This time was a disaster because I could not get ahold of the client's emergency key contact, and when I did, she was also on vacation. So you guessed it, two key contacts are a plus on the contract if that's possible. I scheduled a locksmith to come later in the day because I still had five more days on this assignment. On Father's Day one year, I did the same thing. This was another disaster, for I had to wait forever to get a locksmith to come to rescue me. Being I have always had signage on my car, I never had a problem with gaining access back into the home. Every time I had to use a locksmith, I would show my contract, my license, and I was in, minus a few dollars, which hurt a little. It's now a policy of mine to request two sets of keys or make a spare to leave in the office. I will always check the key that is made to make sure it is cut correctly and works.

It is also possible to have a key break in the lock if it's a sticky lock and you use too much force. Having some tools in the car if this happens and if enough of the key is sticking out of the lock, you might be able to grab it and pull it out. If not, you will have to call a locksmith, and if they can't get it out, the lock might need to be replaced. Be gentle with your locks, or you might be in this situation. This had happened to my daughter on one of her dailies. She was able to get the key out, and I had a spare for her to get back in because she had the client's dog with her when this happened. A sticky lock can work after you spray the key with WD-40 or if you have pencil in the car.

When You Lose a Key

If this ever happens, don't panic. This is why we have key contacts and locksmiths. I have never lost a key but have misplaced a key, and it can become very stressful if you start to panic. It's just another complication that will make for a long and stressful day. Though we have emergency key contact telephone numbers, sometimes we can't get in touch with them right away. And in a case like I had, my client's key contact was on vacation, and my client didn't know. Having had my fair share of being locked out of the home, I have had the opportunity to learn a little about the locksmith trade. I had questioned them on losing a key, and they had told me that they could make another key with certain locks without having to replace the lock. That would cost more money, but at least you're in.

I remember going to get a key one time, and I had a marker that I placed the name of the pet on with permanent marker. So I had done this as soon as I got in the car and placed the key on the shelf of the dashboard to dry. I left and made a left turn, and the key fell to the floor. *Okay, no problem, I'll get it on my next stop*, I thought. It disappeared, and I had to go back to get another key from the client. I swear I ripped my car apart, checked the garbage; it was nowhere to be found. Well, it was about a month later, and I was cleaning out my car. Don't ask me how this happened, but the key had managed to fall to the passenger side of the car, work its way to the back of the car on the driver's side, and go under the rug. So I guess, with all my stops and turns along the way, the key worked its way around my car. I would never have thought that is even possible. Having two sets of keys is the only way to go, just for this purpose and if you lock yourself out.

Working on Holidays

Holidays tend to be a busy time of the year for pet sitting, so you will need to consider how to structure your business. I myself have never charged extra for holidays because I was aware at the start of my business that this was going to be part of the job. This is also the most lucrative time for pet sitters as well. I have considered it, for most business will pay their employees time and a half for major holidays. I am in the process of restructuring my business, and although I have used only ICs in the past, this time around I'm going to have employees.

I want to keep my staff and be fair when it comes to working on holidays, which will be required. So these are some of the busiest holidays that I will charge an additional fee for my employee's services.

- 🐾 Memorial Day
- 🐾 Fourth of July
- 🐾 Labor Day
- 🐾 Thanksgiving
- 🐾 Christmas Eve
- 🐾 Christmas
- 🐾 New Year's Eve
- 🐾 New Year's Day

I am used to working holidays and actually look forward to having hardly any traffic on the roads. I have learned to get out super early to get my assignments finished so I can get back home to get dinner in the oven, open presents, or to enjoy a little downtime. I would say working holidays takes some getting used to, and this was difficult when my children were young. I have been so busy on holidays at times that I haven't been able to enjoy them all that much. But my schedule for holidays are never the same from year to year, so some years can be very busy with not much time for celebrating while others can be very stress-free and relaxing. Pet sitters can't take on an assignment for two weeks and tell their client they have to make other arrangement for Christmas Eve and Christmas day. If this was the case, we would surely lose some clients. So adding an extra fee to holidays should be a good incentive to working on holidays.

Now working holidays may not be the ideal situation, but working in the days before Christmas, especially, are the most difficult of all. There have been times I have had assignments near the local mall or shopping centers. It is in these moments I began to feel like I might go insane, getting stuck in major traffic jams. Everyone is out trying to get last-minute shopping done, and traveling time is doubled, sometimes tripled. Days are long, and nights are even longer, something to keep in mind before the holidays are upon us.

CHAPTER 3

Pet Emergencies

If you plan to become a pet care professional or if you are a seasoned pet care professional, there are basic emergency skills and techniques you need to know. Hopefully you will not need to use this information often. But I can guarantee you that the longer you're in this business and the more pets you care for, there will come a time when you will be faced with an emergency situation. You might be wondering what constitutes a medical emergency; this can be summed up as a situation that requires immediate attention due to some serious disability such as a life or death scenario to the pet in your care where minutes can make a difference. In some of the cases you encounter, you might be able to provide part of the help the pet requires. Some situations will require immediate veterinary care. If you doubt your ability to handle the problem at hand, it would be best to leave the care in the hands of the veterinarians. I will try to cover as many of the signs that can surface while pet sitting.

When I first started in this business and I was faced with a sick or injured animal, I would sometimes panic; this does not help the situation. It is very important to keep a cool head and to do your homework. By that I mean learn as much as you can about illness and their signs. Sometimes the pet owner themselves will not be aware of some signs, and it's our responsibility to be professional and let them know if you suspect a problem. Not only that, but you will be prepared when something goes wrong. Having this knowledge and informing your client of a possible problem (even if the client won't admit to it) will give your business the excellent reputation it deserves. There have been several times I have noticed a problem, informed the client, and either the problem will become apparent immediately or shortly thereafter. I have been told many times, "You were right," and I attribute this to the many years of working with animals, looking for any changes, unusual behavior, or signs. You don't have to be a scientist as most of this is just common sense and being aware of the usual behavior of the pets in your care. After all, that's what our job is all about—caring for animals.

I have compiled some basic pet care tips, transportation of injured or sick animals, recognizing illnesses, and anything that would be helpful for any pet left in your charge. First I would suggest you have a first aid kit to carry in your car. When putting together a kit, choose a container or carrying case that is compact, durable, simple to carry, and easy to open. Plastic tackle boxes, toolboxes, sewing boxes, or a container used for art supplies will work great without you having to spend a lot of money on your kit. Here are the items you will need to carry in your kit:

- Adhesive bandages of various sizes
- Glad cling wrap (for covering bandages in rainy weather)
- First aid tape
- Alcohol wipes or a small bottle of alcohol
- Antibiotic cream, a triple antibiotic ointment
- Antiseptic solution or wipes
- A & D ointment
- Benadryl (plain or children's allergy relief formula)
- Calamine lotion
- Cotton balls
- Q-tips
- Disposable instant cold/hot packs
- Elastic bandage

- 🐾 Flashlight and extra batteries
- 🐾 Hand sanitizer
- 🐾 Hydrocortisone cream
- 🐾 Hydrogen peroxide
- 🐾 List of emergency numbers for poison control and veterinarians
- 🐾 Disposable plastic gloves
- 🐾 Safety pins
- 🐾 Scissors
- 🐾 Soap, washcloths
- 🐾 Sterile gauze
- 🐾 Syringe
- 🐾 Karo syrup (for insulin shock)
- 🐾 Thermometer
- 🐾 Tweezers

The Red Cross offers classes in pet first aid along with manuals that can educate and prepare you for pet emergencies. Pet Tech is an international training center where they teach CPR and first aid for dogs and cats, and they offer PetSaver training, which is a one-day course for pet owners and pet care professionals. They also offer Pet Tech Instructor (PTI) training, which is a three-day course for anyone interested in teaching the PetSaver class in your area. Any of these classes should prepare you for any emergencies that you might encounter while pet sitting.

Signs of Illnesses

As professional pet sitters, we should be prepared. Learn to notice when a pet in your care is acting differently and observe what you've seen as this will help the veterinarian diagnose a possible problem. Learn to notice the most minor changes because many animals tend to mask their pain. That is why it is crucial to ask a lot of questions at the initial consult and have this information included on your contract. Some of the danger signs that you can look for are body temperature, pulse, heart and respiratory rate, gum color, and the way they are breathing. I like to look at their eyes because they will tell you how your pet is feeling. I would describe it as a glazed appearance, and animals tend to communicate with their eyes. With cats you will also see a definite sign of a problem. A normally friendly cat will be hiding. Or a cat that generally hides is out and doesn't have the energy to find its hiding spot. When an animal is in pain, they sometimes tremble as if they are cold and pant as if they were hot due to the stress of their condition.

When we are left in charge, an illnesses can appear rather quickly, sometimes overnight. I like to address some of the signs that you might encounter. And remember, this section is not meant to diagnose or treat but rather help you notice any changes or problems. For me, this is a very important aspect of this business; keeping the pet healthy and safe is my top priority. Most people think that this is a cute little job and that it is not so difficult to care for a pet. This profession is riddled with responsibility and liability. It's obvious that we have the client's home to care for, but I believe that most of my clients would be more concerned about the welfare of their pet. We are entrusted to care for living, breathing creatures, and any behavior that is not the norm for the pet in your care should be addressed immediately.

Urinary Problems

Urination problems can occur in both dogs and cats. Some of the signs can include straining to go and nothing or only a small amount comes out. Blood in the urine is usually a blockage or a urinary tract problem. Decreased urination can be a sign of kidney failure and/or dehydration. Dehydration, most often than not, accompanies kidney failure. If the pet starts to go more frequently, this could be a sign of diabetes, hyperthyroidism, or, in the case of cat's, uterine infection. Cats seem to be susceptible to urinary problems, and while caring for cats, make sure to monitor their litter box. If a cat starts to urinate outside the litter box for no apparent reason, this could also be a sign of a urinary infection or blockage. This can turn into a life-threating scenario, for it might have been going on for some time before the client left for vacation. If you ever see blood in the urine, the pet should get to vets immediately. The pet should be on a good diet and have lots of water daily. If the pet doesn't drink as much water as they should, you can add water to their wet food to make it soupy; this will give the pet added water when they themselves won't drink enough.

Diabetic Pets

If you plan on caring for pets with diabetes, you should be aware that occasionally there might be a pet that will suffer from insulin shock. This is a complication that comes out of giving them too much insulin or not monitoring their sugar. This can occur before a pet is stabilized with regular insulin dosage. Cats differ from dogs when it comes to diabetes because the cat's diabetes will last for a short time and quickly change or disappear altogether.

Meaning a cat that has been diabetic suddenly has no diabetes at all or has to take a smaller dose. If your client isn't monitoring their cat, a normal dose will suddenly put the cat at risk of an overdose and go into insulin shock. Both dogs and cats should have their diabetes monitored, but cats, in particular, should be monitored closely. One of my clients had a special litter box for diabetic cats. The litter that was used was sunflower seeds; the urine would filter through and go into a pan at the bottom of the box. This made it easy to test the cat's urine, but this obviously wouldn't work well in multi-cat households. If your client isn't testing their pet, you would be wise to suggest that they speak with their veterinarian. Dr. Michelle Bamberger, DVM, states, "The signs of insulin shock begin about three to seven hours after the last dose of insulin and include weakness, fatigue, seizures, coma." I myself was not aware of the time frame involved in diabetic shock and used to stay longer after giving the insulin injection. This appears to be irrelevant; if this situation was to occur, a pet sitter would not be there to detect a problem. Or we would walk in on a bad situation. Also, while giving insulin injections, it is best to keep the times to twelve hours in between, and if this is not possible, the later the better. If the pet appears to be drunk or wobbly with a lack of mental alertness, the blood sugar has dropped too low. First, try to get them to eat. If this does not work, you will need to administer light Karo syrup, maple syrup, or honey. Rubbing a small amount of the syrup on the gums and inside the pet's mouth is all that is needed. Do not do this if the pet is having a seizure or is unconscious as this might cause the pet to choke. This can be a life-threatening dilemma.

Diabetic pets are prone to infections, another concern to be aware of. Urinary tract infections are the most common because the sugar in the urine allows bacteria to grow. Any signs of blood in the urine or straining to go will require a trip to the vet as soon as possible. Muscle tremors, agitation, depression, and weakness are some of the other signs that the pet's blood sugar has dropped too low. Some more serious signs are shivering, convolutions, and lastly, the pet could go into a coma. At all times you must monitor the pet in your care as this is a very stressful moment for both the pet and yourself when any of these complications occur.

Color and Texture of Poop

Disgusting, I know! But you can learn a lot about the pets in your care by their poop. And of course, it's important to notice any changes from the normal poop including all the different varieties from the poop that may be indicating a medical problem. The poop will give you a big clue as to what is happening in the pet's gastrointestinal tract. Ask your client what the normal stool looks like, how often the pet goes, and what color it usually is. This can be green, brown, mustard yellow, gray, and whatever other shades, depending on the dyes used in the pet's food. Take notice when the texture, color, quantity, or odor changes; the pet might be having a problem. One sign of a potential problem is the presence of black tarry poop or bright red blood; this could mean the pet is suffering from gastrointestinal bleeding. This was a sign that one of my own dogs came down with, and the cause turned out to be a tumor on her spine that was growing into her other organs. It was very sad as it was inoperable. And of course, when the poop is watery (diarrhea) for an extended amount of time, this will lead to dehydration and could be a sign of an underlying medical problem. So although this topic is gross, it will help when you're trying to assess a situation. And a dog walker or pet sitter cleans a lot of poop during the course of a day; we should be able to notice these changes.

Anal Sac

Both dogs and cats have anal sacs. Cats rarely have problems, but dogs do. And the smaller breeds tend to have their fair share. Pets suffering from an impacted anal gland will usually scoot across the floor and seem to be constantly licking their rear end. Normally these sacs will empty when the pet goes to the bathroom. An interesting fact to the anal gland is that these sacs will produce a liquid that is passed when the pet poops. This lets the other animals know who was there, a type of identification. The vet will need to empty the clogged gland, and if this is not done, the sac can develop an abscess, which can become very painful for the dog. If the abscess breaks, you will see blood and pus draining from the site, and it will become infected. The dog can also have a fever, have poor appetite, and be tired. This will need immediate attention by the vet. Sometimes our clients are so busy they don't always notice even minor behavior changes like scooting along the floor or licking the rear, and we will be left to care for the problem.

Abdominal Swelling

A pet that shows signs of a distended abdomen or an abdominal swelling can have a ruptured or obstructed urinary tract. A hemorrhage in the abdominal cavity from the liver, kidney, or spleen will be another possibility. A ruptured spleen is when blood is filling the cavity and will be accompanied by weakness and pale mucous membranes (pale gums).

One of my daily walk clients who had an energetic older Labrador retriever has suddenly started to look pregnant (this was a male). He also started to not want to go for his long walk, and just like that, his spleen had ruptured. It's been so long ago I can't remember what caused the spleen to rupture, but my client lost her boy. Bloating causes the stomach to fill with water and twist; this in turn cuts off the blood supply to vital organs. Symptoms will include crying, restlessness, and salivating, and if you gently press on their bellies, this will cause the pet severe pain. This is one of the more serious emergencies, and the cause is not clear. Some think it is caused by drinking fluids right after eating. One of my clients insisted on not giving any water to the dog until I was leaving after the pet was fed as she swears this was the cause of her dog getting bloated in the past. You will need to get the pet to the vet immediately as surgery is necessary to save the pet's life. Both dogs and cats alike can get bloated. Cushing's can cause a pet to have a distended abdomen along with tenderness to the touch. Abdominal swelling is never a good sign in a pet.

Vomiting

Vomiting is common in dogs and cats; they usually vomit due to poor food choices or eating nonfood items. If the pet only vomits once in a while and this happens while in your care, withhold food and water for a few hours. After that you can feed them a combination of rice and chicken broth for a day. Then gradually start to add in their normal food to the rice and broth. If they vomit more than two times in a twenty-four-hour period, this could be a sign of an emergency and could lead to dehydration. Chronic vomiting can be signs of food intolerance, inflammatory bowl or kidney disease, intestinal blockage, diabetes, heartworm, parasites, cancer, or an allergy.

Hair balls will make a cat vomit, and if it is chronic, there can also be a blockage involved, causing the cat to vomit more than usual. When taking on cat assignments, one of the questions I will always ask the owner is, how often do they vomit? Some cats will do this more than others because of constant grooming by the cat without any medical problems involved. Cats can also become gluttons and then go on to spit up their food.

In dogs, parvovirus can cause the dog to vomit, and they will also have bloody diarrhea and be dehydrated.

Weight Loss

If you have a pet you care for on a regular basis and you begin to notice that they are losing weight and they won't eat as much as normal, they can be showing signs of inflammatory bowel disease, parasites, or diabetes. A definite sign that there is a problem going on is the lack of an appetite; this is not only for the illnesses listed above but for many others as well.

In cat's, hyperthyroidism will cause weight loss along with a ravenous appetite. A note to the client informing them of what you notice will make them aware of a potential problem. Being we don't always see the pet on a daily basis, we will notice this more than our client. I can't tell you how many times after I mention this to my client that they then admit they thought the pet was losing weight.

Hyperthyroidism

This can affect both dogs and cats but is more common in cats with similar signs. Weight loss can occur even with an increased appetite, and they will also have diarrhea with a nasty smell and or go outside the litter box for cats. Difficulty breathing, a dull dry coat with increased shedding can be other signs. You might also notice increased irritability, or the pet may seem stressed, nervous, or restless. Pets seem to crave cold places. These are all signs of hyperthyroidism in both dogs and cats.

Hypothyroidism

Elderly cats over ten years of age that are gaining weight with no change in their diet could be suffering from hypothyroidism. Although it is considered rare in cats, veterinarians are seeing more cases of hypothyroidism. Symptoms for cats suffering from hypothyroidism are similar to the signs of hyperthyroidism, including soiling outside the litter box and sleeping more than usual, with the exception of weight gain.

When dogs are suffering from hypothyroidism, weight gain without any change in diet could be a sign of a problem. They could be showing irritability with signs of increased aggression. Hair loss around the tail, a dull dry coat accompanied by dandruff, and dry skin are some other signs. The pets also seem to like warm temperatures more as they cannot tolerate the cold.

Nasal Discharge

Nasal discharge in a dog can be a sign of distemper, especially if runny eyes, diarrhea or vomiting, slowness or fatigue, and fever are present. It could also mean something is in the nasal passage and is making the pet scratch at it, and this might be accompanied by sneezing to try to dislodge the object. A tumor, abscess, or a fungus can cause a pus or crusty discharge. If the tumor happens to be cancerous, the pet will sometimes sneeze and will have blood in its mucus. This was the case with a very loving chocolate Lab that I used to care for. It was a sad ending, but we must remember this is part of the job.

If the discharge is also accompanied by trouble breathing, this could mean that the pet has pneumonia. If the discharge is foamy white and the tongue is blue, this could mean heart failure. This was the case for one of my client's dogs that was on heart medication; he walked across the floor and collapsed.

A yellow discharge from a cat's nose can be a sinus infection, which is easily treated with antibiotics. A runny nose in cats could mean an upper respiratory infection and is especially dangerous to kittens. If you think that the cat may have a contagious disease (such as feline herpes virus or cat flu), disinfect your hands and change your clothes before caring for other pets. I will always carry a spare set of clothes in my car including sneakers if I suspect a contagious disease. This is not only for my clients' pets but for mine as well. I have never brought anything home to my pets by being cautious.

Respiratory Problems

Respiratory problems can be determined by the inability of a pet to breathe properly when they are lying down. Short, rapid breaths, restlessness, and tiring easily are additional signs. Extreme respiratory problems can be signs of asthma, heart disease, fluid in the chest, pneumonia, heartworm, nasal congestion, rib fracture, anemia, diaphragmatic hernia (a defect or hole in the diaphragm that allows the abdominal contents to move into the chest cavity), cancer, and upper respiratory infection. Of course, if you see any signs of a respiratory problem, a visit to the vet would be absolutely necessary. Never walk a dog that is having any type of respiratory problem for a long distance. My own dog suffers from sporadic asthma, and being it doesn't happen all the time, my vet isn't too concerned about it. He admitted his own dog has it, and the cause of the attack is unknown.

Seizures

If you are caring for a pet that suffers from seizures, this can be a scary moment, and the seizures can vary in intensity. Some can have only mild head tremors, and others can have full-blown grand mal seizures. The pet's eyes might twitch back and forth quickly, their body will shake, and the pet will not respond to voice commands. The pet might seem confused, scared, or, in extreme cases, become unconscious. Pets with epilepsy might show certain behavior changes before the onset of a seizure. I have cared for several dogs suffering from seizures, including one of my own Labs. Right before they are about to have a seizure, they will become restless and will want to be with you. Then they will become unconscious and have convulsions, which can be mild to severe and last from a few seconds to a few minutes.

It will take some time for the pet to return to normal after the seizure, and they might show signs of anxiety, heavy panting, or attempt to hide. Try to reassure the pet that everything is okay and contact the vet/client even if it was only a mild seizure and ask if anything should be done for the pet. Any seizure lasting more than three minutes is considered an emergency. If the pet stops breathing, you will have to perform CPR procedures, which is a good reason to take a course on pet first aid. I must admit, it is scary to witness, and I am sure the pet is also scared after suffering a seizure.

Choking Pets

If in the event that a pet in your care begins choking, open the pet's mouth and gently look for any type of object that might be causing an obstruction. I once had a dog that had managed to get a small stick lodged in the back of her throat. You have to be careful when trying to get the obstruction out and not force it farther down the throat. If you cannot see any object in the pet's mouth, you might have to perform the Heimlich maneuver because the object might have gone farther down than you originally suspected. Choking happens more frequently with dogs than with cats because of the fact that they manage to sometimes eat things without chewing or eat something that they shouldn't. While pet sitting, I never like to leave the dog alone with a bone as I'm afraid that it might get a portion of the bone stuck in its throat. And I tell my clients so if they instruct me to leave a bone to keep them busy while no one is there. Both dogs and cats are susceptible to choking. This needs immediate attention, and if you do not feel qualified to help the pet, then you must seek immediate veterinary attention.

Heatstroke

While caring for older dogs, you must be careful as not to have them out in the heat too long as they can get heatstroke. This will also apply to very young pets, and although young dogs require a lot of exercise, do not over exercise in extremely hot weather. There are also certain breeds that can be prone to heatstroke, such as dogs with short snouts. Pugs, bulldogs, Shar-Peis, Boston terriers, and Pekingese have narrow respiratory systems and have a tough time when the weather becomes very hot and humid. Overweight dogs and dogs with a double coat such as Chows cannot tolerate the heat as well. Breeds that were bred for the colder climates like the huskies, malamutes, and Newfoundland's should be kept in an air-conditioned home. We actually had a client who had a Newfoundland and wanted her to stay outside during the day and said she would find a cool spot. Well, I constantly disobeyed this particular client and would bring her in the house when I knew the temperature would reach anything above eighty degrees. He didn't like all the hair she would leave around, so what I did was get out the vacuum and cleaned up her hair. I sometimes shake my head in wonder about some of my clients. Also, in the summer months, make it clear to the client that there must be some sort of ventilation or air-conditioning for the pet in the home.

Signs of heatstroke will include noisy, rapid breathing and panting. The pet's gums will be bright red; they will become restless and weak. Vomiting and very thick saliva will be present. If you should take a rectal temperature, anything reading 106 degrees or higher is a definite warning that the pet has heatstroke and can be a life-or-death scenario.

The pet should be cooled down as soon as possible with cold water, and check the temperature every couple of minutes. You must make sure to cool the belly and pads of the feet. If the pet's temperature has gone above 106 degrees, it is important to cool the pet's head and neck as extreme body temperature can cause the brain to swell and kill the pet. A cold water enema will help cool the pet down internally if the pet is near collapse. The body temperature should be brought down to at least 103 degrees. Heatstroke is a life-threatening situation; don't wait for the temperature to go down by itself. After a pet suffers heatstroke, it will need to be rehydrated, and Gatorade or Pedialyte (half water and half Pedialyte) can be added to the dog's water to help with the process. A cat could be reluctant to drink these, so by adding this to a chicken broth, it might encourage the cat to drink. Or you could force the water by using a syringe if the cat resists. A call and visit to the vet would be necessary, and the client should also be notified.

Hypothermia

For pets living in cold regions, there is always a possibility of hypothermia if they are left out for prolonged periods. And the same holds true for hypothermia as with heatstroke; shorter walks when the conditions are very cold and exposure to wet conditions increase the chance for hypothermia. Clients should be made aware that dogs being left out in wet, cold environments can get hypothermia. Symptoms will include disorientation and shivering; in more severe cases, the pet may be extremely tired and weak. A pet must be dried and wrapped in blankets. The temperature in the surrounding environment must be increased. A plastic water bottle filled with very warm water should be placed on the armpits of the pet until the body temperature reaches one hundred degrees. Another thing that would work well is a hair dryer. When the pet starts to recover, rub some Karo, maple syrup, or honey on the gums for quick sugar absorption so that they won't go into shock. Hypothermia can cause the pet's sugar levels to drop, and by using the syrup or honey on the gums, this will help raise the sugar level very quickly.

Constipation

Constipation can be caused by a pet eating bones, rocks, drugs, grass, or a low-fiber diet. It can also be an indication of a problem with the metabolism, a dirty litter box, an obstruction, or a neurological disorder. I have noticed that many of the older cats in my care seem to suffer from this more than the younger ones. Although this is not necessarily a life-threatening problem, attention should be taken. Sometimes adding some pumpkin (use only 100 percent pure canned pumpkin) to their pet food can help to relieve their constipation. I have also used Benefiter to help when the pet becomes constipated, and with cats, one-fourth teaspoon for a small cat and one-half to one teaspoon for a large cat seem to do the trick. Depending on the size of the dog, one teaspoon for each ten to twenty-five pounds will help. Any pet that is constipated longer than three days should be seen by a vet, but in multi-cat households, this is harder to detect. Although I do not usually like to disturb clients while they are away, I will do so if I feel it warrants a telephone call. They are usually grateful that I was concerned for their pet. If they will be home before too much time passes, you can leave a note to let them know as a visit to the vet would be wise to try to determine the problem. Sometimes a pet with long hair will be clogged externally from the dried poo around the rectum. What I usually do is to use some A & D ointment on the area; this will both soothe the area and soften the dried poo. On another visit, I can then clean the area and add more ointment. Your client should ask the groomer to clip the rear close and then use baby wipes to keep the area clean along with applying A & D ointment so the area won't become irritated.

Bee Sting

In the event that a pet you're caring for gets stung by a wasp or bee, it might not be noticeable to the eye because of fur covering the sting. You should see signs that will include swelling, scratching, and sometimes the pet will have difficulty breathing if it has an allergic reaction to the sting. Just like people, some pets can have an allergic reaction to a bee sting and have more severe signs. One of my own dogs once got stung by a bee and developed hives from the sting. The poor girl had hives all over, but it was really noticeable on her face and head. If it wasn't for that, I might not have even noticed the allergic reaction because of her thick coat. What you will have to do is locate the sting and remove the stinger. Be careful and make sure you remove the whole stinger by scraping it. Do not squeeze it. Wrap ice in a towel and apply it to the swollen area. Give Benadryl to relieve symptoms. You could make a paste of baking soda and apply it directly to the sting. The ice should help relieve the pain and swelling, and calamine lotion will help reduce the itch. If your pet has gotten stung on the foot, you can soak it in Epsom salts for about thirty minutes. If after an hour there is no improvement, a vet should be contacted.

Benadryl is an antihistamine, and although it is considered safe for use in cats and dogs, there can be some side effects. If the pet is on other medications, do not use it unless a vet is consulted. Also extreme caution should be taken if the pet has hyperthyroidism, glaucoma, heart or prostate disease.

Snakebite

I'm not an expert on how to distinguish a poisonous snake from a nonpoisonous snake. Depending on your region, you might be able to distinguish the difference of the snakes that are in your area. But unless you are an expert, I would suggest taking the dog immediately to a vet as they have a vaccine that can reduce the risk of death. Signs that a dog has been bitten by a poisonous snake include vomiting with redness and swelling in the area. Waiting a situation like this out could be lethal to the pet. Even if your charge gets bitten by a nonpoisonous snake, if the wound is not attended to, it can become infected. This is why it is important to stay with your dog while outside even if the pet is in their own secure yard. You will be aware of a bad situation immediately and might be able to get a look at the snake that has bitten the dog. Cats are also not immune from getting bitten by a snake, so this is another reason why it would be wise to suggest to the client to leave an indoor cat in the home while they are away or have them sign a waiver to not hold you responsible if they insist on letting the cat out. I myself would not want to worry about cats having access to the outdoors. Horses and farm animals will be difficult to monitor.

Abscess

An abscess is more common in cats than dogs because of the fact that the tough, elastic skin of a cat can seal over a wound. This is another reason to not agree to let the client's cat out while they are vacationing. A cat fight will leave its mark either by being scratched or bitten. It is a collection of pus in the area where a bite has occurred and will usually burst with a discharge of yellow or white pus, but this can take some time. They must be drained and heal from the inside out. A vet should be contacted as they will need to prescribe antibiotics to help with the healing process so that no infection will set in. And I myself will not take responsibility on draining the abscess, not to mention the cat will surely resist.

Coughing

Coughing can be a sign of allergic reaction, asthma, or fluid in the chest. Cancer, heartworm, heart failure, dryness in the air, or parasites such as roundworm could also be a cause. If coughing occurs in a multi-dog household and the cough is more like a gagging cough followed by mucus, kennel cough may be the cause. This is another reason to be cautious when bringing a dog to a day care facility. An added benefit to pet sitting that I have often brought up is that their pet can be safe from contacting kennel cough. I actually had a client who was feeling bad for her dog because of her long work hours. So she kept my service for three days a week and brought the dog to the day care for the other two days. The dog wasn't in the day care for a week when she questioned me about a cough she developed. I suspected kennel cough, and the vet agreed. She now stays at home. Cats may cough due to hair balls or asthma.

Diarrhea

Diarrhea is probably one of the more common problems you will encounter while pet sitting. This could be caused by worm infestation, food intolerance, cancer, liver disease, inflammatory bowel disease, or an infectious disease. If this is a common problem, the owner will usually let me know the cause. Although I have had clients who had gotten a new dog who developed diarrhea, and I would suggest that their vet check for worms. It is very dangerous to puppies and kittens to go for long with diarrhea. If this is a mild case, try withholding food for twelve hours and give plenty of water, and after twelve hours, you can offer the pet some rice with chicken broth. Giving 100 percent pure canned pumpkin will also help to bind the pet. Pepto-Bismol and Kaopectate are recommended by veterinarians to treat dogs but could be harmful to a cat. I myself prefer to treat diarrhea by using a natural remedy such as rice or pumpkin. If the diarrhea is accompanied with bloody stools, vomiting, distress, or being extremely tired, these symptoms are life threatening, and a vet should be contacted immediately. I have cared for nervous dogs that tend to get diarrhea when their owners are away. They stress about everything, and this can bring on loose stools. Although this is not caused by a medical issue, if it persists for more than a day or two, the pet will start to show signs of blood in their stools and will become dehydrated and should be taken to the vet.

Hair Balls

Hair balls are quite common in cats but not life threatening. You can suggest to your client that they get some form of lubricant sold in pet stores. A hair-ball-control food or treats could be another suggestion. A cat with chronic hair balls may mean they are suffering from some type of stomach problem. Ferrets are also prone to hair balls, but unlike cats, they cannot bring them up. So it is necessary to treat the ferret with a lubricant as you would do with a cat.

Bad Breath

Bad breath is not necessarily an emergency but is a sign that an oral infection, dental disease, abscess, kidney failure, or a tumor might be present. A note to the client informing them that there might be a problem present will be needed.

Ear Discharge

An ear discharge in a pet can indicate a yeast or bacterial infection. Ear mites can also be a cause and so can an abscess. Another possibility could be a tumor or polyp that might be present. This would not be considered an emergency, but the client should be made aware of the situation and a vet should be contacted depending on the length of the sitting assignment.

Torn Nail

When I was caring for a` dog while the owners were away on vacation I went in to see blood spots covering the kitchen floor. It turned out he had torn his nail. If a nail bleeds or tears due to an injury this can cause lameness and you should not try to trim the nail but rather wrap it in gauze and get the dog to the vet and let the vet trim or in extreme cases remove the nail.

Hair Loss

Hair loss in areas of a pet's body can be hot spots, fleas, allergies, or skin mites. Cushing's disease causes the pet to loose hair on both sides of their body, or another possibility could be ringworm. With ringworm you will also see a red circle around the hair-loss site, and it is highly contagious to both people and pets. If you suspect a pet in your care has ringworm, wash your hands thoroughly or wear disposable gloves. If you plan on visiting other homes after the sit, I would suggest a change of clothes and shoes. I have cared for households where ringworm has been an issue and have had to put medicated cream on the affected area of the cats. Disposable gloves were supplied by the client for me to use, and I would always wash my hands with antifungal soap left by the client. This soap gives just a little more protection when caring for pets with ringworm. I have never brought ringworm home to my pets or other clients' homes.

A hot spot is sometimes caused by fleas, although one of my Labrador retrievers seemed to always get them in the spring and fall when my other Labs did not get them at all. My vet had told me that he believed the hot spots were caused by exterior annoyances caused by an allergy The signs are clear, a red spot that will have a sticky substance, pain in the area, hair loss, and scratching or itching of the site. Cortisone spray helps to alleviate the scratching and biting. Although I prefer to use A & D ointment. This would soothe the area, and by the next day I would see an improvement. Rescue Remedy is also very effective on treating hot spots and could be applied directly to the spot as long as the area is not so raw as to cause pain when it is applied.

Ear Infection

An ear problem in a pet will show signs of circling and head tilting, which could be caused by an infection. In case your client hasn't noticed this make them aware of this fact and suggests they get the pet to the vet. I usually suggest that if they do not have the time, I will take the pet for them. Floppy eared dogs are susceptible to ear problems, but are not the only ones. Both cats and dogs can suffer from ear infections. If it is not treated can cause the pet to scratch and shake their ears, which can lead them to damage their ear and cause a Hematoma. This is blood and fluids trapped in a type of blister. They are very painful for the pet and would need to be taken to the vet to be lanced and drained. One of my own cats had a hematoma and after the vet had laced it his ear was permanently disfigured, but we still love him.

Head shaking could be an injury to the ear flap such as a Hematoma or an infection of the inner ear canal and could cause permanent damage or even death if not treated. If these symptoms are also accompanied by hearing loss, circling or stumbling, this is a definite sign of an inner ear infection or worse, an infectious disease such as distemper, especially if you are caring for puppies. One of my clients had a pug they had rescued that had a severe inner ear infection for some time and his balance was never the same. He would walk in circles because of this.

Gum Color

Some pets might be showing signs of stress for reasons unknown. You can check their gums to see what color they are. Hot pink or a deep red coloring accompanied by rapid breathing can be an indication of infection. If the gums have a brick-red appearance accompanied by a fever, this will be a sign of a severe bacterial infection. A brownish color means nitrate poisoning from licking or eating fertilizer.

White, pale, or gray gums might indicate anemia or shock. Purple or blue gums and labored breathing will indicate heart failure, especially in a pet that has not been exercising. A yellow gum (jaundice) is a serious sign of gallbladder or liver disease with the destruction of red blood cells. This past summer I had taken over an assignment where the cat that had liver failure, an infection had set in, and he was seriously jaundiced. This was the first time I was able to see the jaundice (yellow color) in the cat's gums.

Fever

If a pet in your care acts like a fever might be present, you will have to take the pet's temperature to make sure. Causes can be a bacterial or a viral infection, inflammation, reaction to a drug, vaccine, or an immune system problem. If your pet seems warm to the touch, a fever might be present.

If the pet feels cold to the touch, this can be due to shock, kidney failure, or heart failure. Shivering and being tired are signs of a low temperature and pain is present.

Canine Influenza

This is a relatively new disease with the first cases arising in 2004. As of the writing of this book, it has been seen in the United States in over thirty states and has been diagnosed in the District of Columbia with the chance of spreading to other regions. As I was speaking to one of my clients that has been a chairperson for one of the rescues in my area, she had told me that all dogs now coming into the kennel where they are held will need to vaccinate against canine influenza along with the kennel cough vaccine. The reason for this is because it is a new virus, and most dogs have not yet built up immunity to the disease. Canine influenza is often misdiagnosed as the signs represent a typical respiratory infection with symptoms of watery eyes, nasal discharge, cough, loss of energy, and loss of appetite. For those of you who offer group walks or runs to the local doggie park, this disease can be contacted by direct contact by sniffing or nuzzling, through the air by coughing or sneezing, or by contaminated surfaces such as clothing or by the hands of a human. Washing your hands after each assignment will help prevent the spread of the disease.

The cough that is present in canine influenza will be persistent, last several weeks, and can lead to pneumonia, especially in young and older dogs. If any of the dogs in your care might be showing signs of canine influenza, before going to another home, be sure to change your clothing and shoes and sanitize your hands. Definitely make your clients aware that a problem might be present. I would more than likely also to touch base with the client's vet while they are away and ask if it would be necessary for the dog to come in immediately.

Poisoning

If you suspect that the pet has ingested some poisonous material, call your local poison control center with the name of the plant or product you suspect. Internationally, you can call Prosar International Poison Control at (888) 232-8870. They require a credit card for the call, which can cost fifty to sixty dollars for the consult. The Poison Control Center can be reached at (888) 426-4435.

Do not induce vomiting if the pet has gotten into anything that says so, bleach or drain cleaner, household cleaning products, any other chemical, or a sharp object. Some clients do not realize some of the plants in their home can be poisonous to pets. Some other common household items can be chocolate; four ounces of baker's chocolate can be deadly to a five- to ten-pound dog.

Dogs are prone to get into things more than cats, but both can get themselves into trouble.

Any human medications including Tylenol or Advil can be fatal in dogs. You will have to induce vomiting to make sure they bring up the pills and get the pet to the vet. For other substances that the pet has ingested, you can give one teaspoon of 3 percent hydrogen peroxide per ten pounds of body weight. Use only 3 percent hydrogen peroxide. You can repeat this a maximum of two times, waiting fifteen to twenty minutes between treatments, but only if they did not vomit enough the first time. Walking a dog around can help speed up the process.

Compressed activated charcoal will help slow the absorption of the poison but only after the pet vomits. The dosage should be one five-gram tablet per ten pounds of body weight. Or if you do not have charcoal on hand, you can burn some bread until black as this can be used as a substitute.

An alternative for less serious cases, you can coat the stomach with egg whites and milk. For a dog weighing ten pounds, you can give one-fourth cup egg whites to one-fourth cup milk, using a syringe to feed the pet. And of course, a visit to the vet will be necessary.

Antifreeze Poisoning

Pets like the taste of antifreeze because of its sweetness, and this can cause kidney failure. Some signs that a pet has ingested antifreeze are vomiting, diarrhea, acting drunk, and an increased thirst. You will have to induce vomiting, and charcoal can slow the absorption of the poison, but this should only be done if the pet is still aware and conscious. An antidote is available but must be given within the hour after ingesting the antifreeze, so the pet must get to the vet immediately.

The information in this section is not to treat, cure, diagnose, or prevent disease but to give insight into potential problems that might arise while pet sitting and the signs to look for. I have always either worked with the client long distance by phone, e-mail, or by text. Call their vet if available, and if their vet is not available, I would get in contact with a vet familiar with my business. Every pet sitter should have a backup vet. Also check to see if you have a Red Cross in your town that offers pet first aid. Attending a class will be very beneficial for you.

CHAPTER 4

Types of Leashes, Collars, and Harnesses

There are many types of leashes, leads, collars, and harnesses, and if you're going to be working with dogs, it would be wise to become familiar with the various types you might encounter. You can do an online search to view what these collars and harnesses look like. Another suggestion that I have is to buy a stuffed dog along with a few of the more complicated collars to practice with. Some of these harness and collars are tough to figure out for someone with little or no experience. One of my clients had used a backup sitter when I was not available, and she was not happy. She had told me that even after she showed her how to put a harness on, the woman couldn't get it right. Every job will be unique, and some newer sitters might need some experience and practice in the beginning. Please make sure, no matter what type of collar or harness is being used, to double-check always before you walk out the door, making sure the dog in your charge is secure and that you have hooked the leash to the D ring and not the flimsy ID tag clip.

Training collars—Chain slip collars or more commonly known as training collars. They are usually reserved for training and should not be left on the dog when your walk is over. With a tug of the leash, they will tighten and then release when relaxed. The correct way to put a chain collar on is to slide one end of the chain through the ring at the end of the collar, making it look like the letter *P*. The top ring should slide through with ease, and when placed on the dog, it should not bend over the other ring. This would defeat the sound created when a quick pop to the leash for correction is taken, not the tightening around the dog's neck. It was not designed to choke the dog, and if this is occurring, perhaps another collar should be suggested. These collars should not be used on puppies, so if you have a client with a puppy and they are using this type of collar, please warm them about health risks to the pup.

Prong or pinch collars—I'm not very fond of these collars for a couple of reasons. One being they have prongs on the inside and will tighten with tension. Second reason being is that if not properly hooked together, you could have a loose dog on your hands. That being said, they are usually used for strong dogs that tend to pull you all over, are highly stubborn, and hard to train. I have had some clients with these collars, but the difference was they bought the ones with rubber tips on the inside prong, making it a little more comfortable to the dog, I guess.

StarMark collar—This collar is better than the prong collar for dogs that pull on the leash. It is made of plastic and is more humane. It should be placed behind the dog's ears. Unsnap any of the links, slide it out to put it on, and do the same to take the collar off. When you pop the leash, it will act like a nip from a mother dog to show who is in charge. This collar imitates a mother dog nipping the pup on the neck to correct bad behavior. I highly recommend these collars for the larger, uncontrollable dogs to correct many forms of behavior issues while walking.

Breakaway collars—They have had these collars for cat care for many years. Recently to the market, they have designed these collars for dogs as well. They have a safety buckle that will release when pressure is applied yet can be worn on walks. This collar protects from strangulation and neck injuries. In the past I would always take the collars off my own dogs when I wasn't home because one of my Labs had gotten stuck on a fence, and if I had not been there, I'd hate to think of the consequences.

Everyday collars—Most owners have these plus the many varieties of training collars. My clients use these to hook ID tags and the dog's license to. Some are a belt style, and others are collars with a metal or plastic buckle with a quick release. They have many different styles including rolled leather, nylon, and a variety of materials. I suggest that you do not use these to walk the dog. Many people do, but I have had dogs slip their collars, and I'm getting too old to be running around, chasing down a dog. Until you experience a dog slipping their collar, you won't believe the amount of stress involved in a situation of this sort.

Martingale collars—They have been known to be called greyhound collars and limited-slip collars. I like these as they prevent a dog from slipping out of their collar. They are also great for use on long-necked breeds or well-behaved dogs that only need a reminder to behave. A light tug will tighten the collar without choking the dog. I always have these in various sizes with a lead attached in my pet sitter sack made by Mendota.

Easy Walk—This harness tightens over the neck and shoulders when the dog pulls forward and has a quick-snap buckle, making this harness easy to put on. I prefer these harnesses over the head halter because the pressure from the dog pulling is across the chest rather than the neck. Some dogs just don't get it because they are so young and eager to go on their walks.

Harnesses—These are great for dogs that pull because they don't put pressure on the neck. Instead pressure will be in the chest area because they go over the dog's chest and abdomen. Harnesses are great for smaller dogs. Some are designed for the dog to step into while others go over the head and under the chest. And despite what many think, dogs can slip out of their harness because it's happened a few times in my career.

Head halter—This is more of a collar than a harness; it has two adjustable straps that are secured on the dog's neck and is fitted to the dog's head with the other strap going around the dog's snout with no pressure being applied to the dog's throat. The neck strap sits high on the dog's head just behind the ears. When the dog feels pressure on the back of his neck, he calms down, and this is great for powerful dogs. The danger to this type of collar is that when the dog lunges, it can injure a dog's neck because of the way the head halter turns the dog's head. And they do not teach the dog not to pull but rather just restrain the dog from pulling. These should not be used if you plan on using a long lead and, of course, should not to be left on the dog when they are alone.

Non-pull mesh harness—I really like these harnesses. My little Italian greyhound wears one. They are comfortable for the dog with a Sherpa cover over the straps going under the dog's legs. This helps prevent irritation. The elastic webbing stretches with the dog's movements. I have used these mostly on smaller dogs, but they are made for the larger breeds as well.

Snoot Loop—The design is similar to the Halti except that the straps going around the dog's snout are thinner, giving more control. Both straps are adjustable, making it hard for the dog to remove, and are good for short-muzzled dogs. It also works for stopping the dog in mid lunge by pulling back and up. These are more difficult to find in local stores but easy to find online.

British slip lead—These leads are my absolute favorite, and I have many in my pet sitter sack. I use these all the time, and I tell all my clients we never lose a dog; the reason being is even if we're using the client's collar and harness, this slip lead is our added protection. This is a great leash because it adjusts to any size dog and is a collar and leash in one. This is a must-have for your pet sitter bag. I have two different lengths, four feet and six feet.

Flexi leads—These are retractable leads that come in a variety of lengths ten, sixteen, twenty-three, and twenty-six feet and sizes for small to large dogs. But I highly recommend that you do not use these while walking. I have gotten burns on the back of my legs and my fingers mangled when reeling in and from the dogs running around behind me. Being they have a plastic handle, I find that it is difficult to have a good hold or grip on your dog. If you are distracted for a second and the dog suddenly lunges, you could lose grip of the handle and watch your dog go running with the handle bouncing along the ground. This could also scare your dog and send him running further away. I find I don't have enough control when extended, and when danger approaches, a dog or car, it could be a close call or too late to reel in. I like to have control on my walks.

Training leads—These leads come in fifteen, twenty, thirty, and fifty feet. Some companies will make these in your desired size. They give a dog freedom to roam and run while still under control and are great to use to exercise a dog. I have a strict policy of keeping a dog on a lead, so if they want the dog to have a run, this is what I use. They should not be used for daily walks.

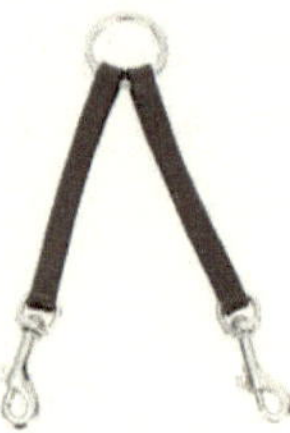

Coupler—These are used to walk two to three dogs on the same leash. I would only use these if the client has already accustomed their dogs to walking in sync while on the lead. It is a great way to walk a few dogs with one lead. I find it provides greater control over a handful of dogs without the dogs pulling in different directions.

Pet Sitter Sack

Being on the road and in unfamiliar homes have made it necessary to be well stocked with supplies. I've had homes with cats and went to clean the litter box with no scooper and no dustpan in sight. Here are some things I have added to my bag. As time goes on you might want to add more. Something I carry in my car but is too bulky to put in my sack is a portable electric Dirt Devil hand vac. This is left in my car for homes with carpeting around the litter box and no working vacuum available. I make sure the pet's area is always clean, even if the client neglects this. I prefer my pet sitter sack to have many separate compartments to keep me organized.

- Plastic dustpan
- Kitty scoopers or plastic dollar-store scoopers—I leave them with my client.
- Disposable booties or dollar-store slippers—This prevents carrying disease; I leave at the client's home.
- Disposable rubber gloves
- Pill crusher and pill popper/gun

- Syringe-This is for hard to medicate cats. Crush and mix with 2 ml. water. Most medications can be crushed except when bottle reads "Do not crush."

- Firewood carrier—This is for helping handicapped pets get up and around.

- Hand sanitizer

- A & D ointment—I use this for just about everything, matted hair with poo by butt, minor cuts and abrasions. I even used it for sticky lock. The laundry list goes on and on.

- Paper towels

- Cleaning supplies (Oxy stain and odor remover, Icky Poo for cat urine, vinegar and water spray bottle)

- Baby wipes

- WD-40—This is great for stiff or hard to open locks.

- British slip lead, harnesses, flashing leash—This is for walking at night.

- Large Ziploc bags—These are for dirty shoes, key organizing, and others.

- Lots of recycled shopping bags, bread bags, newspaper bags—These are for picking up poo.

- Flashlight—This is for power outages; although my cell phone has come in handy when finding my way through the house and out to the car.

- Large blanket—This is for transport.

- Small umbrella—I use this for territorial cats and dogs.

- Empty soda can with pennies—This is for aggressive cats and dogs.

Terrific Tips

After all my years of pet sitting I hope I can give you some helpful tips to make your job just a little easier; here are some that work very well for me.

- To make cleaning cat dishes a breeze, when you first go in, soak them in very hot water. Go about your other duties, and by the time you're finished, the old food has become loose to just sponge out.

- To get a stubborn cat into a cat carrier for transport, turn the carrier upright with the door on top, holding the cat by the nape of the neck with one hand and using your other hand to get the cat's back feet in the carrier. Let the cat go and close the door. It's a very easy method. Now catching the cat is a whole different story!

- To control any size dog with any collar (but works best with training collar or slip lead) place collar high on dog's neck, close to ears, right under jaw. This makes it easy to control the largest and strongest dog. This little trick is called high-collaring and was taught to me many years ago. I have used it throughout my pet sitting career.

- For dogs that get agitated on their walks towards other dogs, people, and cars, I recently purchased some calming caps. They reduce visual annoyances and still allow the dog to go on walks. It filters their vision, making the dog less agitated. This is great for behavior management.

❖ ❖ ❖ ❖ Sometimes clients have ants, and they can be very annoying when it comes to the pet's food. To deter the ants from going after the pet's food, find a saucepan, small pan, or dish larger than the pet's dish. Fill it with a small amount of water and place the pet's dish inside the saucepan. This will create a moat, and ants do not like to swim across to get to the food. No chemicals are involved when water is used and keeps the pets food free from ants.

❖ ❖ ❖ ❖ To keep bugs away while on your walks, try putting some dryer sheets hooked on your shorts or shirt. Or mix up some Listerine and water (half and half) in a water bottle and spray on your arms and legs to keep mosquitoes away. This works well.

❖ ❖ ❖ ❖ For sticky locks or locks that seem broken, try using some WD-40 lubricant before panicking. I can't tell you how many times a client has returned thinking that I hadn't locked their home because the locked opened so easily. You can also use a graphite or lead pencil to help with the lock. Rub the key with the lead, and this should help opening the lock. Although it's not a permanent solution for some locks that are old and need some lubricant to work correctly.

❖ ❖ ❖ ❖ Cat's urine can be difficult to get out. I have found that Icky Poo works great; it can also be used for all pet odors.

❖ ❖ ❖ ❖ For help with a dog that has come into contact with a skunk or has rolled in something hideous, mix 2 oz. Massengill Disposable Douche per gallon of water to eliminate the nasty smell by soaking for 15 minutes, then wash with pet shampoo.

When entering homes with dogs that are somewhat agitated, you can lick your lips to signal the dog to calm down. Yawning reduces stress in dogs as well; yawn and look away. Never directly look the dog in the eyes as this is taken as a threat. By blinking and turning your eyes away, you will be sending out calming signals to the dog. If you turn sideward while approaching the dog to hook their leash, you are letting the dogs know you are not a threat. I'd like to add that you should not smile at a dog; the dog might interpret this as a snarl with teeth being shown. This is only until your dog has become familiar with you.

CHAPTER 5

Pet Sitting Situations: Test Your Knowledge

In this section are actual pet sitting situations and possible solutions for problems that can occur on the job. While every assignment is unique and there might be multiple solutions for the problem at hand, these questions are intended to test your retention of what was talked about in the book.

1. While walking your client's stubborn dog, he begins to plant all four paws firmly and resists your command to follow. What would you do?

    a. Start pulling forcefully on the leash and drag them along.

    b. Yell at the dog to obey.

    c. Wait them out, and when they obey, reward with a treat.

    d. Talk to the dog in a happy voice.

2. What do you do if your dog gets attacked by another dog while out on a walk?

    a. Let go of the dog's leash.

    b. Break up the fight.

    c. Yell for help.

    d. Run away.

3. Upon entering your client's home, a cat that usually hides from you is sitting in plain sight and doesn't run to hide. What would you suspect?

    a. He has suddenly warmed up to you and wants to make friends.

    b. The cat is hungry.

    c. The cat has fallen ill and doesn't have the energy to run.

    d. He's waiting for you to pet him.

4. You reach your client's home and find a window that wasn't open on your last visit now open.

    a. Leave right away and call the police.

    b. Go in and close the window then feed the cat.

    c. Call or text your client and ask if anyone was in to visit the cat.

    d. Check all rooms to see if anything is missing.

5. You get a call from a prospective client who has multiple pets in the home and would like a price quote. What would you tell this client?

    a. I would need to meet with you to be able to give a price.

b.   I need to know what types of pets and exactly how many in order to give a price.

c.   I charge $20 per visit.

6.   Your clients have instructed you to not let their son into the home and he shows up.

    a.   Call the police.

    b.   Call your client.

    c.   Explain to the son that you are not allowed to let anyone into the home regardless of the relationship to the client.

    d.   Let the client's son come in while you supervise his visit.

7.   Your clients have been away on a two-week vacation when their dog starts to show signs of stress and has started to have diarrhea.

    a.   Call the vet immediately.

    b.   Give the dog some rice mixed in their dinner.

    c.   Add extra visits.

    d.   Call your client.

8.   The client has instructed you to set their alarm each time you leave. The alarm has started to go off at all hours.

    a.   Turn it off and do not set the alarm.

    b.   Call the alarm company.

    c.   Call your client and ask what they would like you to do.

    d.   Set the alarm to stay.

9. A cat that needs medication is being extremely difficult to medicate and is starting to stress about having to take his medication.

    a. Call the vet.

    b. Forget about giving him his medication.

    c. Put the medication in his food.

    d. Take him to the vet.

10. Your car breaks down and you have a full schedule.

    a. Cancel all your stops.

    b. Call other sitters for backup.

    c. Rent or borrow a car.

CHAPTER 6

Natural Treatments

With any of these natural treatments, you will want to consult with your client's veterinarian to ensure proper dosage. I will always consult with my clients vet beforehand. Some of the simpler remedies would not harm the pet and help to alleviate minor problems. I have learned from my clients, and in my opinion, natural remedies are better for both humans and animals. I have used these treatments on my own pets; because they are natural, you really can't screw up on the dosage, for the body will just get rid of them through elimination. I would just use caution and check when using in conjunction with conventional medicine as they might interfere with them. Some conventional veterinarians may not agree with these treatments, and you might have to find a holistic veterinarian in your area to consult.

🐾 Milk

A pet's constipation can be treated with some milk. This will loosen the stool. Cats need 2 tablespoons every couple of hours until stools loosen up. Dogs need a bowl of milk according to size.

🐾 Pumpkin

This is high in fiber and helps with constipation and diarrhea. It is also good for pets with upset stomachs or indigestion. What will work to absorb the water in both dogs and cats is 100 percent pure canned pumpkin. Do not use pie filling. Constipation and diarrhea lasting more than 24 to 36 hours requires a visit to the vet.

Small dogs and cats weighing less than 15 lb. need 1–2 teaspoons of pureed pumpkin. Dogs weighing 15–35 lb. need 1–2 tablespoons. Dogs weighing 35 lb. or more need 2–5 tablespoons. Do this 2–3 times a day until stools loosen up or firms up.

🐾 Rice

White rice is used to bind stools of pets with diarrhea. Give your pet the same amount of cooked rice as you would food. And by cooking the rice in low-sodium chicken broth, you can add flavor and nutrients. On the second day you can add some plain yogurt to the rice and some boiled chicken/turkey or chopped meat until the diarrhea has cleared up. Although I would try to stay away from the chopped meat due to the high fat content and this might upset the pet's stomach.

🐾 Probiotics

You can get the same benefits as yogurt with probiotics in a concentrated form. You can purchase a refrigerated probiotic from health food stores. This will help with constipation and diarrhea add half a capsule to food, yogurt, or mix with chicken broth, water, and give with syringe.

🐾 Karo Syrup

This is used to treat insulin shock for pets with diabetes. Rub the syrup on the gums or inside the cheek. Make sure not to give too much at once to avoid choking. Another inexpensive source is honey and molasses for treating insulin shock. Rub a small amount of the honey or molasses on the gums or inside the cheek.

🐾 Natural Sea Salt

This is used to treat ringworm. Mix with small amount of water to create a paste and leave on affected area for about five minutes. An alternative mixture calls for using vinegar instead of water to make the paste. Both are effective home remedies to treat ringworm.

🐾 Orange Flea Treatment

You will need 4 oranges and 1 quart water. In a large saucepan, place the peels from the oranges and boil until the peels are soft. Let cool and place the orange peels in blender with some of the water. Mix well then return the chopped peels to remaining water and strain the mixture into a spray bottle. This mixture can be used on your pet, carpets, bedding, and furniture. This mixture will actually get rid of the fleas because orange peels contain citrus oil that kills them and is not toxic to the pet.

🐾 Hair Ball Remedy

Use papaya capsules. Empty one capsule into cat's food. Mix well. Do this for 3 days. This will help to bring up the hair balls.

🐾 Slippery Elm

This is a nontoxic, homemade treatment used to treat kennel cough or bronchitis, helps soothe and lubricate the urinary tract with urethritis, helps soothe stomach distress with gas, acts as a joint lubricant with arthritis, and helps soothes irritable bowel with colitis.

🐾 Hair Balls

Open 2 capsules of slippery elm and then add 1 tablespoon boiling hot water to dissolve. You can then add to a tablespoon of tuna, wet cat food, or favorite food. Cats don't seem to mind slippery elm when added to their favorite dish.

🐾 Diarrhea Treatment

You will need 1 tablespoon of slippery elm powder (found in health food stores) and 12 oz. hot water. In a bowl, slowly pour hot water over tablespoon slippery elm powder, stirring constantly until smooth. For this recipe, dosage should be as follows:

cats, ½ teaspoon (or 2 cc. by syringe) 3–4 times per day; small dogs, 1 teaspoon 3–4 times per day; medium dogs, 1 tablespoon 3–4 times per day; large dogs, 2–4 tablespoons 3–4 times per day. Unused portions can be stored in the refrigerator up to 3 days.

❖ Constipation Treatment

Use 1 teaspoon of slippery elm powder and follow same mixing instructions and dosage for diarrhea. Slippery elm also makes an excellent herbal dressing or bandage for wounds, sores, or burns. Mix just enough water with the powder to make a paste and apply to the area, and if needed, you can wrap in a bandage.

❖ Rescue Remedy

This treats a variety of anxiety and behavioral disorders and will help the pet relax due to stress from thunderstorms, fireworks, vet visits, and some types of aggression. This can also be used to treat hot spots on dogs and can be applied directly to the spot, that is, if it isn't too raw. Otherwise it will sting. This can be used 3–4 times a day for 2–4 weeks for acute problems. Use 4–8 drops on the gums, tongue, or lips. Use a full dropper to water dish or 4–8 drops in the pet's wet food. A full dropper can also be mixed in a spray bottle of water (distilled water is best) and can be sprayed on bedding. A few drops on your hands can be rubbed onto the pet's head and ears. Any of these applications is acceptable, and there isn't a wrong way to apply Rescue Remedy.

Simple Remedies

With these simple remedies you will want to consult with your client's veterinarian to ensure proper dosage. Caution should also be taken when other medications are being administered to the pet. Definitely ask your clients vet when using Benadryl, but I have used this many times in calming and treatment of allergies among many of the dogs in my care and my own. I had a Labrador retriever that was afraid of thunder and fireworks, and this helps alleviate her fears.

🐾　Benadryl

Make sure that you use only plain Benadryl or Benadryl Children's Allergy Relief Formula (12.5/5ml.). The dosage is 1 mg. per pound every 6 to 8 hours for both dogs and cats

Benadryl is very effective when used properly and is also used to alleviate other problems such as:

Bee stings and insect bites
Snakebites
Vaccination reactions
Motion sickness
Itching
Controls vomiting
Used as a mild tranquilizer

🐾　Dish Detergent

Dish detergent will suffocate the fleas and is not harmful to the pet. My daughter has used this to treat young abandoned kittens less than five weeks old. Fill a cup, half with dish detergent (any dish detergent will work) and half apple cider vinegar. Wet the pet and take out of water. Lather up and let sit for a few minutes. Place the pet back in water and rinse well. Towel dry and use a flea comb to get the dead fleas off the fur. Wash the pet again with pet shampoo as dish detergent is harsh on the skin. If this is a kitten or puppy, make sure that the pet is kept warm during the process.

🐾　Bleach

This is used to treat ringworm, using bleach without sodium hydroxide, which is commonly known as lye. Use one part bleach to six parts water. Patting the affected area will dry the ringworm out.

Tasty Dog Recipes

Alaskan Malamute Meatballs

½ pound ground beef
2 tbs. grated cheese
1 carrot finely grated
½ cup whole wheat bread crumbs
1 egg beaten well
½ tbs. tomato paste

Preheat oven to 350°. Combine all ingredients together and mix thoroughly. Roll into meatballs (whatever size is appropriate for your dog). Place on a cookie sheet, spray with nonfat cooking spray. Bake at 350° for 15–20 minutes or until they are browned and firm. Cool and store in fridge or freezer.

Basset Hound Delight

1 pound ground turkey
1 cup cooked brown rice
1 egg beaten
¼ cup fresh chopped parsley
3 tbs. wheat germ
½ cup carrots

Preheat oven to 350°. Combine all ingredients in large bowl and mix well. Place in lightly greased loaf pan. Bake at 350° for 60 minutes or until done. Slice and serve over dry dog food. Leftovers can be kept in the fridge or frozen.
Parsley will take care of bad breath.

Weight on Meatballs

    1 ½ pounds fatty raw hamburger, minced
    ½ cup wheat germ oil or wheat germ
    3 eggs
    3 cups oatmeal

Form ingredients into meatballs appropriate for your dog's size. Place on cookie sheet and put in freezer. After frozen, place meatballs in containers. Microwave about 30 seconds per meatball, depending on the size. Feed 2–3 per day. This is also great for the finicky eater.

Bow-Wow Birthday Cake

    1 ½ cups all-purpose flour
    1 ½ tsp. baking powder
    ½ cup margarine, softened
    ½ cup corn oil
    1 jar strained beef or liver baby food (2 ½ oz.)
    4 eggs
    3 strips dog beef jerky, crumbled
    plain yogurt or cottage cheese, for icing

Preheat oven to 325°. Sift flour and baking powder together. Set aside. In large bowl, with electric mixer at medium speed, cream margarine until smooth. Add corn oil, baby food, and eggs; mix until smooth. At low speed, gradually beat flour mixture into beef mixture until batter is smooth. Fold in beef jerky. Pour batter into greased and floured 8" × 5" × 3" loaf pan and bake in 325° oven for 70 minutes. Let cool on wire rack a few minutes before removing from pan to cool completely. Ice each slice with yogurt or cottage cheese (yields an 8" loaf cake).

I purchased a bone-shaped pan online and would bake these up for my client's dog birthday. They loved it!

Chicken Cake

> 1 chicken bouillon cube
> 1 cup whole wheat flour
> 2 cups wheat germ
> ½ cup cornmeal
> 2 eggs
> ½ cup vegetable oil
> 2 cups water
> vegetable oil spray, garlic flavor

Preheat oven to 375°. Dissolve bouillon cube in warm water. Combine flour, wheat germ, cornmeal, eggs, oil, and water. Mix well. Spray two cake pans with garlic-flavored oil and sprinkle with flour. Bake for 50 minutes. After removing cake from oven, turn upside down and let cool. This recipe will make two small cakes.

Be creative. Make pup cakes with muffin pans or with dog-shaped bones and ice with yogurt. The dogs really eat them up!

Tasty Cat Recipes

Chicken Delight

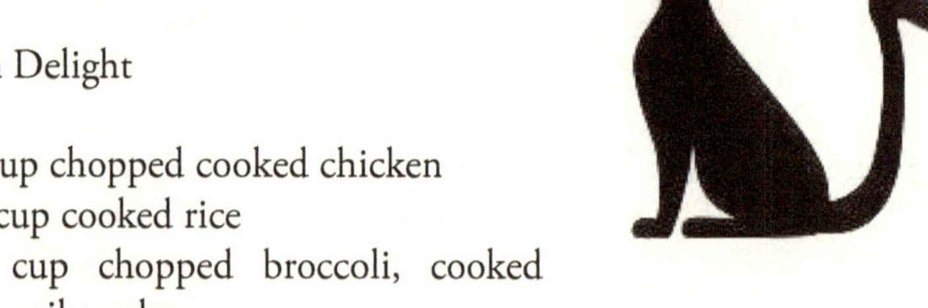

> 1 cup chopped cooked chicken
> ½ cup cooked rice
> ½ cup chopped broccoli, cooked
>   until tender
> ¼ cup chopped carrot, cooked until tender
> chicken broth

Process all ingredients in a food processor or blender with enough chicken broth to hold together. This recipe must be stored in an airtight container in the refrigerator and feed 2–3 tbs.

Feline Dream Feast

> 2 cans sardines packed in oil
> 2/3 cup cooked brown rice
> 2 chicken livers, cooked in water and drained
> ¼ cup chopped parsley

Combine all ingredients in a food processor or blender and mix until mixture is well blended. Store in refrigerator.

Kitty Sole Food

> ½ lb. fillet of sole
> 2 tbs. chopped parsley
> Water
> 1 tbs. margarine
> 1 tbs. all-purpose flour
> ½ cup milk
> ¼ cup shredded cheddar cheese
> 2 tbs. chopped liver
> ½ tsp. nonsalt salt
> 2/3 cup cooked rice

Preheat oven to 450°. Place sole in small greased baking dish. Sprinkle with parsley. Add enough water to cover the bottom of the dish. Bake in 450° oven for 10 minutes. Cool and shred with fork.

Melt margarine in small saucepan. Stir in flour and heat until it bubbles. Gradually stir in milk and cook, stirring constantly, until mixtures thicken. Remove from heat and add cheese, liver, and salt, stirring until cheese is melted.

Add the flaked fish, rice, and cheese sauce and stir well. Cool and store in airtight container in the refrigerator.

Tiny Tuna Treats

> ½ cup whole wheat flour
> ½ cup nonfat powered milk
> ½ can tuna in oil, chopped into small pieces
> 1 tbs. vegetable oil
> 1 egg beaten
> ¼ cup water

Preheat oven to 350°. In large bowl, mash tuna, add the four and powered milk, and mix well. Stir in water, oil, and egg and mix well. Mixture should be sticky.

Shape mixture into ½ inch balls. Place on greased cookie sheets. Press balls with fork to flatten. Bake for 10 minutes at 350°. Remove treats from oven; let sit 5 minutes and then turn treats to bake another 10 minutes or until golden brown. Cool completely on wire rack. Store in airtight container in the refrigerator.

You can substitute ½ cup canned chicken in place of the tuna to make a tasty chicken treat.

Angel Baby Bites

> 3 jars 2 ½ ounce baby food, beef or chicken
> ¼ cup nonfat powdered milk
> ¼ cup wheat germ or cream of wheat

Preheat oven to 325°. In large bowl, combine all ingredients and mix well. Roll into small balls and place on greased cookie sheet. Flatten slightly with fork. Bake for 10 minutes or until golden brown. Cool on wire rack and store in refrigerator and can also be placed in freezer for longer storage.

This recipe can also be microwaved to make bite-sized drops. Microwave on medium heat for 3–4 minutes but keep a check on the cookies. They come out chewy and are great for older cats (dogs too) with dental problems.

Answers to Pet Sitting Situations

1. While walking your client's stubborn dog, he begins to plant all four paws firmly and resists your command to follow. What would you do?

   Wait them out, and when they obey, reward with a treat. It might take a couple of tries with a really stubborn dog, but after a couple of times, they will begin to understand that when they obey your command, they will be rewarded. Never give the treat unless they obey your command.

2. What do you do if your dog gets attacked by another dog while out on a walk?

   There is no right answer for this question and only two that I would encourage depending on your personality and abilities to handle a dangerous and stressful situation as we all differ in our abilities. I highly advise about running or letting go of the leash as both could become disastrous.

   Break up the fight and prevent it from escalating out of control. Yell for help if you feel that you cannot handle the situation at hand

3. Upon entering your client's home, a cat that usually hides from you is sitting in plain sight and doesn't run to hide. What would you suspect?

   The cat has fallen ill and doesn't have the energy to run. A cat that usually hides and is now out, sitting in a corner, by a chair, or in plain sight is acting out of character. He should be taken to the vet as soon as possible as this could be an illness that has progressed while the owners are away.

4. You reach your clients home and find a window that wasn't open on your last visit now open. What do you do?

   Leave right away and call the police. Although a client's friend, relative, or neighbor might have stopped in to check on the cat, there is a strong possibility that an intruder has broken into the home. Always think of your safety first and get out immediately.

5. You get a call from a prospective client who has multiple pets in the home and would like a price quote. What would you tell this client?

    I need to know what types of pets and exactly how many in order to give a price. When quoting a price over the phone, always quote higher whether you charge per pet or by your time. Many times the client will not give all information needed over the phone, and you will be held to your quote. If, on the other hand, you get to the client's home and it's not too involved, it is always easier to lower your rate than increase it. There have been times I undercut my fee over the phone and the potential client was quite upset to hear a higher rate.

6. Your clients have instructed you to not let their son into the home and he shows up. What do you do?

    Explain to the son that you are not allowed to let anyone into the home regardless of the relationship to the client. Being firm in your decision as the client obviously has reasons as to why they do not want their son in their home. I would then proceed to call or text my client to inform them that their son was around and what transpired, always respecting the client's requests.

7. Your clients have been away on a two-week vacation when their dog starts to show signs of stress and has started to have diarrhea. What would you do?

    Give the dog some rice mixed in their dinner, half rice and half pet food. Wait a day before contacting the vet. If after twenty-four hours there is no improvement or the dog has gotten worse, a visit to the vet would be required and a call to the client informing them on the situation.

8. The client has instructed you to set their alarm each time you leave. The alarm has started to go off at all hours. What do you do?

    Call your client and ask what they would like you to do. Being your client has given strict instructions on setting the alarm, I would contact the client before calling the alarm company. You might suggest setting the alarm to stay if the client has a motion detector in place. Then follow the client's instructions on what they would like before authorizing the alarm company to come in and check the alarm.

9. A cat that needs medication is being extremely difficult to medicate and is starting to stress about having to take his medication. What would you do?

    Put the medication in his food. Most pill forms of medication can be crushed, and you could call your clients vet to make sure this would be an option. If this could not be done, the cat would then have to be taken to the vet for boarding.

10. Your car breaks down and you have a full schedule. What do you do?

    Call other sitters for backup if you have an emergency plan and pet sitters that can help in an emergency. If not, you would have to borrow or rent a car because the show must go on.

RECOMMENDED READING

How Dogs Learn by Mary R. Burch and Jos S. Bailey
The Dog's Mind by Bruce Fogle
The Truth about Dogs by Stephen Budiansky
The Domestic Dog by James Serpel
The Evolution of Canine Social Behavior by Roger Abrantes
Dog Language by Roger Abrantes
Canine Body Language by Brenda Aloff
Petiquette: Solving Behavior Problems in Your Multipet Household by
    Amy D. Shojai
On Talking Terms with Dogs: Calming Signals by Turid Rugaas
Learning to Hear What Animals Tell You by Carla Schack
Click to Calm by Emma Parsons
Cat Training in 10 Minutes by Miriam Fields-Babineau
The Total Cat by Carole Wilbourn
Cat Owner's Home Veterinary Handbook by Delbert G. Carlson and
    James M. Griffin
Psycho Kitty by Pam Johnson-Bennett
Twisted Whiskers by Pam Johnson-Bennett
Cat vs. Cat by Pan Johnson-Bennett
Think Like a Cat by Pam Johnson-Bennett
Dr. Pitcairn's Complete Guide to Natural Health for Dogs and Cats by
    Richard H. Pitcairn and Susan H. Pitcairn
The First Aid Companion for Dogs and Cats (Prevention Pets) by Amy
    D. Shojai

ABOUT THE AUTHOR

Geri Laverie is the founder of Soft Paws Pet Sitting Service which was established in 1994. While continuing to run her business, she has compiled a handbook to pass along her many years of experience in the pet care industry. During her career she has cared and learned about the many behavior and medical conditions some pets have. When caring for animals, you're constantly facing the many challenges of running the business itself. She has combined all her years of experience in hopes of helping anyone interested in starting a pet sitting service. Being involved in the pet sitting industry for twenty years has been an enlightening experience for Laverie. In 1987 she started a breeding program and obtained very nice Labrador Retrievers from some reputable breeders. She produced a handful of wonderful companion dogs, a few Seeing Eye Dogs and a few field and obedience trail dogs In 2005, Laverie served as Pet Sitters International (PSI) New York State Ambassador.

www.ingramcontent.com/pod-product-compliance
Lightning Source LLC
Chambersburg PA
CBHW051041250726
48656CB00001B/83